Writing for Inclusion

Writing for Inclusion

Literature, Race, and National Identity in Nineteenth-Century Cuba and the United States

Karen Ruth Kornweibel

FAIRLEIGH DICKINSON UNIVERSITY PRESS

Vancouver • Madison • Teaneck • Wroxton

Published by Fairleigh Dickinson University Press
Copublished by The Rowman & Littlefield Publishing Group, Inc.
4501 Forbes Boulevard, Suite 200, Lanham, Maryland 20706
www.rowman.com

Unit A, Whitacre Mews, 26-34 Stannary Street, London SE11 4AB

Fairleigh Dickinson University Press gratefully acknowledges the support received for scholarly publishing from the Friends of FDU Press.

British Library Cataloguing in Publication Information Available

Library of Congress Cataloging-in-Publication Data

Includes bibliographic references and index.
ISBN 978-1-68393-097-6 (cloth : alk. paper)
ISBN 978-1-68393-098-3 (Electronic)

♾™ The paper used in this publication meets the minimum requirements of American National Standard for Information Sciences Permanence of Paper for Printed Library Materials, ANSI/NISO Z39.48-1992.

Printed in the United States of America

In loving memory of Gladys Anne Kornweibel

Contents

Acknowledgments

This book would not have been possible without the influence and support of a considerable number of amazing teachers, colleagues, friends, and family. The anonymous reviewer for Fairleigh Dickinson University Press offered me invaluable suggestions that strengthened my argument and helped me to better situate it in both historical and critical context. At East Tennessee State University, I work with incredible people in both the Department of Literature and Language and the Honors College. There are too many to list them all, but particular thanks go to the late Karen Cajka for no-nonsense advice, Phyllis Thompson and Norma Honaker for moral support and for reading and commenting on chapter drafts in our reading group, and Judy Slagle for having read part of my manuscript and for being a mentor and unwavering supporter. Additional thanks to graduate assistants Katie Lea, Leslie Mullins, and Alexandria McQueen for editing and the unenviable task of converting the manuscript from MLA to Chicago. Thanks to my excellent former colleagues in the Department of African American Studies at Ohio University, particularly Vibert Cambridge and Robin Muhammed. During my PhD program at UT Austin I had the good fortune to work under Helena Woodard and Cesar Salgado and to be taught by many excellent professors; others who significantly influenced the trajectory of study that would lead to this book include Sonia Labrador-Rodríguez, Benigno Trigo, Katherine Arens, and Janet Swaffar. As an undergraduate at UC San Diego, the matchless teaching and mentoring of Frances Smith Foster set me on this path.

When people ask me what I do for a living, I am tempted to say I went into the family business; my father, Richard Kornweibel, was a Latin American history professor and my uncle, Theodore Kornweibel Jr., was also a historian and a professor of Africana Studies. Their example piqued my interest in both African American and Latin American history and culture. I am thankful for my siblings, Mark and Tolithia Kornweibel, who know better than most others where I am coming from. Our mom, to whose memory this book is dedicated, influenced all I do as she quietly taught by example that every single person on the planet has innate and incalculable value and should be treated accordingly. I have immense gratitude for lifelong friend and fellow academic Gina Marie Pitti who always, always reminds me to believe. Finally, this project would never have been completed without the faith and intellectual, moral, and practical support of my husband, Daniel Newcomer. To have found a true partner is a rare and wonderful gift. I am also grateful for the patience of our son, Benjamin, who may or may not yet understand just exactly what his busy mama is up to.

Chapter One

Reflections on Afro-Cuban and African American Discourses of Identity

In 1850, Emilia Margarita Tuerbe Tolón y Otero, the first woman ever exiled from Cuba by the Spanish, sat down in a New York City boarding house to sew what would become the Cuban flag. In the previous year during conversations regarding the future of their native land, Tuerbe Tolón's annexationist husband Miguel Tuerbe Tolón and two other important Cuban exiles, filibuster Narciso López and political activist and author Cirilo Villaverde, had determined the design that guided the hands of this Cuban woman. The flag imagined by these Cuban exiles and pieced together by Emilia Tolón y Otero represented their desire to free their island from Spanish Colonial rule and write their nation into existence. Significantly, in creating this flag they decided to draw upon the power and inspiration of an established symbolic language. López wanted to follow the example of the United States in gaining independence from a European colonial power; additionally, as he was a proponent of the annexation of Cuba by the US, he insisted the Cuban flag contain many of the colors and symbolic elements of the flag of the United States and the flag of Texas, then recently annexed by the United States.[1] The white background of the Cuban flag was intended to highlight the other figures. In a nod to the stripes of the Stars and Stripes, the three blue stripes were chosen to depict the three states into which Cuba was then divided. The red equilateral triangle symbolized their union since it was the Masonic symbol of union, and, in a nod to the flag of the Republic of Texas, a white

1

star was placed in the center of the triangle to represent the star of Cuba rising up over a field of blood.[2]

The Cuban flag is a narrative of national identity written in cloth and thread rather than with paper and ink. The fact that the Cuban flag, a symbol of proto-national Cuban identity, was first sewn in the United States echoing the strong symbolic language—the colors, stars, and stripes—of two flags from its northern neighbor indicates the complex and intertwined nature of ideas of national identity in Cuba and the United States during the nineteenth century.[3] The United States had a significant influence on Cuba from the way in which Cuban nationalists looked to the American Revolution as a model of breaking free of colonial rule, to the fact that proximity meant many important nineteenth-century Cuban intellectuals and statesmen spent time exiled in the United States, to the Spanish–American War of 1898.[4] While Miguel Tuerbe Tolón, Emilia Tolón y Otero, Narciso López, and Cirilo Villaverde all ended up making significant contributions to the formation of Cuban national identity, the figure who most clearly represents the importance of the United States as a staging ground for the Cuban independence movement is, of course, José Martí. The hope inherent in the flag sewn in 1850, a symbol created *in anticipation of the nation that exiled Cubans hoped it would represent*, is a yearning echoed by Martí in his *Versos Sencillos*:

> Yo quiero, cuando me muera,
> Sin patria, pero sin amo,
> Tener en mi losa un ramo
> De flores, —y una bandera![5]

> I want, when I die,
> Without country, but without master,
> To have on my grave a bunch
> Of flowers, —and a flag![6]

The Cuban flag sewn by Emilia Tolón y Otero and Martí's poem are two instances of the nation as idea—as narrative as well as sociopolitical, geographical, or historical reality—and both serve as reminders of the importance of symbols and of literature in the creation of the nation and in the construction of national identity.

Just as the United States played a crucial role in imagining and negotiating versions of Cuban national identity as they were being developed in the nineteenth century, Cuba played a significant role in the intense *renegotiation* of the conception of US national identity during that same time period. This was particularly true among various groups who believed that it was the "Manifest Destiny" of the United States to place a Cuban star on their own Star-Spangled Banner. As Louis A. Pérez Jr. explains in his book *Cuba in the America Imagination: Metaphor and the Imperial Ethos*, in the early nineteenth century the American imagination became fixed upon Cuba to the extent that "awareness of Cuba" became important for "the ways that it acted on the formation of the American consciousness of nationhood. The destiny of the nation seemed inextricably bound to the fate of the island. It was impossible to imagine the former without attention to the latter."[7] In 1848, just two years before Emilia Tolón took up needle and thread to help in the project of Cuban independence, President James K. Polk had offered Spain $100 million for Cuba. In 1854 President Franklin Pierce tried again, this time raising the offer to $130 million.[8] Cuba was considered a desirable addition to the nation because of its strategic location and lucrative cash crops, and also because it might be annexed in an effort to keep the balance of slave and free states in the period leading up to the Civil War, a time of intense flux in terms of ideas of US national identity. Cuba became a part of the intense negotiation between two very distinct versions of US identity, the competing versions that would come to be represented by two flags: the Stars and Stripes on one side and the Southern Cross on the other. However, interest in Cuba did not diminish with the end of the Civil War. As Pérez explains, after the Civil War, and increasingly after 1898, Cuba was essential to American formulations of national identity because it became the "overseas adversary" perpetually available to unite Americans in "a common cause;" this common cause ultimately "fixed permanently how Americans came to think of themselves: a righteous people given to a righteous purpose," an image that Pérez refers to as "an exalted manifest destiny." [9] Thus, as Pérez explains, in the nineteenth century Cuba became firmly located within the way in which Americans imagined their national identity, even if it was a matter of definition by juxtaposition.

On both sides of the straits of Florida at various times throughout the nineteenth century, members of the Cuban *criollo* elite like Miguel Tuerbe Tolón and Narciso López considered annexation to the United States as a politically and economically preferable alternative to their continued status as a Spanish colony.[10] The fact that most of those involved in the conception of the Cuban flag were annexationists points to the issue of slavery and Cuban anxieties about the feared "Africanization" of Cuba. Furthermore, Villaverde's participation in these conversations, particularly since he wrote the most important nineteenth-century Cuban antislavery novel, reminds us of the role of literature in the formation of paradigms of national identity and demonstrates the centrality of issues of slavery and race in constructions of national identity in both nations.[11] Even after 1865 when the abolition of slavery in the United States complicated the issue of Cuban annexation, some members of the Cuban landowning (and even slave-owning) elite argued that abolition would be a small price to pay in order to achieve independence from Spain. While proposals for the outright annexation of Cuba never came to fruition, the United States played an essential role in the Cuban struggle for independence. Much of the theorizing, planning, and financing of the Cuban independence movement took place in the United States. When Cuba finally achieved independence from Spain in 1898 as a result of the Spanish–American War it ironically, in the eyes of those who had fought for independence rather than annexation, fell under the imperial rule of the United States. When Emilia Tolón sewed the first Cuban flag in 1850, she did not merely piece together white, blue, and red fabric. Her work was at the nexus of shifting paradigms of national identity encompassing the possible annexation of Cuba by the United States, the balance of power in the United States between slaveholding and non-slaveholding states, the future of Cuban slavery, anxieties about race and the future of the then just imagined Cuban nation, and anxieties about race and the future of the United States.

Before the unique cultural and political relationship between Cuba and the United States in the nineteenth century, a number of similar political and economic experiences and institutions created strong ties between the two geopolitical entities. The "analogous sociopolitical and historical circumstances"[12] experienced by Cuba and the United States which influenced later paradigms of national identity began with European colonization and continued when the slave trade followed ocean and market currents from Africa to the Caribbean to the United States. John Lowe describes the fluidity of the "age of contact, exploration and conquest" in the New World, and, speaking specifically about the circumCaribbean, notes the "many geopolitical similarities between the two realms [Caribbean and US South], which for centuries were in fact contiguous, sans national boundaries, and . . . part of the same juridical and cultural control."[13] Significantly for this study, Lowe further emphasizes "similarities (in spite of the myth of a bichromatic U.S. South) in hybrid populations."[14] Similarities in the plantation societies established in both Cuba and the United States, as well as proximity and a complicated flow of citizens, slaves, sugar, and ideology between the two further affected the national, social, and literary production of both nations. The issue of slavery and conceptions of race are particularly important in their impact on constructions of national identity in the United States and Cuba. Each country has a legacy of African slaves who were forcibly brought into hostile environments and forced to forge a place and an identity within a forming nation, fighting to be included in constructions of national identity. As Pérez describes, by the 1840s African slaves and their descendants constituted the majority of the Cuban population. This fact led to a social anxiety about blacks, and particularly about the racial constitution of the imagined nation, which contributed to Spain's hold on the colony.[15] In the United States, although independence had been achieved long before Cuba broke free of Spain, and despite the fact that the population of color never constituted a majority, much thought and action were focused on alleviating social anxieties about color and the fate and face of the nation. White supremacy and the protection of racial purity were strong forces in society. In both Cuba and the United States, abolitionist movements, the processes of emancipation, and the biological and cultural integration of the "African" population into the nation involved complicated controversies regarding race and national identity. From the colonial experience, to the slave trade, to the pre–Civil War plans to annex Cuba as a slave state, to post-emancipation issues, to the Spanish–American War of 1898 and the resulting US involvement in Cuban government, much of the complex history between the two countries cannot be separated from the presence of people of African descent in the New World and their role in the process of forming national identities.

As Cuba and the United States have gone through the processes of national formation, of becoming in Benedict Anderson's terms, "imagined political communities" that are "both inherently limited and sovereign,"[16] geopolitical entities that understood themselves as having both physical and theoretical boundaries that separated them from all other nations, they have shared reciprocal roles influencing the terms by which each nation negotiated its physical and ideological territory. Historian Louis A. Pérez Jr. borrowed the phrase "Ties of Singular Intimacy" from William McKinley's 1899 State of the Union message as the subtitle for his 1990 monograph *Cuba and the United States*. Indeed, while it is certainly possible to focus on patterns of contradistinction between Cuba and the United States, in terms of nineteenth-century stories of race and nation told through literature by and about the people of the African diaspora in these two nations, what emerges is a picture that, like the flags of the two countries, includes a shared set of issues, overlapping symbolic language, analogous discursive threads, and similar literary genres.

This book examines what I am defining as Afro New World *discourses of identity*; it creates case studies to comparatively explore common genres that arise in both Cuba and the United States in which individuals from both nations negotiate (with) ideas of nation and national identity. On one level these discourses of identity challenge constructions of individual identity based on the notions of racial identities held in their societies. On a larger level, these works both explicitly and implicitly challenge and potentially transform more "official" and exclusionary versions of national identity. The common genres under discussion contain many similarities—common symbols, tropes, discursive threads, and concerns—that arise not only from the stripes and stars of an overlapping symbolic language, but also from commonalities of experience in two New World nations engaged in continuing struggles to raise banners of national identity from under the shadows of both colonialism and slavery. The nineteenth-century Afro-Cuban and African American authors represented here had to negotiate cultural identities within these shadows, hoping that they could one day be free of the institutions of colonization and slavery, and also of their long-lasting effects. Unlike Martí, who prophetically feared that colonial rule would outlive him, they imagined a day when they had both a flag *and* a country that would welcome them as full citizens.

SECOND REFLECTION: LITERATURE AND THE REALITIES OF RACIALIZATION

This comparative study of literature that engages issues of race and national identity is intended to highlight the contested nature of both terms. Since the beginning of African slavery in the New World, strict and powerful paradigms of racial identity have served to draw, define, and police the boundaries between different socially constructed categories, such as nonhuman and human, slave and free, black and white. Individuals and groups created narratives as part of the process by which they negotiated their identities in light of the strict and exclusive paradigms of humanity, race, and citizenship prevalent in their nations. In other words, authors of Afro-Cuban and African American texts like the ones at the center of this study wrote in response to and in conversation with ideas of race in their nations, and particularly as they related to both humanity and citizenship. Alexander G. Weheliye defines "race, racialization, and racial identities as ongoing sets of political relations that require, through constant perpetuation via institutions, discourses, practices, desires, infrastructures, languages, technologies, sciences, economies, dreams, and cultural artifacts, the barring of nonwhite subjects from the category of the human as it is performed in the modern west." [17] Racialization specifically, for Weheliye, should be understood not as either a "biological or cultural descriptor," but rather "as a conglomerate of sociopolitical relations that discipline humanity into full humans, not-quite-humans, and nonhumans"; [18] it operates like a "master code" that equates human exclusively with the "western Man," creating a "global color line" that distinguishes human from not-quite-human and simultaneously makes such categorizations appear to be natural. [19] He uses the term racializing assemblages to designate the forces that enact racialization. [20] The issue of masculinity is an overlapping concern related to humanity. A global gender line separating human from nonhuman or not-quite-human based on sex exists such that individuals, like the male authors to be examined in this volume, must negotiate with concepts of masculinity as they try to make arguments for their humanity. As a consequence, when they argue for their own inclusion in the nation, the argument does not automatically apply to women. [21]

I would add that conceptions of national identity in both the United States and Cuba in the nineteenth century were based on the idea of the Western Man, as the citizen should "naturally" be the full human. For example, those on the other side of the color line in the United States—those not-quite-human or nonhuman—had trouble, in William L. Andrews's terms, proving they were "of 'the people,' the American chosen" and had to demonstrate that they could master the "rituals of Americanization" necessary to be perceived as self-determining subjects and citizens of the nation.[22] Andrews's argument implies two important things. First, while Andrews is writing specifically about the United States and African American literature, what he refers to as the "rituals of Americanization" occur across the Americas as peoples of African descent struggle for incorporation into their nations on their own terms. Second, his description notes that "those marked by racial heritage as other"—those subject to racialization—have to negotiate their identities by adhering to, manipulating, and/or destroying these "rituals of Americanization"—the means of participating in paradigms of identity which determine who is Cuban, for example, and who is not.[23] That is, people who have been defined by the culture as not-quite-human must struggle against the paradigm of the fully human and the "cultural laws," to use Weheliye's term,[24] that condition and construct ideas of humanity.

Weheliye's work is based on his desire to "pose the problem of subjection qua agency in different ways" and to determine "what different modalities of the human come to light" if we see how the idea of the human is imagined by those traditionally excluded from the category.[25] Along these lines, my examination of the nineteenth-century works in this book attempts to see what ideas of human and national identity come to light when we examine how these ideas are transformed by those traditionally excluded from the categories. It is important to note, however, that these authors operate within, rather than outside, the process of racialization and participate to varying degrees in the "rituals of Americanization" or Cubanization which loomed large over their own ideas of humanity and citizenship. They had been racialized and acculturated. As Langston Hughes famously described, they need to fight against the powerful "urge within the race toward whiteness, the desire to pour racial individuality into the mold of American standardization," which is the urge toward conformity with the human/Man ideal as posited along hierarchical lines.[26] This compulsion holds so much power since "blackness designates a changing system of unequal power structures that apportion and delimit which humans can lay claim to full human status and which cannot."[27] As this book will make clear, the literary production of individual discourses of identity within the African diaspora in the Americas during the nineteenth century was one way by which the "proof" of participation in the rituals of national identity could be achieved; it was also a way in which the impulse toward the "mold" of "standardization" could be subverted. These texts, created during the process of cultural incorporation in Cuba and the United States, complicated the racializing assemblages that struggled to maintain the distinction between those included in the social and cultural paradigm and those whose exclusion often made such a paradigm possible.

Following Fanon's psychological analysis, I see these authors as having to radically resist being defined from outside, having to resist being "[s]ealed into that crushing objecthood" of being named by others, having their attitudes and actions fix them "in the sense in which a chemical solution is fixed by a dye."[28] The vivid image employed by Fanon illustrates the way in which racializing assemblages "fix," or enforce, particular identities or traits on individuals. The fact that Fanon focuses on an individual being named according to the ideology of another points to the importance of language in the process of identity negotiation. In Bakhtin's essay "Discourse in the Novel," he signals the fact that language is a site of contention, that it has to be appropriated by the speaker and forced to serve the speaker's intention. Bakhtin argues that before language is appropriated, it is neither "neutral" nor "impersonal."[29] Rather, the word "exists in other people's mouths, in other people's contexts, serving other people's intentions: it is from there that one must take the word, and make it one's own. . . . Language is not a neutral medium that passes freely and easily into the private property of the speaker's intentions; it is populated—overpopulated—with the intentions of others."[30] When the others who overpopulate language with their intentions are those in power and the person attempting to make the word "one's own" or the object of the discourse belongs to a marginalized group (i.e., s/he is nonhuman or not-quite-human), the experience of resistance and alienation is heightened. In the case of the texts in this book, the clear categories defined and justified by racialization become complicated as words are appropriated in order to construct new possible conceptions of human and citizen.

THIRD REFLECTION:
FRAMING A COMPARATIVE STUDY

As previously discussed, the nineteenth century was a time of great flux concerning conceptions of national identity in both the United States and Cuba. The texts to be examined in this book are Afro-Cuban and African American texts engaged in these issues drawn from the literary archives of nineteenth-century Cuba and the United States. While my work engages specifically with Afro-Cuban and African American authors, it rests on the foundation of comparative work by critics like Martha Cobb, O. R. Dathorne, Vera Kutzinski, Lois Parkinson Zamora, Gustavo Peréz Firmat, José David Saldívar, Paul Gilroy, Deborah Cohn, George B. Handley, Ifeoma Kiddoe Nwankwo, and John Wharton Lowe.[31] While not all of these authors specifically or exclusively address the literature of the African diaspora in the Americas, they stand as a foundation for my comparative project because they elucidate many of the important connections between the literature of the United States and that of Latin America.

In addition, a number of important studies have linked fiction and nationalism, most notably in the case of Latin America, Doris Sommer's *Foundational Fictions*. Sommer examines "national romances," suggesting at moments the hostile nature of the rhetoric of national identity created in these novels to the racial other.[32] She writes that the "pretty lies of national romance" may be "strategies to contain the racial, regional, economic, and gender conflicts that threatened the development of the Latin American nations," noting that the texts "were part of a general bourgeois project to hegemonize a culture in formation" and create a "culture that bridged public and private spheres in a way that made a place for everyone, as long as everyone knew his or her place."[33] While the novel is the literary form most often seen as aligned with and constructive of national identity, counterdiscourses that challenge this hegemonic bourgeois project do not always use the novel form. This is particularly true of early African American and Afro-Cuban texts engaging issues of national identity; very few Afro-Cuban or African American authors had the opportunity to publish a novel during the first half of the nineteenth century. For this reason, a consideration of other genres—slave narratives, poetry, speeches, plays, and novellas—is necessary to examine the ways in which these authors attempted to enter into conversations about national identity.

Several previous comparative studies are at least partially justified on the basis of the similarities they find in texts across national boundaries, although they understand the similarities they find in texts from different national and cultural traditions in different ways. George Handley writes of "moments when texts resonate synchronically with one another."[34] Influenced by Édoard Glissant, John Wharton Lowe employs the metaphor of rhizomes, or multiple roots, that connect beneath the surface of texts.[35] Deborah Cohn analyzes "recurrent themes and preoccupations" and "convergences, similar features and strategies."[36] Other authors focus on more specific themes. For example, Valérie Loichot's *Orphan Narratives* focuses on how "black or white, women or men, complexly interwoven into the history of slavery," authors from different New World nations "illustrate similar complications of linear time and subversions of genealogy."[37] Catherine Russ focuses on the twentieth-century development of "a trans-American poetic imaginary that has emerged from the brutal, dehumanizing past" of the plantation.[38] Part of the initial motivation for this study was my having noted similarities in African American and Afro-Cuban texts both in terms of genre and in terms of the issues, overlapping symbolic language, and analogous discursive threads within them. In his discussion of diaspora studies, Weheliye cautions that "reliance on comparison frequently affirms the given instead of providing avenues for the conjuring of alternate possibilities."[39] Comparatively examining nineteenth-century texts from the archives of the United States and Cuba with a focus on examining racialization and constructions of national identity highlights the unnaturalness of these constructs as well as allowing us to see alternate visions of the nation and the human.

Two of the most relevant comparative works to this project deal specifically with African American and Afro-Cuban literature: George B. Handley's *Postslavery Literatures in the Americas: Family Portraits in Black and White* (2000) and Ifeoma Kiddoe Nwankwo's *Black Cosmopolitanism: Racial Consciousness and Transnational Identity in the Nineteenth-Century Americas* (2005). Handley, whose book focuses primarily but not exclusively on works from the United States and Cuba, discusses what he terms postslavery literatures from Plantation America and interrogates the common emphasis on genealogy within many of these works. Handley points out that many authors in postslavery Plantation America create family histories to "expose the historical roots of social contradictions that have yet to be transcended" in order to finish the process of decolonization in their nations.[40] Handley understands how literature impacts ideas of nation, encouraging readers to "avoid the temptation to see in any given work what the nation already is; rather, we can see in the text evidence of resistance to a textual discourse that has come before and a projected image into the future of what a revised version might look like."[41] As part of her study, Nwankwo's volume engages the works of slave writers from Cuba, the United States, and the West Indies. Her work focuses on the way enslaved black writers negotiated ideas of modernity in their quest to be perceived as equals by the dominant society and also on how individual writers related to transnational ideas of the black community arising after the Haitian Revolution.[42]

The discourses of identity examined here include works from both the pre-abolition nineteenth-century Cuba and the postslavery period, from both the antebellum and postbellum United States. The main works are two slave narratives, Juan Francisco Manzano's *Autobiografía de Juan Francisco Manzano* and Frederick Douglass's *Narrative of the Life of Frederick Douglass, An American Slave*, and two second-generation mulato/a[43] fictions, Martín Morúa Delgado's *Sofía* and Charles W. Chesnutt's *The House Behind the Cedars*. This project reflects Handley's in its focus on comparative readings of texts whose comparability arises in part from the "uncannily similar . . . cultural quandaries" existent during their production.[44] What this study offers to complement the work of previous critics is an interrogation of the continuity between works produced in the slavery and postslavery periods. The choice to pick two central genres, one on either side of this gap, is also based on a desire to interrogate the extent to which common symbols and discursive threads are transformed over time. As Saidiya V. Hartman explains regarding her study on terror, slavery, and selfhood spanning the antebellum period, reconstruction, and the gilded age in the United States, there were "tragic continuities in antebellum and postbellum constitutions of blackness."[45] This interrogation helps deepen our understanding of the continuing story of how individuals of African descent in Cuba and the United States negotiate for inclusion in paradigms of national identity and write against the reality and legacy of racialization.

FOURTH REFLECTION: SLAVE NARRATIVES AS DISCOURSES OF IDENTITY

Slave narratives are both life stories told in the first person and powerful self-writings in which slave authors negotiate the culturally sanctioned paradigms of identity in order to allow for their humanity, freedom, and potential incorporation into the nation. The men and women who wrote slave narratives in Cuba and the United States literally had to write themselves free before they could write themselves into the nation. Early slave narratives from the late eighteenth and early nineteenth centuries published in Britain and the United States like those of Gronniosaw, Marrant, and Jea were very closely tied to conversion and captivity narratives and were often written down by an amanuensis. They were examples of "autobiography simplex," narratives that centered on one overriding pattern or metaphor, which was usually the narrative of spiritual salvation for the slave narrator.[46] Exceptions during this early period include Equiano's text, noted as one of the first to include not just the spiritual trajectory of the narrator but also a clear renunciation of slavery.[47] Another exception was Ottobah Cugoano's text notable for his political philosophy.[48] The two texts in this study, *Autobiografía de Juan Francisco Manzano* and *Narrative of the Life of Frederick Douglass, An American Slave*, were later texts that engaged in more complex forms of autobiography.

As Weheliye's work indicates, slavery was more than a political or economic relationship. Because blackness signified a lack of full human status, slave narrators were radically marked as other and excluded from consideration in the human family and the nation. Patterson's concept of social death, which influenced Weheliye, is useful here in considering these texts. According to Patterson, not only were social, psychological, and cultural power employed to enslave individuals in both Cuba and the United States, but this process also forced slaves to change how they saw themselves and their interests as the exercise of these powers transformed "force into right, and obedience into duty."[49] One of the most significant aspects of social death as described by Patterson is the fact that "natal alienation"—the severing of any ties to previous or subsequent generations—meant that the socially dead slave was not part of a family, and, by extension, was not part of the social order at all.[50] Patterson further discusses the radical loss of honor that was a result of slaves' exclusion from humanity and community.[51] The US south was one of many slave societies that became a timocracy, a society governed by rules motivated by concepts of honor, manliness, and chivalry, concepts that work to reinforce the boundary between human and nonhuman.[52] He cites a "Confederate soldier who described his flag as the symbol of 'an adored trinity—cotton, niggers and chivalry.'"[53] One thing about Weheliye and Patterson's analyses that is helpful is that they are not culturally specific, considering racialization and slavery, respectively, in ways that transcend national borders. While it is possible to make distinctions between the Cuban and American systems of slavery, and particularly the de jure justifications behind them, whether it was the paternalistic Spanish system that technically upheld the humanity of the slave and considered the slave subject to the Spanish monarch and Catholic Church, or the chattel system that reduced slaves to moveable property, the reality is that as a result of racialization slaves in both Cuba and the United States experienced social death and were considered if not nonhuman, then not-quite-human. Often, they were not considered persons; they were *never* considered *of the people*.

As William L. Andrews explains, early slave narratives employed, among other strategies, appeals to pathos and metaphor-making arguments, and centered on questions of identity and veracity,[54] questions that are related to social death and lack of honor. The nonhuman or not-quite-human who did not really belong to society was making a case regarding his/her identity— that s/he was human and part of society and that s/he spoke the truth, particularly about slavery. The reality of slavery and the rhetoric that maintained it created the necessity, in Davis and Gates's terms, "for the slave to write himself into the human community through the action of first-person narration."[55] The slave narrator had to construct him/herself in such a way as to become a person with a voice that could be recognized. The slave narrative represents a discourse of identity in which a historical individual negotiates his/her place within larger paradigms of national identity and culture. More than merely an autobiography, the slave narrative is similar to what a nation's intellectuals accomplish when they write the histories of their homelands. The way in which a national history envisions the nation and the story of how the nation became what it is in the present help to define its possible future identity. Like formal histories, the nonfiction slave narrative is simultaneously an account of the past, an indication of the present, and a discursive act intended to create a desired future for the author, such as acceptance and participation in society.

In his study of slavery, Patterson emphasizes that symbols are "a major instrument of power" in that authority comes when those who can control "appropriate symbolic instruments" use symbols to transform their power into a right.[56] Slave narratives engage with and challenge both the processes of racialization and the symbols that were used to justify slavery. Within this system, the manipulation of language, specifically the control of literacy, was one of the most critical tools used to maintain slavery; as critics including William L. Andrews and John Sekora have demonstrated, one way slaves vied for citizenship within societies rhetorically constructed to deny it to them was by writing their own life stories.[57] In many instances the slave narrative functioned as an act of self-writing by which the slave narrator challenged some of the basic beliefs of his/her society and made a case for his or her inclusion in it. In other words, although masters and slaves shared the same geography, the two groups existed as two separate nations divided not by a physical boundary, but racializing assemblages that worked together to keep the slave in his/her place.

While the de facto reality of slavery in Cuba, especially on the sugar plantations, systematically stripped slaves of their humanity, the discussion of the Cuban slave narrative tends to address the need for citizenship and freedom, accepting that in the nineteenth century the de jure humanity of the slaves was largely accepted in Cuba. In North American narratives and the criticism that surrounds them, on the other hand, the denial or defense of the slave's humanity is as common a consideration as his/her freedom. Despite this difference, Miriam DeCosta-Willis finds "striking similarities" in the form and content of Spanish and English language slave narratives. As she explains, they both focus on three themes: a search for identity—here both humanity and citizenship could apply—, a desire for freedom, and a sense of alienation in a hostile society.[58] In both Cuba and the United States, slaves and ex-slaves wrote to defend themselves from the dehumanizing and disenfranchising racializing assemblages that excluded them from their societies. They wrote in order to bridge the rhetorical gap between bondage and freedom and all that this difference in legal status implied. They wrote to define for themselves a future identity as a free human member of society.

While the United States has a long history and large body of slave narratives—of which the *Narrative of the Life of Frederick Douglass, an American Slave* (1845) [59] is one of the most famous and influential—Cuba has only one such narrative, *Autobiografía de Juan Francisco Manzano* (written in 1835). Many North American slave narratives like Frederick Douglass's were explicitly abolitionist. Douglass's *Narrative* was chosen for this study because it is his first, written while Douglass was a fugitive slave, because the fact of its writing under the patronage of William Lloyd Garrison in some ways makes more apparent the racializing assemblages he is negotiating, and because it is closest in time to Manzano's text. Like Douglass, Manzano was also a fugitive slave during the time of his writing, although more of an urban truant/deserter than a *cimarrón* in the traditional Cuban sense, and wrote his autobiography at the behest of his own powerful patron, Domingo del Monte.

Neither Manzano nor Douglass began their public engagement with slavery, freedom, and racialization in their slave narratives. In order to more fully understand these two works and how they engage with racialization and national identity, chapter 2 introduces these individuals and gives a brief overview of some of their previous works—Douglass's antislavery speeches and Manzano's poetry—as well as discussing their relationships with their patrons and the politics surrounding the production of their slave narratives. Chapter 3 consists of a comparative reading of the narratives of Juan Francisco Manzano and Frederick Douglass; in these autobiographical texts, they negotiated and troubled the paradigms which policed the lines between the categories of slave and free, nonhuman and human, black and white. The common symbolic language and narrative threads within these two texts indicate certain similarities of situation, and highlight the realities of exclusionary paradigms of national identity. Examining these autobiographies and their common threads additionally reminds us of the various and powerful ways in which slave writers within the Afro–New World literary tradition laid a foundation for the struggle to reclaim their dignity in the face of the tyranny and violence of Plantation America. Finally, a discussion of two later texts by these authors, Manzano's play *Zafira* and Douglass's novella *The Heroic Slave*, examines how the use of the trope of the rebellious slave further articulates their resistance to being defined as not-quite-human and allows them to imagine new conceptions of human and citizen.

FIFTH REFLECTION: SECOND GENERATION TRAGIC MULATA NOVELS AS DISCOURSES OF IDENTITY

The many fictional figurations of the mulato/a and his/her place in society are a second significant discourse of identity produced by and about those marked by racial heritage as *other* in both Cuba and the United States. Since the "fear of the dark" leads to both the demonization of difference and the desire for control, racializing assemblages worked to "place" individuals according to racial categories that were defined as necessarily distinct and exclusive in order to ensure the "purity" of national identity. In both Cuba and the United States, fictional representations of the liminal, often ambiguous figure of the mulato/a demonstrated the ways in which the figure became a site of contention in defining identities. Many of the earliest fictional representations of the mulato/a appeared in both Cuban and North American antislavery novels such as *Sab*, *Cecilia Valdés*, *Uncle Tom's Cabin*, and *Clotel, or the President's Daughter*; many of these first-generation tragic mulata fictions were written by white authors.[60] The depiction of mulato/a characters in these novels worked to destabilize racially based justifications of slavery, but they often also reinforced stereotypical ideas of racial identity. In post-emancipation literary representations of the mulato/a, the figure represents a liminal space in which strict paradigms of identity could be complicated and questioned.

After slavery, as social integration of the African and African-descended populations in Cuba and the United States continued, and their struggles for human and civil rights took on new parameters, each nation had to deal with the fact of miscegenation and the status of mixed race offspring. In both Cuba and the United States, those in power strove to identify and thus control those marked by racial heritage as other. The "fear of the dark" leads to the demonization of mixed-race individuals and the desire to be able to "place" all individuals according to racial categories that are seen as necessarily distinct and exclusive to ensure the "purity" of national identity. The figure of the mulato/a stands at the crossroads, challenging the color line by undermining society's ability to identify, place, and control the mobility of the racially marked *other*. Vera Kutzinski explains that writers in the United States in the periods before and after the Civil War were, like their Cuban counterparts, "particularly fascinated by women of ambiguous racial origin" because "the iconic mulata" acted as "a symbolic container for all the tricky questions about how race, gender, and sexuality inflect the power relations that obtain in colonial and postcolonial Cuba."[61] Lauren Berlant's observations about the postbellum mulata figure in the United States echo Kutzinski's ideas. Berlant writes, "By occupying the gap between official codes of racial naming and scopic norms of bodily framing conventional to the law and general cultural practices, the American mulatta's textual and juridical representation after 1865 always designates her as a national subject, the paradigm problem citizen."[62] In both Cuba and the United States, fictional representations of the liminal, often ambiguous figure of the mulato/a demonstrated the ways in which the figure became a site of contention in establishing the boundary between citizen and alien.

Mulata fictions highlight the "repeated pattern of guilt" of white society in regard to the sexual exploitation of black women and the dehumanization and commodification of whites' own mixed-race children.[63] The great irony is that in order to keep silence about the transgressions of white males, the mulata is figured as sexual predator rather than product of sexual abuse. In both Cuba and the United States, the mulata was scripted as degenerate because she was forced to bear the stain of her own engendering and her body was over-determined as sexualized. In Cuba, at times the emphasis on women engendering children whiter than themselves was so strong that promiscuity and secrecy were both tolerated, and implicitly accepted. In the United States, since laws against interracial marriage encouraged rather than discouraged illicit sexual relationships between the races and since the power of whiteness also meant that often paternity was unknown or at least unspoken, more fundamental social institutions and mores were threatened. In some cases, white male privilege and the project of whitening replaced a more explicit emphasis on traditional values like marriage and paternal responsibility. This reality reinforced and legitimized the sexual abuse and violence done to black women, slave and free. In the more extreme cases, this protection of white male sexual privilege enabled sexual violence and potentially led to situations in which individuals lacked the knowledge of kinship necessary to avoid extremes such as incest. Incest was only the most extreme case of a set of anxieties about social position that arose from miscegenation. Julio Ramos suggests that hybridity itself is the most important threat of miscegenation because it problematizes hierarchy, ruining notions of purity and separation.[64] By his/her very existence, the nineteenth-century mulato/a violated the boundary between categories and threatened social hierarchies.

While many narratives focusing on the figure of the mulato/a worked to reinforce existing ideas of race and the existing power structure, after the abolition of slavery the mulato/a was reinvigorated as a site of contention regarding definitions of racial identity and control. In his work examining the history of mixed-race characters in fiction, Werner Sollors goes through an extensive history of the tragic mulato stereotype and the variety of critical attitudes toward it. Sollors's examination is particularly useful to this study in that it is not limited to literature written in the United States (nor to literature written by black authors) and provides a suitably comprehensive contemplation on the mulato/a figure for the present comparison of works from Cuba and the United States. Sollors points out many problematic aspects of the trope, from its clichéd or stereotypical nature, to the danger of an "underlying racialism" and focus on biologically determined identities, to its racist appeal to write readers.[65] However, his reading also makes clear that he joins other critics in their assessment that the figure, particularly after emancipation, was used in potentially transgressive and/or transformative ways. Sollors speaks of a "counter-tradition" in which the mulato/a character is "a most upsetting and subversive character who illuminates the paradoxes of 'race' in America."[66] If racialization worked to create a clear line between human and nonhuman or not-quite human, the mulato/a inherently challenged that line.

Second generation mulato/a novels written after abolition in both nations engage the trope of the tragic mulata for new purposes, purposes which often relate to constructions of national identity particularly as the mulata became the symbol for all that was uncertain regarding racial identity even as forces in Cuba and the United States worked to strengthen racializing assemblages that would allow them to maintain the color line in order to assign individuals their proper "place" in society and ensure the "purity" of national identity. In both nations, these literary figures symbolize anxieties about either developing or changing ideas of national identity.

This book performs a comparative reading of two representative works from this genre, Martín Morúa Delgado's *Sofia* (1891) and Charles W. Chesnutt's *The House Behind the Cedars* (1900), within the context of their authors' ideas regarding race and national identity and with an emphasis on the shared symbolic language and common discursive threads that run through the texts. These novels are of particular interest due to the ways in which they reflect ideas of national identity and citizenship espoused by their authors in other contexts. Morúa and Chesnutt wrote both fiction and nonfiction works centered on the complex issues of racial identities, miscegenation, and national identity. In order to elucidate the ways in which these novels operate as embodiments of ideas and ideologies, chapter 4 provides an examination of their authors' political nonfiction, focusing primarily on Martín Morúa Delgado's "Ensayo politico o Cuba y la raza de color" [Political essay or Cuba and the colored race] and several of Charles W. Chesnutt's essays, most notably "The Future American." Chapter 5 examines commonalities in the postslavery reworking of the mulato/a narrative in Morúa's *Sofía* and Chesnutt's *The House Behind the Cedars*. As these novels demonstrate, racial difference has been maintained not only by laws and social conventions, and by a rhetoric of national identity that draws, defines, and polices the boundaries between different racial categories. As a necessarily illegitimate, unplaceable, and thus transgressive figure in nineteenth-century Cuban society and nineteenth- and turn-of-the-twentieth-century North American society, the mulato/a is the most visible "site" at which this blurring occurs. A reading of their essays and novels helps us to understand the ways in which Chesnutt and Morúa Delgado employ the figure of the mulato/a as a liminal space in which strictly exclusionary paradigms of human and national identity could be confronted in order to expand those included as citizens.

One clarification needs to be made regarding the choice of texts for this book. The texts under consideration were not chosen based on the influence they had at the time they were written. In the case of Manzano and Douglass we see a stark difference given the significant contemporary influence of Douglass's text and the relative obscurity of Manzano's. As Frances Smith Foster explains, Douglass's *Narrative* sold 30,000 copies in the first five years it was in print.[67] Manzano's manuscript was not published in nineteenth-century Cuba, but rather passed around among del Monte's associates. Del Monte gave the text to Anselmo Suárez y Romero to revise and then included the revised version in a dossier of materials he gave to Richard R. Madden, an Irish abolitionist. Madden included a translated and re-edited version of Manzano's text in *The Life and Poems of a Cuban Slave*, published in London in 1840. This text erased Manzano's name, abridged and rearranged the story, and sandwiched the narrative between texts written by Madden. It was not until 1937, in fact, that Manzano's manuscript was rediscovered and published in Spanish in Cuba. However, that is not to say that Manzano's text did not have an influence, although its influence was not as significant as that of Douglass's narrative. William Luis explains that Manzano's life as described in his text was "a model for and a generator of narrative production" which also served as an inspiration for many other

Cuban antislavery writers.[68] On the other hand, when it comes to Martín Morúa Delgado and Charles W. Chesnutt, Morúa's ideas and writings had much more influence on his society than anything produced by Chesnutt, largely due to the Cuban author's subsequent role in politics. Influence was not the criterion; all the texts in the book were chosen as artifacts from the literary archive that provide evidence of the negotiations of identity taking place as both Cuba and the United States emerge from slave societies into nations in post-plantation America in which definitions of national identity remain significantly entangled with ideas of race.

The discussion of the Afro–New World discourses of identity, and their contexts, in this volume will delineate common narrative threads within the literature of the African diaspora in the Americas, common threads that arise as individuals negotiate paradigms of national identity in Cuba and the United States. These commonalities are the result of the questioning, transgression, and explosion of terms and boundaries within the rhetoric of national identity. The resonances within the Cuban and North American canons imply a greater connectivity than previously imagined and allow for a richer analysis of the tradition of Afro–New World resistance to racism and injustice. Not only does an investigation of ideas of national identity and race in the past challenge us to reexamine our comfort with considering these ideas "natural" in the present, but doing so across national boundaries further highlights the constructed nature of such concepts. It also allows us to more fully understand systems of oppression and exclusion by examining these responses to racializing assemblages in an extra-national context.

NOTES

1. It is worth mentioning here that the US flag has the same color scheme as the British Union Jack, so the Cuban example is in an iterative process of imaging national identities based on existing symbols.

2. Clara Emma Chávez Alvarez, "La boradora de la bandera cubana," *Revista de la Biblioteca Nacional José Martí* 1 (January–June 1993): 31, 35.

3. Although it lies outside the scope of this book, it is interesting to note that the Puerto Rican flag was first displayed in New York in 1885 at the founding of the Puerto Rican section of the Cuban Revolutionary Party. The Puerto Rican flag, which mirrors the Cuban flag but switches the red and blue sections, was first constructed as part of the conversation regarding Cuba and Puerto Rico's common struggle against Spain, but also reflects the complex relationship between Puerto Rico and the United States. For an interesting argument regarding flags and Puerto Rican nationalism, see Juan Manuel Carrión, "The War of the Flags: Conflicting National Loyalties in a Modern Colonial Situation," *Centro Journal* 18.2 (Fall 2006): 100–123.

4. Of course, this process did not end in the nineteenth century, although that is the focus of my argument. From the Platt Amendment and its implications, to the Cold War, to ongoing embargoes, in the twentieth and twenty-first centuries Cuba and the United States continue to be mirrors and foils for one another in terms of their conceptions of national identity.

5. José Martí, *Martí Vol. XI: Ismaelillo, Versos Sencillos, Versos Libres* (Habana: Rambla, Bouza y Compañia, 1918), 185.

6. Unless otherwise cited, translations from the Spanish are my own.

7. Louis A. Pérez Jr., *Cuba in the American Imagination: Metaphor and the Imperial Ethos* (Chapel Hill: University of North Carolina Press, 1998), 1.

8. Louis A. Pérez Jr., *Cuba and the United States: Ties of Singular Intimacy* (Athens: University of Georgia Press, 1990), 43.

9. Pérez, *Cuba in the American Imagination*, 11.

10. Pérez, *Cuba and the United States*, 36.

11. One curious aspect of Clara Emma Chávez Alvarez's telling of the story of the woman who sewed the Cuban flag is the fact that Chávez Alvarez refers to Emilia Margarita Tuerbe Tolón y Otero as "una joven *trigueña* y bella" (31, my emphasis). The word trigueña comes from the root *trigo* (wheat) and can be translated as wheat-colored. It connotes racial mixture, generally indicating a person who is lighter than a mulata clara, but it is an ambiguous term that has been used to denote a range of racial identities. Thomas M. Stevens, *Dictionary of Latin American Racial and Ethnic Terminology* (Gainsville: University of Florida Press, 1989), 238–239. There is nothing in Chávez Alvarez's article, which does trace how Emilia Tolón y Otero's family came to Cuba from Spain, to indicate why she chose this word to refer to this young woman. There is certainly no indication in the article that the woman who sewed the Cuban flag had African blood. However, from my point of view, it would be particularly fitting for the reality of racial admixture in Cuba to be part of the story of the way in which Cuba's national identity was symbolically stitched together.

12. Deborah N. Cohn, *History and Memory in the Two Souths: Recent Southern and Spanish American Fiction* (Nashville: Vanderbilt University Press, 1999), 7.

13. John Wharton Lowe, *Calypso Magnolia: The Crosscurrents of Caribbean and Southern Literature* (Chapel Hill: University of North Carolina Press, 2016), 4.

14. Ibid.

15. Pérez, *Cuba and the United States*, 32.

16. Benedict Anderson, *Imagined Communities: Reflections on the Origin and Spread of Nationalism* (New York: Verso, 1991), 6.

17. Alexander G. Weheliye, *Habeas Viscus: Racializing Assemblages, Biopolitics, and Black Feminist Theories of the Human* (Durham: Duke University Press, 2014), 3.

18. Ibid.

19. Ibid., 27.

20. Ibid., 4.

21. This is certainly even more relevant for the gender nonconforming, though that is outside of the scope of this book.

22. William L. Andrews, *To Tell a Free Story: The First Century of African American Autobiography, 1760–1865* (Chicago: University of Illinois Press, 1986), 126.

23. Ibid.

24. Weheliye, *Habeas Viscus*, 27.

25. Ibid., 2, 8.

26. Langston Hughes, "The Negro Artist and the Racial Mountain," in *Voices from the Harlem Renaissance*, ed. Nathan Irvin Huggins (New York: Oxford University Press, 1995): 305.

27. Weheliye, *Habeas Viscus*, 3.

28. Frantz Fanon, *Black Skin, White Masks*, Trans. Charles Lam Markmann (New York: Grove Press, 1967), 109.

29. Mikhail Bakhtin, "Discourse in the Novel," in *The Dialogic Imagination*, ed. Michael Holquist, trans. Caryl Emerson and Michael Holquist (Austin: University of Texas Press, 1981), 293.

30. Ibid., 293–294.

31. Here I am thinking of works such as Martha Cobb's *Harlem, Haiti, and Havana: A comparative critical study of Langston Hughes, Jacques Romain, and Nicolás Guillén* (1979), O. R. Dathorne's *The Dark Ancestor: The Literature of the Black Man in the Caribbean* (1981)—which focuses on the Caribbean, but includes references to "the southern rim of the United States, eastern Mexico, and the Caribbean regions of Central America, Brazil, Venezuela and the Guyanas" (Dathorne 1)—Bell Gale Chevigny and Gari Laguardia's collection *Reinventing the Americas: Comparative Readings of Literature of the US and Spanish America*

(1986), Vera Kutzinski's *Against the American Grain: Myth and History in William Carlos Williams, Jay Wright, and Nicolas Guillen* (1987), Lois Parkinson Zamora's *Writing the Apocalypse: Historical Vision in Contemporary U.S. and Latin American Fiction* (1989), Gustavo Peréz Firmat's collection *Do the Americas Have a Common Literature?* (1990), José David Saldívar's *The Dialectics of Our America: Genealogy, Cultural Critique, and Literary History* (1991), Antonio Benitez Rojo's *The Repeating Island: The Caribbean and the Postmodern Perspective* (1992), Paul Gilroy's *The Black Atlantic: Modernity and Double Consciousness* (1993), Deborah Cohn's *History and Memory in the Two Souths: Recent Southern and Spanish American Fiction* (1999), George B. Handley's *Postslavery Literatures in the Americas: Family Portraits in Black and White* (2000), Carlos Hiraldo's *Segregated Miscegenation: On the Treatment of Racial Hybridity in the U.S. and Latin American Literary Traditions* (2003), Elizabeth Christine Russ's *The Plantation in the Postslavery Imagination* (2009), and John Wharton Lowe's *Calypso Magnolia: the Crosscurrents of Caribbean and Southern Literature* (2016).

32. Doris Sommer, *Foundational Fictions: The National Romances of Latin America* (Los Angeles: University of California Press, 1991), 29.

33. Ibid.

34. George B. Handley, *Postslavery Literatures in the Americas: Family Portraits in Black and White* (Charlottesville: University Press of Virginia, 2000), 30.

35. Lowe, *Calypso Magnolia*, 9–10.

36. Cohn, *History and Memory in the Two Souths*, 2, 7.

37. Valérie Loichot, *Orphan Narratives: The Postplantation Literature of Faulkner, Glissant, Morrison, and Saint-John Perse* (Charlottesville: University Press of Virginia, 2007), 1.

38. Elizabeth Christine Russ, *The Plantation in the Postslavery Imagination* (Oxford: Oxford University Press, 2009), 3.

39. Weheliye, *Habeas Viscus,* 30.

40. Handley, *Postslavery Literatures in the Americas*, 5, 16.

41. Ibid, 18.

42. Ifeoma Kiddoe Nwankwo, *Black Cosmopolitanism: Racial Consciousness and Transnational Identity in the Nineteenth-Century Americas* (Philadelphia: University of Pennsylvania Press, 2005).

43. Because I will discuss different aspects related to mulatos vs. mulatas, I have chosen to use the Spanish spelling of the terms and to use a slash when I am referring to both.

44. Handley, *Postslavery Literatures in the Americas*, 5.

45. Saidiya V. Hartman, *Scenes of Subjection: Terror Slavery, and Self-Making in Nineteenth-Century America* (New York: Oxford University Press, 1997), 7.

46. Andrews, *To Tell a Free Story*, 36.

47. Ibid., 56.

48. Anthony Bogues, "The Political Thought of Quobna Cugoano: Radicalized Natural Liberty," in *Black Heretics/Black Prophets: Radical Political Intellectuals* (New York: Routledge, 2003), 25–46.

49. Orlando Patterson, *Slavery and Social Death. A Comparative Study* (Cambridge: Harvard University Press, 1982), 1–2.

50. Ibid., 5.

51. Ibid., 79.

52. Ibid. 96.

53. Ibid.

54. Andrews, *To Tell a Free Story*, 1.

55. Charles T. Davis and Henry Louis Gates Jr., *The Slave's Narrative* (New York: Oxford University Press, 1985), xiii.

56. Ibid., 37.

57. See William L. Andrews' *To Tell a Free Story* and John Sekora's "Black Message/White Envelope: Genre, Authenticity, and Authority in the Antebellum Slave Narrative," *Callaloo* 10, no. 3 (Summer 1987): 482–515. As I will discuss later, there is a striking difference in the volume of slave narratives produced in Cuba versus the United States.

58. Miriam DeCosta-Willis, "Self and Society in the Afro-Cuban Slave Narrative," *Latin American Literary Review* 16, no. 31 (January–June 1988): 7.

59. Throughout the course of his life, Frederick Douglass wrote three autobiographies: *The Narrative of the Life of Frederick Douglass, An American Slave* (1845), *My Bondage and My Freedom* (1855), and *Life and Times of Frederick Douglass* (1881). Douglass engaged in continual negotiation regarding not only his own place within society but also the place of his people. In print and in speeches, Douglass argued for the full participation of African Americans in American society. For the purposes at hand, *Narrative of the Life of Frederick Douglass, An American Slave,* represents the clearest example of a discourse of Afro–New World identity coming into conversation with the master narratives of the day. Further, it is the only autobiography written while Douglass was still legally a slave and the text most contemporary to Manzano's. Luis A. Jiménez's 1995 article began a comparison of these two texts. Jiménez writes of a "hidden unity" between the two men based on his reading of the silences within the two texts. Luis A. Jiménez "Nineteenth Century Autobiography in the Afro-Americas: Frederick Douglass and Juan Francisco Manzano," *Afro Hispanic Review* 14, no. 2 (Fall 1995): 47.

60. In Cuba, Gertrudis Gomez de Avellaneda's *Sab* and Cirilo Villaverde's *Cecilia Valdés* are the two most famous. In the United States, Lydia Maria Child's "The Quadroons" and "Slavery's Pleasant Homes" and Harriet Beecher Stowe's *Uncle Tom's Cabin* are works that engage the tragic mulato/a character type. William Wells Brown's *Clotel* is another example, this time written by an African American author.

61. Vera Kutzinski, *Sugar's Secrets: Race and the Erotics of Cuban Nationalism* (Charlottesville: University Press of Virginia, 1993), 21, 7.

62. Lauren Berlant, "National Brands/National Body: Imitation of life," in *The Phantom Public Sphere*, ed. Bruce Robbins (Minneapolis: University of Minnesota Press, 1993), 113.

63. Quoted in Sollors, *Neither Black Nor White*, 235.

64. Ramos, "Cuerpo, Lengua, Subjetividad," 233.

65. Werner Sollors, *Neither Black nor White yet Both: Thematic Explorations of Interracial Literature* (New York: Oxford University Press, 1997), 223–225.

66. Ibid., 234.

67. Frances Smith Foster, *Witnessing Slavery: The Development of Ante-Bellum Slave Narratives* (Madison: University of Wisconsin Press, 1994), 147.

68. William Luis, *Literary Bondage: Slavery in the Cuban Narrative* (Austin: University of Texas Press, 1990), 39.

Chapter Two

Countering Negation in Juan Francisco Manzano and Frederick Douglass's Early Texts and Patronage Relationships

On the third of November, 1845, Frederick Douglass delivered an address in Cork, Ireland, on the topic of the annexation of Texas. In the speech, Douglass criticizes the United States' annexation of Texas. As Douglass tells the story, the conflict arose when Mexico abolished slavery in Texas, but the "Texicans" introduced slaves despite the legal proscription.[1] He excoriates the United States for "pretending" good relations with Mexico while encouraging the Texicans to rebel and claims the annexation of Texas was done in "indecent haste."[2] His final and most cogent critique is that the main reason the United States allowed Texas to add their star to the Stars and Stripes was to expand the market for slaves in North America in order to keep prices high and the slave trade profitable.[3] While for the creators of the Cuban flag, Texas was a symbol of freedom from Spanish rule, for Douglass it was a symbol of the hypocritical and unconscionable power of the United States and its commitment to the peculiar institution. This is an example of the sustained campaign waged by Douglass in speeches and in written texts to expose the evils of slavery and American society and to fight for the abolition of the former and the transformation of the latter. It is also an example of how authors like Douglass appropriate and reinterpret national symbols in order to challenge ideas of national identity that exclude them.

Cuban slave author Juan Francisco Manzano also had a sustained public discourse that, often much more obliquely, challenged the institution of slavery and the social mores of his day. In his most famous poem *"Treinta años"*

23

["Thirty Years"], Manzano writes of fate and the struggle that he has had to undergo as someone who was born to misfortune and who has suffered his entire life.[4] While the narrator never identifies himself as being a slave, the assumption made both in the nineteenth century and today is that the poem is autobiographical, and nineteenth-century Cuban readers would likely have known Manzano was a slave. I agree with Azougarh's assessment that while Manzano may not have been able to directly refer to slavery in many of his poems, his focus on his terrible destiny, impious fortune, unhappy birth, and sad misfortune are euphemisms for his enslavement.[5] The choice not to mention slavery also makes the poem more universal and by doing so, invites readers to empathize with the narrator and thus with the slave. The final stanza of *"Treinta años"* concludes with the poignant idea that even more difficult than the suffering and misfortune of his first thirty years is imagining the hardships he is destined to face in the future. The narrative voice's apostrophic cry to God in this stanza heightens the emotion of the description of his sufferings, both past and projected.[6] The lament makes clear that as someone who suffers the tragic fate of being considered not-quite-human in his society, he has little hope that his situation will change. He makes an implicit critique of a society that would doom anyone to the fate of the slave, let alone someone who can so eloquently write about his destiny; the existence of a slave poet in and of itself is an argument against much of the dehumanizing discourse associated with racialization and slavery. By both its very existence and its content, Manzano's literary production represents a sustained campaign against tyranny and racialization in Cuba.

This chapter centers on the politics, circumstances, texts, and relationships surrounding the production of slave narratives by these two authors serving as a background against which the *Autobiografía de Juan Francisco Manzano* and *Narrative of the Life of Frederick Douglass, An American Slave* can be read as transformative discourses of Afro–New World identity. Both Manzano and Douglass were born into slavery and both men wrote these versions of their life stories after having become fugitives, but before legally gaining their freedom.[7] Both men were also known for producing texts before writing their autobiographies: Manzano for his poetry and Douglass for his anti-slavery speeches. Poetry and oration were part of the process by which they came to understand their societies and their own identities. They are also fora that the men used to further anti-slavery arguments. Finally, Manzano's poetry and Douglass's oratory are what brought them to the attention of their patrons. Manzano wrote the story of the first part of his *Autobiografía* in 1835 at the request of Domingo del Monte, a member of the *criollo* elite in Cuba who had befriended the slave after having read his poetry. Douglass's text was written in 1845 as part of his participation in William Lloyd Garrison's American Anti-Slavery Society, participation which started after Garrison saw him speak at an anti-slavery meeting. Both

Douglass and Manzano had to negotiate the complexities of these patronage relationships during the production of their autobiographical slave narratives. What becomes evident from looking at the historical context, the complex relationships Manzano and Douglass had with their patrons, and their early works is that both men intentionally entered into dialogue with ideas of racial and national identity to challenge the exclusionary nature of these constructs.

LAW, CUSTOM, AND STEREOTYPE IN THE SOCIAL CONSTRUCTION OF THE SLAVE

The need for patrons rose in part from the status of the slave in the nineteenth-century Plantation America of which Cuba and the United States were a part. The legal, social, economic, and cultural line between enslaver and enslaved created in part through the process of racialization was intended to be an unambiguous demarcation. Although not all New World slave systems defined the same relationship between enslaver and slave, while there were free people of color in both nineteenth-century Cuba and the United States, and while the slave systems in both countries developed loopholes like the ability for a slave to buy his or her freedom, the distinction between slave and citizen in these two societies was intended as an impassable boundary. In each of these lands, racializing assemblages worked to ensure that slaves and enslavers were not able to switch roles. This in part explains the way in which slavery and race became inextricably linked in the Americas. As Waldo E. Martin explains, race was a "potent human myth" that "in nineteenth-century America clarified the status quo among various known peoples and underlaid America's national identity."[8] This was also true in Cuba where legal, civil, and religious authorities worked to identify and control slaves, and the slave who desired freedom faced overwhelming physical barriers, and the daunting task of overcoming social negation, of crossing the socially constructed barrier between slave and enslaver, subject and citizen, nonhuman and human. The laws governing slavery and the social structures involved in its maintenance were further strengthened by the fact that racialization occurred on every level, permeating society's customs, common sayings, religious discourse, literature, and other cultural expressions.

Although the practice of slavery did not always correspond to the rhetoric, the discourses surrounding slavery in Cuba and the United States appear to have been framed and complicated by different legal and ideological concerns. Slave codes in Spanish colonies were based on *Las Siete Partidas del rey Alfonso el sabio*, a set of laws compiled at the direction of King Alfonso X between 1263 and 1265. Under this system, the humanity of the slave was legally upheld. Spanish colonial law considered slaves as human beings and subjects of the Spanish monarch who fell under the jurisdiction of the Catholic Church.[9] One implication of this structure was the belief that slaves had souls and should be taught religion. These layers of hierarchy—monarch, church, and slaveholders—created a paternalistic ideology of slavery that in theory protected some basic rights of the slave. The United States, on the other hand, had a different set of complex ideas regarding the status of slaves. The difference in attitudes towards slavery in the United States did not come solely from the fact that the British system had a different history and rhetoric than the Spanish. Another significant difference arose from the fact that Cuba remained a colony for more than a century after the United States became a sovereign nation. In the United States, the rhetoric of slavery was negotiated and constructed within the context of the American Revolution and the establishment of an independent republic. While it seems overdone to mention the irony of the coexistence of slavery with the ideals of life, liberty, and the pursuit of happiness, it is nonetheless relevant. Slaves were legally nonhuman; they were considered chattel, moveable property, things. From the time the United States *Constitution* was ratified in 1789 until the passing of the thirteenth and fourteenth amendments in 1865 and 1868 abolishing slavery and conferring citizenship upon former slaves, another way that slaves were legally not-quite-human came from their definition in the three-fifths clause of the constitution as mathematically less than a full person for purposes of representation. The legal codes of the United States continually reinforced the dehumanization and consequent stripping of rights of African American slaves. In addition, the major denominations of the protestant church in the southern states often supported the institution of slavery. Just as Cuban slaves were understood within a rhetoric of paternalism, slaves in the United States came to be understood within the legal system of chattel slavery which increasingly defined them as property rather than persons, and which had a clearly defined place for them as objects located within rather than subjects of the nation. Any slave who wished to redefine his or her status had to negotiate within these paradigms.

However, despite the de jure differences, the de facto realities in the United States and Cuba were much more reflective of each other. One similarity is in the construction of slaves as being like children. In Cuba, the monarch and the church theoretically worked to ensure some basic rights but, more importantly, slaveholders were expected to treat their slaves as less-developed human beings—metaphorically akin to children. For example, one passage from *Las Siete Partidas* describes the legal consequences of the violent death of a slave as a serious matter because although "[t]he father may punish his son moderately, and the master his slave," he should not be "so cruel and so excessive in doing this, that they do evil."[10] Here we see the analogy: master is to slave as father is to son. Certainly, it would be foolish to argue that all enslavers considered and treated their slaves like children or that the slaves themselves believed or felt that way, but, within the rhetoric of slavery in Cuba, the idea of slavery as based on a pseudo-family relationship served to make the institution more palatable to slaveholders without, as we shall see in the discussion of Manzano's text, improving the lives of the slaves. In his discussion of natal alienation, Patterson explains many of the rituals associated with this practice, among which are the denying of natal kin ties and the creation of "fictive kin bonds to the master and his family."[11] In the United States, one small example of this practice was the identification of slaves with their masters through the imposition of the master's last name. These were not empowering kin bonds, as the fictive kinship was "quasi-filial"; that is, the metaphor of kinship was used "as a means of expressing an authority relation between master and slave, and a state of loyalty to the kinsmen of the master."[12] Additionally, these fictive kinship ties were sometimes ironically and hypocritically coexistent with the actual biological kinship of masters and slaves that occurred due to the rape of slaves by their masters. In both Cuba and the United States, because slaves were seen as perpetual children, they were by definition considered incapable of full participation in society. The equation of slavery with people of African descent was so entrenched that the same problem obtained for free blacks within both nations. This meant that even if Douglass and Manzano became emancipated, they would still not be considered a part of society and would not be considered citizens.[13]

In addition, nineteenth-century black authors had to negotiate a hostile field of other socially accepted conventions of African American and Afro-Cuban identity. One important aspect of the construction of slaves as nonhuman or not-quite-human which mired the slave in his/her status was the assumption of and stubborn belief in the slave's intellectual, spiritual, and moral inferiority. This believed inferiority can be clearly seen in the stereotypes associated with people of African descent in both the United States and Cuba. Patterson explains that symbols are a major instrument in creating and maintaining power and he locates the site of authority in the ability to "control (or at least be in a position to manipulate) appropriate symbolic instruments."[14] In the US context, as John W. Blassingame writes, "[m]ost antebellum whites firmly believed that Africans were ignoble savages who were innately barbaric, imitative, passive, cheerful, childish, lazy, cowardly, superstitious, polygamous, immoral, and stupid."[15] Patterson discusses the "ideology of 'Sambo,' the degraded man-child that, to the southerner, constituted the image of the slave."[16] The characteristics he describes are similar to those detailed by Blassingame: docility, irresponsibility, laziness, immorality, silliness, and childishness; Patterson quotes Stanley Elkins as indicating that "this childlike quality . . . was the very key to his being."[17] Significantly, Patterson adds that "[a]n almost identical stereotype of the slave existed in the Caribbean."[18] The construction of the slave as child in Cuba is closely related to the myth of the "degraded man-child" in the United States. In writing of Cuba, Julio Ramos echoes some of the ideas of these stereotypes when he argues that slave testimony was considered invalid in nineteenth-century Cuba due to the belief that Africans were immoral and lacked basic reason.[19] Most importantly for this study, Patterson concludes that this kind of stereotype is "an ideological imperative of all systems of slavery"; the stereotype is "an elaboration of the notion that the slave is quintessentially a person without honor," someone defined by "the total absence of any hint of 'manhood.'"[20] The emphasis on manhood here points to the particularly masculine nature of constructions of national identity in the nineteenth century and adds yet another layer to the ways in which slaves, both corporately and as individuals, were excluded from the nation. Individuals like Douglass and Manzano were considered as negations; they were nonhuman or not-quite-human, not free, not white, not participants in "manhood," and therefore, for all of these reasons, not citizens.

African Americans and Afro-Cubans in the nineteenth century were also seen as embodying the threat of physical and sexual violence. Not only did slaves face the assumptions inscribed upon them as people of African descent—that they were for all intents and purposes nonhuman beings incapable of the intellectual and spiritual sophistication of whites—writers like Douglass and Manzano had to further counteract the rhetoric of rebellion and criminality implied by their status as fugitive slaves.[21] William Luis describes slaves in general and fugitives in particular as being represented in Cuban fiction as "morally corrupt," "libidinal," and threatening[22] —this last so significant in Cuba because of the proximity and precedent of Haiti. This is evident in how free people of color were treated on the island and in the intense anxiety felt by the white *criollo* elite regarding the increasing Africanization of the population of Cuba in the nineteenth century. Along similar lines, according to Blassingame's reading of antebellum literature in the United States, the recurring character Nat was "[r]evengeful, blood-thirsty, cunning, treacherous, and savage . . . the incorrigible runaway, the poisoner of white men, the ravager of white women."[23] As fugitive slaves, Douglass and Manzano would have to overcome the stigma of rebellion and the implied threat of violence in their struggle to create an effective ethos, to garner for themselves the credibility to write about their identities and their lives. Particularly for Douglass, to present himself, even in the North, as a fugitive slave in the antebellum United States was to enter into an occupied rhetorical landscape evoking images of the murderous rage of violent slave rebellions and the fear of the consequences to the purity of the white race and society should blacks be granted freedom.

MANZANO, THE *DELMONTINOS,*
AND RICHARD ROBERT MADDEN

All of the stereotypes produced as a byproduct of racialization made it difficult for current and former slaves to have their stories heard and to enter into public conversations about both personal and national identity in their homelands. Since a large part of the power of masters lay in their control of "symbolic instruments," it "effectively persuaded both slave and others that the master was the only mediator between the living community to which he belonged and the living death the slave experienced."[24] Douglass and Manzano were considered nonhuman or not-quite human beings so it was difficult on their own to write autobiographies that would be read by others. Unsurprisingly, in this context both Juan Francisco Manzano and Frederick Douglass negotiated relationships with patrons who could serve as the mediator between the slave and society. While in neither case are the relationships unproblematic, without figures like Domingo del Monte and William Lloyd Garrison we would likely not have these texts to consider. Examining the manner in which patronage relationships simultaneously open space for and hem in the discourses of identity created by Douglass and Manzano aids in developing a richer understanding of some of the choices made by these authors in their texts. In the case of Manzano, his relationship with Domingo Del Monte and the members of Del Monte's *tertulia,* and their desire for him to write his own story gave him the discursive space in which to write himself, but the presence of Del Monte and others complicated the production and reception of the text. For a century the text became what they intended it to be. In the case of Douglass, not only did his patrons support and encourage him, they also added framing narratives which invested Douglass with certain characteristics, prefiguring him for the reader as the free man of moral standing he was to depict within his text. For both Douglass and Manzano, the support and framing by patrons was according to the patrons' agendas, not the slave narrators' own. In both cases, Douglass and Manzano received a certain amount of authentication, but at the cost of accommodating their patrons and being subsumed into larger political projects which overlapped with, but were not identical to, their own.

Juan Francisco Manzano was born in Cuba in 1797. He grew up in a time when the Cuban economy was increasingly dominated by sugar production due to the boom of sugar demand in the early nineteenth century, the decline of Haiti as a sugar producer following the Haitian Revolution, and the importation of English and American technology. These changes transformed Cuban slavery and Cuban culture.[25] The effects were far reaching, from increased importation of slaves which changed the racial makeup of the island, to deforestation, to a revamped Spanish bureaucracy brought about through the Bourbon Reforms to further modernization of production, efficient colonial administration, and consolidation of Spain's economic and political power. The efforts by Spain to strengthen their power over their colonies led to a backlash by Cuban creoles and an increase in Cuban nationalist sentiment. Manzano's patron, Domingo del Monte, was engaged in the nationalist project. Del Monte has been called "the first great patriarch of Cuban *belles lettres*."[26] A proponent of independence, Del Monte believed that the production of a national literature was necessary to the creation of a free and independent Cuban nation. As "a reformer intent on building a Cuban literary tradition,"[27] he hosted a *tertulia* of writers which contained almost the entire Cuban intellectual class of his time.[28] Del Monte served as bibliographer, literary critic, and patriarch for his intellectual community; he is credited with introducing neoclassicism, romanticism, and realism to Cuba, and also with persuading the writers in his *tertulia* to focus on "New World and Cuban motifs" in literature, including slavery.[29] Domingo del Monte increasingly supported abolition and the production of anti-slavery literature, including Manzano's life story, during the peak of Cuban slavery and Cuba's domination of world sugar production.[30] Like many of his contemporaries, del Monte feared that too large a percentage of the population of Cuba was black, and his vision for the imagined Cuban nation was based on the ideal of the Western Man.

Although he thought that slavery would have to end for the good of Cuba, del Monte proposed a plan under which Cuba would first end its participation in the slave trade, and then gradually abolish slavery while importing free white workers to offset the perceived racial imbalance on the island. In "Cuban Whites and the Problem of Slavery," Robert Paquette explains that "[d]uring the first half of the nineteenth century, no Cuban-born white, or at least no Cuban-born white of standing, held anything near to the uncompromising, immediatist abolitionism of a . . . William Lloyd Garrison."[31] Del Monte was not entirely altruistic and his vision for a proposed Cuban nation did not necessarily have room for former slaves.[32] He wanted to see a free and independent Cuba *with his class in power*; for this reason, among others, del Monte wanted to ease into abolition by ending the slave trade and reimplementing a paternalistic model of slavery, the less virulent slavery that Spanish slave codes, based on *Las Siete Partidas*, suggested. Domingo del Monte's primary focus was the constitution of a Cuban nation, a nation that did not necessarily include free black citizens. Sonia Labrador-Rodríguez points out that as the incorporation of blacks in Cuban society and in the foundation of a Cuban national identity was not part of the *delmontine* agenda, Manzano was mainly important to the *Delmontinos* as a slave-poet providing testimony that would justify their fight against the slave trade. The members of the Cuban *criollo* elite gathered in del Monte's *tertulia* asked Manzano for his testimony precisely to support their plans to create a whitened Cuban society and culture.[33]

The fact that del Monte was younger than Manzano is striking because it underscores the extent to which Manzano's slave status invalidated him in the eyes of society and made him dependent on the intervention of those with social status. In negotiating a relationship with del Monte, Manzano gained readers that desired to hear his story and whose social, political, and economic agendas allowed space for his own personal project. The *delmontinos* were also crucial in collecting the money needed to eventually buy Manzano's freedom. In terms of the need for patronage, one aspect of Cuban society which worked to Manzano's advantage was the fact that *criollo* intellectuals like del Monte looked on slavery not only as an economic system, but also as it related to the relationship between colony and colonizer. Cuban planters like del Monte ultimately felt conflicted in supporting slavery because they saw the master/slave relationship as analogous to the metropolis/colony relationship.[34] The anxiety inherent in a colonized position strongly influenced the ideas of *criollo* intellectuals regarding slavery. Their anti-colonial vision and the perceived need for the transformation of the Cuban slave system led del Monte and his *tertulia*—men who represented intellectual authority in Creole Cuban society—to provide a readership for Manzano's discourse of identity.

While del Monte did not pick up a pen and author Manzano's life history, he did authorize the text and appropriate it into his own national project once it was produced. As various critics have already detailed, Manzano's text was revised and corrected by a member of del Monte's *tertulia*, anti-slavery novelist Anselmo Suárez y Romero,[35] and included in a dossier of materials del Monte gave to the Irish abolitionist Richard R. Madden. Madden included a translated and re-revised version of Manzano's text in *The Life and Poems of a Cuban Slave*, published in London in 1840. This text erased Manzano's name and sandwiched the highly abridged narrative in between texts written by Madden. Manzano's original manuscript was not rediscovered and published in Spanish in Cuba until 1937, more than a century after its composition. Manzano's text was co-opted into del Monte's desire for a Cuban nation and Madden's abolitionist project. In addition, his testimony was, in William Luis's words, "a model for and a generator of narrative production" by those in del Monte's *tertulia*; many of the ideas and themes in Manzano's writings were repeated in other anti-slavery texts produced by members of this group.[36] Another symptom of the fact that Manzano had to overcome having his humanity, freedom, manhood, and citizenship negated by society was his lack of control of his own autobiography. Within that life story, as we shall see in the next chapter, are various negotiations with and challenges to the very rhetoric that constructed him as a negation, an object of discourse rather than a speaking subject.

DOUGLASS AND THE
GARRISONIAN ABOLITIONISTS

The paradigms of identity—of manhood, freedom, and citizenship—that branded Douglass a slave, a brute, a fugitive, and, most devastating for his political cause, a necessarily unreliable witness, were significant difficulties for Douglass to overcome, particularly since he hoped to reach a much wider audience with his text than Manzano had. Early slave narratives from the late eighteenth and early nineteenth centuries published in Britain and the United States like those of Gronniosaw, Marrant, and Jea were very closely tied to conversion and captivity narratives and were often written down by an aman- uensis. They were examples of "autobiography simplex," narratives that cen- tered on one overriding pattern or metaphor, which was usually the narrative of spiritual salvation for the slave narrator.[37] They made implicit arguments against slavery in that the salvation of the narrator implied his humanity which then challenged many justifications for slavery. The slave narratives of the 1840s in the United States, Douglass's most notably, were distinct in their North American, antebellum, fugitive consciousness that presented a new kind of conversion narrative; rather than focusing on the slave narrator's conversion from heathen to Christian (and from slavery to freedom through the workings of Providence), the texts present an opportunity for the reader to be converted to action for the cause of abolition.[38] They were part of the larger abolitionist movement that, while it clearly focused on the abolition of slavery, was also a movement that challenged many aspects of American society and posited the need for a radical change in national identity. In writing his life story, Douglass was associated with William Lloyd Garrison and the American Anti-Slavery Society. Garrison championed the use of moral suasion rather than political means to defeat slavery, advocating im- mediate and total abolition. He "believed that slavery was based on a racism that pervaded the structure of society—including its fundamental political and religious institutions."[39] However, although Garrison imagined a trans- formed America with different institutions, Garrison was not a radical and never proposed social equality for blacks. He had a very particular vision for how Douglass, whom he met in 1841 after hearing Douglass's first speech at an Anti-Slavery meeting, should be incorporated into the abolitionist cause. Garrison knew the movement could benefit from Douglass's eyewitness tes- timony so he worked to imbue the man and his 1845 *Narrative* with the authority necessary to be accepted as a credible witness.

From the perspective of a nineteenth-century reader, given the lack of authority of the fugitive slave, the first step in the process of accepting Douglass's discourse of personal and social identity occurred during the process of reading the texts which frame and introduce Douglass's 1845 *Narrative*, the paratext. Douglass's text is introduced by two documents: a lengthy preface by Garrison and a shorter letter from Wendell Phillips, Esq., another well-known abolitionist. Several critics have demonstrated the extent to which Garrison and other white abolitionists limited and subsumed slave narrators into their own political projects. For example, Beth A. McCoy's work on paratexts in the African American struggle for freedom persuasively demonstrates that they "have functioned centrally as a zone transacting ever-changing modes of white domination and of resistance to that domination."[40] McCoy emphasizes that the paratexts do not serve the author or the text, but rather function as "an indirect white supremacy . . . that interferes with the fugitive writer's authorial primacy."[41] Both Garrison and Phillips character-ize their slave witness as part of their attempt to control the narrative. Al-though the two introductory texts address the need for true accounts of slav-ery, their main focus is on Douglass himself. Following the logic of their own agendas, these paratextual authors achieve four major discursive ends: Garrison and Phillips describe Douglass's moral and religious character, as-sert the former slave's intellectual ability, defend Douglass's right to speak, and define him as possessing a non-threatening manhood. These aspects highlight the need to overcome the ways in which racialization has negated Douglass's identity and credibility.

In his preface, Garrison invests Frederick Douglass with many important characteristics to give him credibility and empower him to persuade his audience. Garrison first and most thoroughly addresses the subject of Doug-lass's religious and moral sophistication. The famous abolitionist discusses at length Douglass's "virtuous traits of character" [42] to counteract the common stereotype produced by racialization which defined slaves as naturally lazy, promiscuous, deceitful, and devious. In the preface, Garrison blames the institution of slavery for any perceived depravities in the slave. The subject of morality resonates strongly in the preface as Garrison imbues Douglass with the characteristics necessary to make him a reliable witness and critic of the system of slavery. Similarly, Wendell Phillips, Esq. validates his "Dear Friend" Douglass when he asserts "we have known you long, and can put the most entire confidence in your truth, candor, and sincerity."[43] Phillips writes a character reference for the fugitive slave, carefully describing Douglass as one of "God's children." [44] The moral standing constructed by and witnessed to in the introductory texts framing his *Narrative* helps authorize Douglass's denunciations of the immorality of slavery and simultaneously increases the rhetorical, political, and social force of his self-description as a free (hu)man.

Although imbuing Douglass with the proper moral and religious character was important in order for him to be believed as a credible witness against slavery, Garrison's text also works to promote Douglass as an intellect ca-pable of social comment. To this end, Garrison speaks of Douglass not just as intelligent, but as a "prodigy" in "natural eloquence," stating that "[a]s a public speaker, he excels in pathos, wit, comparison, imitation, strength of reasoning, and fluency of language."[45] The repetition of characteristics also serves to underscore the mental capabilities demonstrated by Douglass. Garrison's account paints Douglass as a figure with the "wit," "reasoning," and "fluency" to write himself into history.[46] Although he emphasizes Douglass as gifted, Garrison does not describe Douglass as unusual or unique. As Frances Smith Foster explains, since slave narratives were written to "expose the perfidy of slavery, the tension between the depiction of the protagonist as individual and the protagonist as every slave becomes obvious."[47] Garrison lays the foundation for a more general attack on slavery supported by a discourse of inherent African American intellectual ability. According to Garrison's logic, blacks needed time and opportunity in order to attain the highest human achievements, and, considering the extent to which slavery caused the debasement of the people, it was surprising how well they had done.[48] With this line of reasoning, Garrison addresses Douglass's intellectual ability in order to validate his text.

As a chattel slave, property and not a person, Douglass faced perhaps his greatest obstacle because he dared to speak against his condition. Racialization defined him as being outside of humanity and society, denying him the right to enter into the conversation about his moral, intellectual, and social status. Since many nineteenth-century readers might have considered it a great impropriety for an ex-slave to dare to write about his own life, Garrison argues that it is both reasonable and proper for Douglass to write an account of his life as a slave. Garrison works to further circumvent the possible argument that the work is not Douglass's own by stating that it is "entirely his own" and once again underscores how "creditable" this achievement is to Douglass's moral and intellectual standing.[49] Wendell Phillips, Esq. uses both religious and patriotic rhetoric to demonstrate Douglass's right to speak. Phillips "was glad to learn, in your story, how early the most neglected of God's children waken to a sense of their rights, and of the injustice done them."[50] Phillips puts Douglass on the side of God and justice, considering natural the fact that as one of "God's children" he has rights. Phillips later directly compares Douglass to the greatest icons of the rhetoric of American citizenship, the founding fathers. Speaking of the danger Douglass faces by publishing his name and the facts of his life, Phillips compares him to the signers of the Declaration of Independence who signed "with the halter about their necks."[51] Phillips's statement points to the very real physical danger that Douglass was in as a fugitive slave. More importantly, by metaphorically equating Douglass with the founding fathers, slave owners with the oppressive English colonial government, and Douglass's *Narrative* with no less than the Declaration of Independence, Phillips awakens the patriotism of his audience and prepares them to accept Douglass as a witness and spokesman for the "new" American cause—abolition. Phillips counteracts the power of the three-fifths clause through the use of a metaphoric comparison between

Douglass and the founding fathers, opening up a rhetorical space in which Douglass and other former slaves can be considered citizens of the American nation.

Since the fear of rebellion was a significant barrier for fugitive slaves and the cause of abolition, Garrison took great care in his preface to present Douglass as possessing an acceptable, non-threatening manhood. Garrison describes the kind of man Douglass is in order to calm the fears evoked by the specter of Nat, the savage black male. Garrison describes Douglass as industrious, intelligent, and talented but emphasizes that "He has borne himself with gentleness and meekness, yet with true manliness of character."[52] Garrison's discourse emphasizes not Douglass's manhood, which might have seemed threatening, but rather his "gentleness" and "meekness," leaving the adjective "manliness" to apply not to the man himself, but to his character. The rhetoric of humility posits Douglass as a safe figure who would never, as some whites feared, try to kill the master or rape the mistress. Like all aspects of the picture of Douglass painted by Garrison and Phillips, the rhetoric of humility is a careful construction designed to weaken the objections that readers schooled in the dominant paradigms of nineteenth-century social identity would likely raise in relation to the fugitive slave's *Narrative*.

MANZANO AS POET AND DOUGLASS AS ORATOR

Lest a discussion of the patronage relationships obscure the significance of Manzano's and Douglass's abilities as creators engaged in ongoing conversations about their identities and their place in the nation, it is important to remember that both men produced numerous texts prior to the writing of their slave narratives. Douglass's speech on the annexation of Texas at the beginning of this chapter, although it closely postdates the publication of the *Narrative*, was one in a series of speeches given on the abolitionist lecture circuit and Manzano's previously discussed sonnet "*Treinta años*" is representative of his wider poetic production. Both men were already using language to engage with the possibilities and problems of romantic ideals like freedom and equality and citizenship as they were debated in their homelands. However, they did so from very different positions. Manzano was an individual poet writing of his life in Cuba. He had started composing verses by memory as a young man even before becoming literate. Before meeting Domingo del Monte he had published two collections of poetry, *Poesías líricas* (1821) and *Flores pasageras* [sic] (1830). Beginning in 1841, Douglass was a speaker participating in the anti-slavery movement in the northern United States.[53] One obvious difference is that their texts were produced in very different rhetorical situations. Where Manzano's emphasis appears to be artistic and personal, Douglass's was very clearly argumentative and political. While the genre and style of the works may be different, there are both significant similarities and interesting differences in the main themes and ideas expressed in their works.

One common theme in both Douglass's speeches and Manzano's poetry is religion. In Douglass's early speeches, "[n]o theme . . . occupied his attention more than religion."[54] When referring to religion, Douglass's focus is social and political; he calls out Christian hypocrisy, denounces the abusive nature of Christian slaveholders, and highlights the hypocrisy in the American church's support of slavery.[55] Douglass argues against slavery in two ways, by seeking to undermine religious justifications for it and by showing how it corrupts true religion. Manzano also engages the theme of religion in his poetry, most notably in the poem "Oda a la religión" ["Ode to Religion"]. The genre named in the title indicates right away that Manzano's approach is different than Douglass's; where Douglass is critical of religion as it is practiced in the United States, Manzano's poem is a more personal expression of the value of religious faith that not only lends him credibility, but also implies the injustice of his situation. The poem begins with a narrator who looks to God in his tribulations and who, while praising God, expounds on the sweet comfort that Christianity gives to the disgraced one who finds himself undone by the insane afflictions of life.[56] On first examination it appears that Manzano's approach is a personal and emotional expression rather than a social critique. As with *"Treinta años,"* the insane afflictions that cause the narrator to cry out to God for comfort in "Oda a la religión" can be read as code for his enslavement and the fact that he is disgraced can also be attributed to the lack of honor, social position, and humanity attributed to the slave. Thus the poem, like Douglass's speeches, does perform a social critique and presents an argument against slavery.

Manzano's work is replete with appeals to pathos like those in *"Treinta años"* and *"Oda a la religión."* Things can be so pitiable in the world of Manzano's poetry that the narrator in *"A la muerte"* ["To Death"] detests his own existence[57] and another lyric poem is titled *"Una hora de tristeza"* ["An hour of sadness"]. The influence of romanticism is evident, but Manzano's focus on the pathos of his situation clearly relates to being a slave. Manzano is not the only one to focus on the pathos of the slave's situation. Douglass's speeches also involved a number of appeals to pathos, including eyewitness descriptions of the horrors of slavery[58] and laments regarding the separation of slave families.[59] Manzano takes on the theme of separation in *"La esclava ausente"* ["The Absent Slave Woman"] in which the title character expounds upon the strength of love even in the face of separation.[60] Reminiscent of Douglass's critiques in his speeches of the horrors and sufferings of slaves,[61] Manzano's narrator speaks of the horrors of slavery and calls the master both inhuman and terrible both for his treatment of the slave and also for separating the lovers, pointing out that loving was never a crime.[62] Both authors appeal to the values of their audiences when they call them to witness physical abuse and the severing of family relationships.

As one might expect, Manzano has a number of poems that contain a very different register and different themes than Douglass's speeches. Romanticism was a significant influence, and among his poems are odes to roses and music, among other things. However, even Manzano's ability to participate in the genres and tropes of romanticism is an implicit argument against his perceived lack of humanity and reason. The subject matter for the majority of Manzano's poems can be attributed to the reality that slaves faced in Cuba; they are in the tragic mode and emphasize destiny, suffering, and pain.[63] His poem "A la calumnia" ["On Slander"] stands out because it directly addresses the topic of honor (or the lack thereof) that Patterson highlights in his discussion of slavery. The first stanza of the short poem speaks of the power of slander; in the second stanza the narrator warns that the one who is prepared to slander another should be wary because slander often hurts the one who commits it.[64] While it can be read as a simple proverbial poem, how interesting for the slave, a being so maligned and negated by society, to warn that those who slander are likely to be the ones who suffer the consequences in the end.

One final poem by Manzano that is more overtly political and anti-slavery is "*Un sueño*" ["A Dream"]. In the poem, dedicated to one of his brothers, Manzano's narrator expresses the pathos of his separation from family due to slavery, seeks solitude, and then dreams of growing wings and trying to escape Cuba carrying his brother in his arms. Flight is a common trope in Manzano's poetry and is predictably symbolic of escape, perspective, and freedom. For Rachel Price, distance and even exile are presented in the poem as "the longed for *antidotes* to a nightmarish reality of sugar mills and death."[65] Unfortunately, in "*Un sueño*," like Icarus who is cited in the poem, the brothers are unable to fly to freedom. This is partly due to the fact that they cannot return to the island which is "enemigo suelo" [enemy ground].[66] The ground itself is suspect because of its association with the plantation economy and slavery.[67] Manzano's is a variation of the exile consciousness that marks the period of the development of Cuban national identity. Emilia Tuerbe Tolón y Otero and her compatriots are physically in exile but still able to claim their homeland while rejecting Spanish rule. As a slave, Manzano is an internal exile, alienated from the land and the proto-nation due to the association of land and plantation slavery. In the poem he cannot necessarily imagine the island as a safe place. Despite the inability to help his brother escape slavery and the problematic nature of the "suelo," references to the mountains and to the *palenque* give the poem the consciousness of a *cimarrón*.[68] It includes reference to an alternate space in which the slave might become free and be able to affirm his identity beyond society's negation. This is also a poem in which we see a glimpse of Manzano's desire for freedom for someone other than himself—in this case, his brother. While his writings might appear personal rather than political, the "dream" of trying to save his brother can be read as representative of his desire to see the chains of slavery fall.

Topics in Frederick Douglass's speeches that were more overtly political rather than personal include the identity of the slave in the eyes of the Constitution, the need for northerners to dissolve their union with slaveholders,[69] and the issue of prejudice against color in the North.[70] Some of these themes came from the Garrisonian anti-slavery agenda, but Gary S. Selby effectively argues that although many read the early speeches as mere accommodation to the Garrisonian agenda, a close reading gives evidence that Douglass's ideology was often at odds with it.[71] Selby identifies several "points of tension" between the Garrisonian agenda and Douglass's speeches, including Douglass's depiction of slave identity.[72] Selby focuses on passages in which Douglass indicates slaves' self-awareness and their ability to negotiate the difficult realities of slave life and argues that Douglass presents slaves not as passive victims, but as astute negotiators of their social positions.[73] There are other aspects of the slave's perceived identity that Douglass highlights and challenges which further support Selby's assessment. In an address from 1842, Douglass makes a statement reminiscent of the previous discussion of how slaves were considered negations. Indicating his experiential knowledge of how slavery and racialization denied slaves an identity, Douglass states, "They are goods and chattels, not men. They are denied the privileges of the Christian—they are denied the rights of citizens. They are refused the claims of the man. They are not allowed the rights of the husband and the father. They may not name the name of Liberty."[74] Here Douglass details how humanity, religion, citizenship, manhood, family ties, and freedom are denied to slaves. He clearly hopes to evoke sympathy from his audience and to challenge them to question their own assumptions about slaves. The passage also indicates the difficult position from which he speaks/writes: how can a negation dare address society? His use of the pronoun "they" instead of "we" shows a grammatical distancing from this negation. The statement as a whole also indicates the scope of the task he hopes to achieve. Although ostensibly Douglass's project was that of the anti-slavery society, it was more than freedom that he wished to win for himself and his brethren. Douglass's speech implies that he imagines a future in which all Americans are free and have all the rights they deserve as (hu)man, Christian citizens.

Another example of how Douglas challenges the perceived identity of slaves can be found in his address to the Twelfth Annual Convention of the American Anti-Slavery Society in New York City. Douglass gave this speech on May 6, 1845, days before the publication of the *Narrative*. In it he makes a radical statement about his identity when he states, "These hands—are they not mine? This body—is it not mine? Again, I am your brother, white as you are. I am your blood-kin."[75] Through references to his hands and body—standing there right before the audience—he makes a claim to self-ownership. More than that, he makes even more radical the abolitionist slogan "Am I not a man and a brother?" by his statement, "I am your brother, white as you are. I am your blood-kin." Douglass's use of the rhetoric of family can be read as metaphorical here: he and his audience may appear to be different, but they are brothers. They have a shared nature, a shared nation, and a shared religion. However, Douglass is all too well aware of the sexual abuse and exploitation of slave women and the realities of miscegenation in slavery. Seen in this light, his statement may also be a critique of this exploitation and a realistic assessment that the bloodlines of white and black America are intertwined.

One of the larger points in this section of the speech is that northerners who "continue in the Union" are just as culpable for slavery as slaveholders. After his statement about being blood-kin to his audience, Douglass continues by making a promise and reminding them of the reality of his status in the United States. "You don't get rid of me so easily," he promises, "I mean to hold on to you."[76] They are claimed, accountable. "And in this land of liberty, I'm a slave. The twenty-six States that blaze forth on your flag, proclaim a compact to return me to bondage if I run away, and keep me I bondage if I submit. Wherever I go, under the aegis of your liberty, there I'm a slave."[77] By invoking the flag, Douglass presents a symbol of the Union and of his audience's union with slaveholders. He also invokes all of the romantic ideals associated with the flag and the country, including liberty, in order to highlight the hypocrisy of American ideals versus American actions.

COMMON THREADS OF AMBIVALENCE AND RESISTANCE

Manzano's poems and Douglass's speeches give evidence of the thought and consideration they had given to their own sense of identity vis-à-vis their social construction as negations who did not possess any of the characteristics of the Western Man. They use religion, appeals to pathos, and notions of kinship to counter the dehumanizing force of slavery. They resist their negation at the hands of the racializing assemblages of society as they continually assert themselves as subjects rather than objects of discourse. Nevertheless, the patronage relationships surrounding the production of their slave narratives make them much more complex in terms of how to interpret Manzano and Douglass's accommodation versus resistance to the power and projects of del Monte and Garrison. According to Sonia Labrador-Rodríguez, if the promise of manumission became an incentive for writing, then master/slave roles could be been reinforced since this incentive could have compelled the slave writer to do what the patron wanted.[78] This contention raises the question as to whether in their slave narratives, despite their previous works which demonstrated radical ideas regarding their own identities, patronage relationships allowed either Douglass or Manzano to write anything, in Garrison's words, "entirely his own."

What is evident from the discussion of Manzano's poems and Douglass's speeches is that both men boldly entered into discourse in order to challenge their perceived status as negations. They contest the idea that they and other slaves and people of African descent in their lands are not free because they are nonhuman, nonwhite, non-"men," who have no honor nor family ties and are, for all of these reasons, not citizens. As we shall see in the following chapter, in his *Narrative*, Douglass exceeded Garrison's expectations, producing a text that narrated his life and denounced the evils of slavery, a text that negotiated both his identity as perceived by his readers and the status of his people within the nation and that echoed the themes from his speeches. While the 1835 *Autobiografía* is not unproblematic, it is also a text that works to serve the interests of both the author and his audience. The text emphasizes Manzano's identity as a creator and an intellectual, challenges many of the ideas of his society regarding Afro-Cuban identity, and echoes themes from his poetry. As the examination of *Autobiografía de Juan Francisco Manzano* and *Narrative of the Life of Frederick Douglass, an American Slave* in the next chapter will show, their adaptation and manipulation of some of the recurring ideas of this discussion allow these slave narrators, these nineteenth-century black intellectuals, to reimagine ideas of citizenship and national identity. Their slave narratives act as discourses of identity positing new ideas of national identity, ideas that are even more radically explored in their later works *Zafira* and *The Heroic Slave*.

NOTES

1. Frederick Douglass, *Frederick Douglass Papers, Series One: Speeches, Debates, and Interviews, V olume I (1841–1846)*, ed. John W. Blassingame (New Haven: Yale University Press, 1979), 73.
2. Ibid.
3. Ibid., 73–74.
4. Juan Francisco Manzano, *Juan Francisco Manzano: Autobiografía del esclavo poeta y otros escritos*, ed. William Luis (Madrid: Iberoamericana, 2007): 137–38.
5. Abdeslam Azougarh, *Juan Francisco Manzano: Esclavo poeta en la isla de Cuba* (Valencia: Ediciones Episteme S.L., 2000), 34.
6. Ibid.
7. After the production of his narrative, Manzano's patron Domingo del Monte collected money to buy Manzano's freedom. Similarly, in 1846 Douglass received the official documents that legally conferred the freedom he had taken when he became a fugitive. His legal freedom was bought by several of his English abolitionist friends who collected the money to buy his freedom. Some of Douglass's abolitionist contemporaries argued that the transaction was

counterproductive since it "recognizes [*sic*] the right of slaveowners to buy and sell persons." Frederick Douglass, *Autobiographies* (New York: Library of America, 1994), 1057.

8. Waldo E. Martin, *The Mind of Frederick Douglass* (Durham: The University of North Carolina Press, 1986), 197.

9. Herbert S. Klein, *Slavery in the Americas: A Comparative Study of Virginia and Cuba* (Chicago: University of Chicago Press, 1967), 66, 87.

10. Ibid., 60.

11. Patterson, *Slavery and Social Death*, 54.

12. Ibid.

13. Infantilization was also used to exclude women from full participation in society during the nineteenth century, which meant that the status of female slaves had a further layer of exclusion and negation.

14. Ibid., 37.

15. John W. Blassingame, *The Slave Community: Plantation Life in the Antebellum South* (New York: Oxford University Press, 1978), 227.

16. Patterson, *Slavery and Social Death,* 96.

17. Quoted in Patterson, *Slavery and Social Death*, 96.

18. Ibid.

19. Julio Ramos, "La ley es otra: Literatura y constitución de la persona jurídica," *Revista de Crítica Literaria latinoamericana* 20, no. 40 (1994): 308–9.

20. Patterson, *Slavery and Social Death*, 96. This discourse of immorality and exclusion from the norm (i.e., manhood/personhood) also applied to female slaves, who had a complicated and ironic relationship to the cult of true womanhood. Female slave narrators such as Harriet Jacobs knew that, compared to the pure and asexual angel of the house, they would be considered wanton. In trying to gain acceptance as free (human) women, they faced the added burden of having to defend their morality despite the fact that they had lived in a position which did not give them the power to protect their sexual purity. For a more detailed analysis of female slave narrators in the United States, see Frances Smith Foster's *Written by Herself: Literary Production by African American Women, 1746–1892.*

21. Manzano had also fled slavery, although not in the standard way of a *cimarrón* fleeing to a *palenque* in the mountains. The *cimarrón* did not get a voice until Miguel Barnet's *Biografía de un cimarrón* (1969) in which Barnet presents the story of Esteban Montejo. As with Douglass and Manzano, the presence of Barnet as patron and midwife for Montejo's story frames the narrative with a complicated set of issues regarding agency, agenda, and legitimacy.

22. William Luis, *Literary Bondage*, 3.

23. Blassingame, *The Slave Community*, 220.

24. Patterson, *Slavery and Social Death*, 8.

25. See chapter 2 in Franklin Knight's *Slave Society in Cuba During the Nineteenth Century* for a detailed look at "The Sugar Revolution of the Nineteenth Century" (Knight, 25–46). See also Manuel Moreno Fraginals's *El ingenio: Complejo económico social cubano del azúcar*, 3 vols. (Havana: Editorial de Ciencias Sociales, 1978).

26. Sylvia Molloy, "From Serf to Self: The Autobiography of Juan Francisco Manzano," in *At Face Value: Autobiographical Writing in Spanish America* (New York: Cambridge University Press, 1991), 37.

27. Gera C. Burton, *Ambivalence and the Postcolonial Subject: The Strategic Alliance of Juan Francisco Manzano and Richard Robert Madden* (New York: Peter Lang, 2004), 24.

28. Cesar Leante, "Dos obras antiesclavistas cubanas," *Cuadernos Americanos*, 207 (1976): 76.

29. Jerome Branche, "'*Mulato entre negros*' (y blancos): Writing, Race, the Antislavery Question, and Juan Francisco Manzano's *Autobiografía*," *Bulletin of Latin American Research* 20, no. 1 (2001): 69.

30. Luis, *Literary Bondage*, 1.

31. Robert L. Paquette, "Cuban Whites and the Problem of Slavery," in *Sugar is Made with Blood: The Conspiracy of La Escalera and the Conflict between Empires over Slavery in Cuba* (Middletown, CT: Wesleyan University Press, 1988), 96.

32. Branche, "Mulato entre negros," 72. Branche explains that although Del Monte has often uncritically been described as an antislavery humanist, "Delmontine opposition to slavery as an altruistic vindication of the rights of the enslaved . . . is a highly questionable proposition" (73).

33. Labrador-Rodríguez, "La intelectualidad negra," 23.

34. Paquette, "Cuban Whites and the Problem of Slavery," 90–91.

35. For one example of a change made by Suárez, see Labrador-Rodríguez (17). As a result of his experiences in del Monte's *tertulia*, most notably his work on Manzano's text, Suárez y Romero went on to write the anti-slavery novel *Francisco: El ingenio, a las delicias del campo* [*Francisco: The Sugar Mill, or the Delights of the Countryside*], a text that was also commissioned by del Monte and given to Richard Robert Madden.

36. Luis, *Literary Bondage*, 39.

37. Andrews, *To Tell A Free Story*, 36.

38. Andrews, *To Tell A Free Story*, 99–100.

39. Gary S. Selby, "The Limits of Accommodation: Frederick Douglass and the Garrisonian Abolitionists," *The Southern Communication Journal* 66, no. 1 (2000): 53.

40. Beth A. McCoy, "Race and the (Para)Textual Condition," *PMLA* 121, no. 1 (2006): 156.

41. Ibid., 157.

42. Frederick Douglass, *Narrative of the Life of Fredrick Douglass, an American Slave.* (New York: Oxford University Press, 1999), 3.

43. Ibid., 13.

44. Ibid., 12.

45. Ibid., 4, 5.

46. Ibid., 5.

47. Foster, *Witnessing Slavery*, 68.

48. Douglass, *Narrative of the Life of Fredrick Douglass*, 6.

49. Ibid., 7.

50. Ibid, 12.

51. Ibid., 13.

52. Ibid., 5.

53. In what follows, I will focus on the recorded speeches from 1841 to right before the publication of the *Narrative* in 1845.

54. Gary S. Selby, "Mocking the Sacred: Frederick Douglass's 'Slaveholder's Sermon' and the Antebellum Debate over Religion and Slavery," *Quarterly Journal of Speech* 88, no. 3 (2002): 330.

55. Douglass, *Frederick Douglass Papers*, 11, 16, 19, 20, 24, 25.

56. Manzano, *Autobiografía del esclavo poeta*, 140–41.

57. Ibid., 167–68.

58. Douglass, *Frederick Douglass Papers*, 3, 16, 29, 31.

59. Ibid., 5, 25, 33.

60. Manzano, *Autobiografía del esclavo poeta*, 170–71.

61. Douglass, *Frederick Douglass Papers*, 3, 16, 31.

62. Manzano, *Autobiografía del esclavo poeta*, 171, 172.

63. Jose R. Jouve-Martin, "En la urna del destino: Zafira y el modo trágico en la obra de Juan Francisco Manzano," *Revista de estudios hispánicos* 43, no. 3 (2009): 505.

64. Manzano, *Autobiografía del esclavo poeta*, 151.

65. Rachel Price, "Enemigo Suelo: Manzano Rewrites Cuban Romanticism," *Revista Canadiense de Estudios Hispanos* 38, no. 3 (2014): 538.

66. Manzano, *Autobiografía del esclavo poeta*, 148.

67. Price, "Enemigo Suelo," 538.

68. Ibid., 542.

69. Douglass, *Frederick Douglass Papers*, 6, 16, 33.

70. Ibid., 5, 9, 11, 12, 17.

71. Selby, "The Limits of Accommodation," 60.

72. Ibid.

73. Ibid.

74. Douglass, *Frederick Douglass Papers*, 16.
75. Ibid., 33.
76. Ibid.
77. Ibid.
78. Sonia Labrador-Rodríguez, "La intelectualidad negra," 19.

Chapter Three

Common Narrative Threads in the
Autobiografía de Juan Francisco Manzano and *Narrative of the Life of Frederick Douglass, An American Slave*

After wars in the Atlantic in the eighteenth century changed the relation of colonists in the Americas to Europe, even more radical shifts took place due to the American, French, and Haitian Revolutions. By 1835 when Juan Francisco Manzano wrote his *Autobiografía*, Cuba was still a colony and had transformed into a major sugar producer with nearly as many slaves as free whites on the island, not to mention the free population of color. Spanish rule had been reinvigorated so that the metropolis could take full advantage of the economic benefits of the colony. The "fear of the dark" on the island was growing more acute, a fact that was particularly troubling for those like Domingo del Monte who wanted to create a new nation independent of Spain but who based the vision for that new nation on a bourgeois nationalism centered on the Western Man. Manzano's text was specifically requested to be used to make an argument against the slave trade—the mechanism by which even more Africans were brought to Cuba—rather than as a part of an abolitionist movement. Frederick Douglass similarly wrote his *Narrative* in a time of flux, which partially explains why his text, responding as it did to his time, signified a new era in the slave narrative genre. In the United States, the wars and revolutions cited above led, among other things, to a questioning of what it meant to be an individual in a republic and what role slavery played in the nation. The first half of the nineteenth century in the United States was characterized by expansion—eleven new stars were added to the Stars and Stripes between 1818 and 1837—and other events that changed the physical, philosophical, and biological landscape of the nation including the ending of the African slave trade, the Indian Removal Act, Nat Turner's Revolt, and the Trail of Tears. As the nation grew, those in power grew more anxious about who was found within the nation and what the status of various groups was within it. In both Cuba and the United States, racializing assemblages worked to keep the white, male, Western ideal as the standard of humanity and to exclude all others from true participation in the nation.

In *The Signifying Monkey*, Henry Louis Gates Jr. singles out a passage from Douglass's *Narrative of the Life of Frederick Douglass* regarding slave songs. For Gates, the importance of this passage is not merely that the songs are indecipherable to whites, but rather that they were "full of meaning" to the slaves; these meanings stand out to Gates because the slave singers were "literally defining themselves in language, just as did Douglass and hundreds of other slave narrators."[1] This reworking of language resonates with Bakhtin's insistence that language is "not a neutral medium," but that it serves another until the speaker "populate[s] it with his own intention, his own accent" and "appropriates the word, adapting it to his own semantic and expressive intention."[2] Just as the slaves had to create new expressions to sing of their true identities and to counteract their negation by society, Douglass and Manzano had to appropriate various narrative threads in order to possess the terms, tropes, and language necessary to negotiate their identities, not as the ideas of the day demanded, but as their desire for acceptance as free people demanded. Their works stand as important artifacts in the archive of resistance not only to slavery, racism, and oppression, but also to the exclusionary nature of many constructions of national identity. These slave narratives can be read for the tropes they adopt and adapt, for the words their authors appropriate, in a Bakhtinian sense, and try to populate with intentions not previously within the discourse of national identity. In the case of both Douglass and Manzano, it is useful to follow Wendy Ryden's lead in reading their texts both in the context of Bakhtinian negotiations and in the context of Mary Louise Pratt's idea of transculturation. Ryden reminds us of Pratt's focus on "the production of texts as they occur in 'social spaces [contact zones] where cultures meet, clash, and grapple with each other, often in contexts of highly asymmetrical relations of power.'"[3] Following Pratt, Ryden goes on to argue that it is useful to read a text like Douglass's—and I would add Manzano's—as "autoethnographic" in that they represent "a selective collaboration with and appropriation of idioms . . . to create self-representations intended to intervene in metropolitan modes of understanding."[4] That is, these texts are discourses of identity that allow their authors to intervene in and destabilize hegemonic, exclusionary ideas of humanity and citizenship and to challenge the global color line.

The majority of this chapter examines a series of similar narrative threads that can be found in *Autobiografía de Juan Francisco Manzano* and *Narra-*

tive of the Life of Frederick Douglass, threads which are part of their discourses of identity and part of their intervention into hegemonic, metropolitan modes of understanding both individual and national identities. Despite the similarities in the texts, they have had different national and literary influence because they occupy different places in their respective national canons. The circumstances surrounding Juan Francisco Manzano's autobiography were much different than those surrounding Douglass's, particularly since there was no plan to publish his work in Cuba when it was produced. While several significant nineteenth-century Cuban novels deal either directly or indirectly with the issue of slavery, including Gertrudis Gomez de Avellaneda's *Sab*, Anselmo Suarez y Romero's *Francisco*, Antonio Zambrana y Vazquez's *El Negro Francisco*, and Cirilo Villaverde's *Cecilia Valdés*, Manzano's text is the only known Cuban slave narrative. According to Ivan Schulman, the lack of literary material by and about slaves in Cuba was due in part to "the racial and social prejudices of the colonial period's master discourse which dissuaded writers from representing marginalized peoples or the theme of slavery in their texts."[5] The Spanish colonial government also suppressed such materials since they had an interest in maintaining slavery in Cuba so as to protect the profitability of their colony. On the other hand, Douglass's text was a significant contribution to a rich genre.[6] The most obvious reason that North American authors produced so many slave narratives is that the United States was a nation deeply divided on the issue of slavery, a divide which included the free North to which fugitive slaves could escape; further, abolitionist groups encouraged the production of slave narratives and other texts as part of their political agenda and the free states of the North provided a large readership.

Clearly Douglass and Manzano, in response to their own politics and the influence of their patrons, had different foci in their writing. Susan Willis has argued that "perspectival limitations are particularly strong in the slave narratives of the Caribbean, where the influence of abolitionists . . . is not a strong factor;" she argues that North American slave narrators who participated in the abolitionist movement had a "broadened perspective" and could write not "raw data, but a meaningful narrative."[7] While Manzano's narrative indicts slavery from his own particular experience, it can be seen as being more limited to the "raw data" of his individual life. However, the coded language of suffering in his poetry challenges us to look beyond the fact that Manzano's narrative appears to be exclusively focused on his individual experiences rather than presenting an overarching critique of slavery. Certainly, in the text Manzano in no way makes an overt claim that his is a representative portrait of Cuban slavery. In fact, he emphasizes the opposite by highlighting his uniqueness and unusual abilities. In his narrative, Manzano consciously presents himself as a slave-poet, defining for himself an individualized intellectual manhood.[8] But this fact in no way diminishes his text as an anti-slavery one. Any reader with compassion and imagination will be moved by his experiences of cruelty and injustice, and in encountering an individual's account would also be forced to imagine the many other evils associated with the institution of slavery.

Where Manzano sought to find a code, a language in which to imagine the slave intellectual so that he could gain his individual freedom and make implicit arguments against slavery, Frederick Douglass tells his life story in such a way as to make an impassioned plea for abolition. Joining an existing tradition of antebellum texts intimately linked with the abolitionist movement, Douglass carefully constructs his narrative to meet both his discursive ends of self-expression and the abolitionist agenda.[9] In his *Narrative*, Douglass constructs an image of himself as a free (hu)man with all of the necessary rhetorical, moral, and intellectual attributes entailed in such a portrait while simultaneously writing a narrative that dismantles the rhetoric of dehumanization that served to support American slavery. Roberto Friol argues that while both Manzano and Douglass's narratives depict the atrocities of slavery with similar intellectual honesty, the difference in the scope of the texts arises from the fact that when Douglass escaped from slavery he was fully aware of his rights as a human being and of his obligation and commitment to all those who remained in slavery.[10] Douglass's autobiography overtly targeted the entire system of slavery in America instead of merely addressing his personal experience in it, creating a narrative that had, from its inception, a larger intention than that of the simple retelling of the life and sufferings of one individual former slave. He wrote to name names and to give concrete identifying facts such as places and dates which would prove that he was not an imposter created by the abolitionist movement to defame enslavers and the system of slavery, as had been suggested by opponents. Douglass's book supported both his lecturing career and the abolitionist movement by insisting upon his authenticity as a witness.

Several scholars have either outlined or engaged in comparative readings of Manzano's and Douglass's texts. While all scholars recognize the differences in agenda, scope, and reception of the two texts, in most cases, critics who engage both *Autobiografía de Juan Francisco Manzano* and *Narrative of the Life of Frederick Douglass* focus on structural, generic, and thematic similarities like the works' "common origin in African oral literature" and the writers' shared "oppressive experiences."[11] On the theme of oppression, Mullen notes that the two texts "appear to be informed by a similar alienating vision of society" as they "project a similar portrait of psychological and physical torment, one firmly rooted in the alien/exile theme."[12] Luis Jiménez emphasizes silences in the texts and how what is not said invites the reader to "decode" what is implied in the text.[13] Jiménez ultimately argues that both Douglass and Manzano's texts are important because "they place the voiceless at the core of their autobiographical space in nineteenth century America."[14] The idea of the alien/exile and of the silent resonates with the radical and multivalent negation of the slave as a result of racialization. Other critics also refer to the idea of negation. Ifeoma Kiddoe Nwankwo compares Manzano's "fundamental desire to be recognized as human, and by extension as an individual," with Douglass's "quest for being" à la the reading of Houston A. Baker[15] and DeCosta-Willis identifies "the search for identity, the desire for freedom, and alienation in a hostile society" as the principle themes uniting these narratives, with "secondary themes includ[ing] education, morality and religion."[16] These analyses overlap with the previously discussed themes in Douglass's oratory and Manzano's poetry, particularly the ideas of negation, suffering, family, honor, and religion.

Although separated by ten years, written in different languages, written under significantly different political systems (nation vs. colony), under different slave codes, within very different literary canons, and by individuals with distinct experiences striving to achieve different ends, the authors of *Autobiografía de Juan Francisco Manzano* and *Narrative of the Life of Frederick Douglass* manipulate some of the same main narrative threads in order to engage with the major paradigms used throughout the New World to negate the humanity of slaves and justify and maintain the institution of slavery. In writing their life stories, Douglass and Manzano engage with four common narrative threads: religious rhetoric, literacy, family, and the complexities of racial identity.[17] Intertwined in all of these are two others, the threads of "manhood" and the pervasive thread of violence which seeks to destroy both manhood and humanity in the slave. As Patterson writes, under slavery the "peculiar role of violence" both creates and maintains a relation of domination that disempowers the slave and empowers the master.[18] The focus on religious rhetoric, literacy, family, and racial identities aids in their self-constitution within their discourses of identity and in their narratives' arguments both against slavery and for the inclusion of the narrators in the nation. Although they do not use the common narrative threads in exactly the same way, both Manzano and Douglass posit the use of religious rhetoric as a higher source of identity for the slave, the control of literacy as a means to undermine the enslaver's monopoly on meaning-making, the trope of family as a problematic and problematizing aspect of the rhetoric of slavery, and rhetorical constructions of whiteness as a mask which, when removed, reveals the hypocrisy and illogic of slavery. A sustained comparative reading of these four narrative threads allows us to deepen our understandings of two texts within the tradition of anti-slavery literature. It also allows us to develop a more nuanced understanding of the ways in which slaves and former slaves were negated and excluded from the nation and how they used discourses of identity to affirm alternate ways of understanding self and nation.

FIRST NARRATIVE THREAD:
RELIGIOUS RHETORIC

Christianity, as one of the most powerful paradigms upon which Western civilization was built, is one of the most important social institutions and racializing assemblages used to define the relationships between peoples in the New World. In the nineteenth century, to be a human and a citizen—to be considered a full participant in either Cuban or American society—meant being a Christian. The term Christian "seems to have conveyed the idea and feeling of *we* as against *they*: to be Christian was to be civilized rather than barbarous, English [or European] rather than African, white rather than black."[19] As implied by this statement, Africans were considered inferior and non-Christian and, by definition, excluded from citizenship. Lack of religion—assumed or real—was used to invalidate the humanity of slaves. Because of this, the use of Christian rhetoric had the potential to validate slave authors for a variety of reasons. First, the worldview of the majority of nineteenth-century Cubans and Americans were fundamentally Christian and in writing discourses of identity making an argument regarding inclusion in the nation, it made sense for slave narrators to emphasize their Christian faith. Second, despite the difference between a Catholic and a Protestant society, Christianity and Christian doctrines were used in both countries to justify slavery.[20] Furthermore, Christianity provided a number of archetypical liberation narratives that could serve as models for projected narratives of liberation. The use of religious rhetoric in Douglass and Manzano's narratives in some ways mirror the difference in their approaches to the topic in the poetry and speeches—the one more personal and the other more political—but there are also similarities. Douglass and Manzano use religious rhetoric to shed light on their positions, to help demonstrate their own legitimacy and credibility, to depict themselves as being worthy of sympathy, and to implicitly argue for their inclusion in the nation.[21]

In her article "Atlantic Countercultures and the Networked Text: Juan Francisco Manzano, R. R. Madden and the Cuban Slave Narrative," Fionnghuala Sweeney points out that "[t]he kind of negotiation required of a Catholic colonial subaltern seeking representation . . . is different in kind to that which takes place against an Anglo-Protestant ethical framework."[22] Three of her insights are helpful to keep in mind while we examine the use of religious rhetoric in Douglass and Manzano. First, Sweeney argues that while in the Anglo-American slave narrative tradition we see "a high dependency on both the underlying principle of individual moral judgement [*sic*] and the individual slave's right to exercise it," in the Catholic context hierarchies "often curtail the exercise of individual moral judgment."[23] Second, Sweeney points out that while Anglo-Protestant texts and the selves they represent are presented "according to a developmental model along which progress—

moral, economic, intellectual, or otherwise—is charted," in the Caribbean/ Catholic context there is less emphasis on developmental and positivist ideas.[24] We shall see this clearly in the difference in the emphases, structures, and organizing metaphors in Manzano's and Douglass's texts. Sweeney also sees "a strong tendency towards rational argumentation" in the US tradition versus an emphasis in places like Cuba on the non-rational and the mystical, including the importance of syncretism.[25]

The use of religious rhetoric by Manzano and Douglass reflect these differences, as well as sharing what Sweeney refers to as "points of overlap and comparison."[26] Sweeney's second point regarding the extent to which these narratives use a developmental model is most easily apparent. *Narrative of the Life of Frederick Douglass* follows the pattern of a linear, practically teleological narrative of development leading to enlightenment and freedom. It is also a prophetic narrative in the tradition of the "jeremiad," that is, the discourse of "prophets crying in the wilderness of their own alienation from prevailing error and perversity."[27] On the other hand, *Autobiografía de Juan Francisco Manzano* is neither teleological nor developmental. Manzano presents a story in which "the metaphor of his life was a fall—a fall from grace, a precipitous, downward, descent into a dark pit where the human self disintegrated into an invisible non-being."[28] Manzano's description of his religious activities and spiritual sensitivity initially work within the text to establish his identity as a good Catholic, and also to reinforce his image as a special child, a chosen son adopted into the master's family, an idea that will be further explored later in the chapter. This early childhood experience is the "garden" from which Manzano will depict his fall. The childhood "garden" can be read, as Ilia Casanovo-Marengo does, as a "metáfora/raíz" [metaphor/root] in which Manzano creates not only the idyllic past from which he will fall, but also creates himself as a subject, as an individual in control of his own writing.[29] The pathos of the fall, then, like the pathos expressed in his poetry, is an integral part of Manzano's discourse of identity. His depiction of his childhood and his spirituality within it are important because of how he uses these strategies to establish his humanity and credibility, to constitute a self that mitigates his social negation, and to gain the sympathy of readers.

In his autobiography, Manzano establishes his identity as a Catholic through a number of episodes. He first relates that even as a child he knew his catechism well and that by age ten he had memorized the longest sermons of Fray Luis de Granada.[30] While these facts work to give Manzano credibility, they do not, in themselves, constitute an argument against his condition as a slave nor promote him into citizenship status since technically masters under the *Siete Partidas* were to Christianize their slaves. The fact that Manzano is taught his catechism by a white woman who takes on the formal religious familial relation of godmother to him illustrates to his readers that he was the recipient of more than the typical Christian instruction provided to slaves, implying that he is more than merely a slave. While Patterson's examination of how the quasi-filial relations between master and slave reinforces the power of the master is relevant here, Manzano consistently promotes an image of himself as having had a special status. In the early pages of his text, Manzano lays a foundation of spiritual sensitivity to show he is not a brute, not merely a body. Manzano's self-presentation as spiritual also makes more poignant the scenes of punishment and abuse that he will later describe for his readers due to the inevitable thread of violence that will enter the text. In speaking of his childhood, Manzano relates that he often recited memorized sermons to guests of his mistress's house, clearly illustrating his intelligence and charisma and relates that he was baptized in the same robe in which one of his masters was baptized.[31] Manzano includes a mention of his baptism to show that he is one of God's children and once again encourages his reader to see him as the chosen son of his first mistress. This status, as well as his intelligence and charisma, blurs the rhetoric of slavery just enough to make the subsequent events of his life, most notably his mistreatment at the hand of another mistress, trouble his nineteenth-century *criollo* readers. Because of the hierarchy of masters, church, and crown, he has already been adopted into the Spanish national family through the actions of his mistress and godmother who provided an atypical religious instruction and can be eligible for inclusion in the Cuban nation that seeks to separate itself from its European parent.

Frederick Douglass presents himself as having been chosen not by a mistress or master, but rather by the hand of Providence.[32] Douglass says that being chosen from among many slave children to be sent to Baltimore from the plantation "laid the foundation, and opened the gateway, to all my subsequent prosperity."[33] Douglass attributes his good fortune to the "special interposition of divine Providence in my favor."[34] Like Manzano, Douglass posits himself as a chosen son, but implies that he has been chosen by one whose authority is much greater than the enslaver whose love and attention give Manzano a sense of entitlement. In a passage reminiscent of scenes from nineteenth-century spiritual autobiographies, Douglass writes of the "deep conviction" he had from childhood "that slavery would not always be able to hold me within its foul embrace;" even in the worst of times, he was comforted by "this living word of faith and spirit of hope" which "remained like ministering angels to cheer me through the gloom."[35]

After implying that God performed a special interposition in his life, marking him for a better future, Douglass goes further, arguing that his very quest for freedom was inspired and nurtured from on high. Douglass uses a very personal spiritual language, speaking of his "deep conviction." He also emphasizes divine involvement in his life, invoking all three aspects of the Trinity. Douglass speaks of God (the Father), the "living word" (Jesus Christ, the Son), and the "spirit of hope" or "good spirit" sent to him from God (the Holy Spirit). Unlike Manzano, who uses his faith and participation in religious activities to establish both his credibility and his special relationship with the master's family (and perhaps, by extension, the nation), in a particularly protestant move that voids all levels of hierarchy above him, Douglass includes as a foundational moment in his narrative his special relationship with God Himself. In discussing how throughout his narrative Douglass appropriates scriptural language and ideas, removes them from their exploitative uses, and employs them for his own "prophetic purposes," Cynthia Nielsen likens Douglass's actions to Foucault's "reverse discourse" which "is productive," able to create and shape social identities and social realities.[36] William L. Andrews reads Douglass's text as a special kind of American jeremiad that condemns society's evils, but that rather than predicting God's condemnation and punishment for the nation's sins, posits a hopeful American future "sustained by the conviction of the nation's divinely appointed mission."[37] The idea of special Providence in Douglass's life might therefore be linked to the American mythos of manifest destiny, and more specifically to Peréz's idea of an *exalted manifest destiny*, an idea obviously predicated on the assumption that the nation and its people had been *chosen*. By depicting himself as chosen, Douglass implicitly but powerfully includes himself in the nation's identity.

One of the most powerful ways that Juan Francisco Manzano challenges the rhetoric of slavery in his *Autobiografía* is through his descriptions of his sufferings and his spiritual response to that suffering. Both Lorna V. Williams and Ivan Schulman mention that Manzano depicted himself in letters to del Monte and in his narrative as a martyr who was not debased, but rather purified, by having been tortured.[38] He often emphasizes his piety and expresses his gratitude for being a Christian, saying that in adverse situations "me tranquilicé porque desde mi infancia mis Directores me enseñaron a amarlo y temer lo [a Dios]"[39] [I was comforted because since my infancy my spiritual directors had taught me to love and fear God]. Manzano describes himself as nightly praying to God to ease his suffering, particularly since his enslavers regularly punish him in capricious and outrageous ways. Ironically, in the Cuban context even the torture Manzano suffers lends him credibility. According to *Las Siete Partidas*, a slave's testimony was not considered valid until "después de que la tortura 'purificara' su palabra y garantizara la fidelidad del testimonio"[40] [after torture 'purified' his word and guaranteed the fidelity of the testimony]. The main reason behind this logic, according to Ramos, is the fact that the right to testify came with citizenship. The slave was thought incapable of telling the truth because, as a "body" rather than a citizen, s/he possessed neither morality nor reason.[41] Torture purportedly purified testimony by overcoming the lack of reason in the slave. In addition, due to the rhetoric of slavery in nineteenth-century Cuba, the scene of his

torture also ironically "purifies" his narrative, adding to the validity of Manzano's testimony and standing as potential evidence of both his morality and
his reason. Just as in the poem "Oda a la religion," Manzano's use of the
narrative thread of religious rhetoric in his autobiography forces his readers
to rethink the propriety of slavery in general and his own status as slave in
particular. It implies that as a moral and rational being, he should be a citizen
rather than a body and his torture is tragically unjust.

As potentially radical as Manzano's narrative is, it is still a personal
account that does not make explicit arguments against slavery. As a jeremiad, Douglass's text functions not merely as an autobiography, but also as a
discourse to help his readers "distinguish between true and false Americanism and Christianity."[42] As a prophet, Douglass testifies that true Americanism and a pure American Christianity could only exist if slavery was abolished. His argument includes the thread of violence when Douglass claims
that religious slaveholders are the worst in their treatment of slaves; he uses
an example he had employed in speeches of a master who uses religion to
justify his cruelty and of his master whipping a "lame young woman" bloody
while intoning the verse, "He that knoweth his master's will, and doeth it not,
shall be beaten with many stripes."[43] Douglass relates such episodes in order
to condemn slave-owning Christianity and to further the argument from his
oratory that slavery corrupts true religion. His attitude is such that he adds an
appendix to the narrative, making sure that it is clear to his readers that he is
only speaking against what he calls the "the *slaveholding religion* of this
land" and not against "the Christianity of Christ."[44] Douglass is careful to
avoid the appearance of attacking Christianity to avoid discrediting himself
in the eyes of his readers. Whether out of piety or social awareness, Douglass
is wise enough to know that although Christianity is used to justify slavery,
he must attack slavery without appearing to attack Christianity. [45] In pointing
out the differences between the two Christianities and aligning himself with
what he calls the Christianity of Christ, Douglass works not merely as an
abolitionist, but as a prophet for a new kind of American identity. Cynthia R.
Nielsen call Douglass a "sociopolitical, religious critic 'from below,' one
whose prophetic voice cries out from the underside of modernity in order to
expose the exclusivity, injustice, and monochrome hue of 'We the People'
and the utter irrationality and duplicity of the whitewashed necropolis pro-
claiming itself 'the City on a Hill.'"[46] Douglass's discourse of identity challenges this whitened version of the People, implying a new and more inclusive "We" as the subject of the nation.

One of the most interesting points of intersection between *Autobiografía
de Juan Francisco Manzano* and *Narrative of the Life of Frederick Douglass*
is in their authors' use of the figure of Jesus Christ. While the structural
backbone of his narrative may be the metaphor of the fall, Manzano is not the
guilty Adam who eats the fruit. Manzano's poetry includes numerous exam-

ples of his sufferings and the pathos of his misfortunes. In his autobiography, he emphasizes his piety and innocence when he invites his readers to associate his sufferings not just with a generalized martyr type, but with the *archetypal* Christian martyr. When Manzano describes the physical and emotional torture he suffered as a young boy for the dubious crime of having picked a leaf off a geranium plant (a plant the mistress insists is her property he has stolen), he describes how his hands were tied "como las de Jesu Cristo" [like those of Jesus Christ]; before giving gory details regarding the thread of violence, he apostrophizes, "¡Oh Dios! Corramos un velo sobre esta escena tan triste. ¡Ay!, mi sangre se derramó y perdí el sentido. Cuando volví en mí, me hallé en la puerta del oratorio en los brazos de mi madre, anegada en lágrimas"[47] [Oh God! Pull a curtain over this sad scene. Oh! My blood poured out and I lost consciousness. When I came to, I found myself in the door of the chapel in the arms of my mother who was overcome with tears]. Manzano hopes that his readers, who most likely have meditated on the sufferings of Christ, will be more sympathetic to his cause because of his association with Christ. Sylvia Molloy argues the passage was important and radical, citing as evidence the fact that in his English translation, Richard Madden takes out the comparison to Christ, describing Manzano's hands as being tied not "like those of Jesus Christ," but rather "like a criminal."[48] Madden's version makes Manzano potentially guilty in the figurative comparison to a criminal. Manzano's original version evokes sympathy because in being punished so severely for picking a geranium leaf he implies that he, like Christ, was innocent. Not only is he tied like Christ, but also "he rises to consciousness in a scene reminiscent of the Pieta—his tormented body in the arms of his mother."[49] Thus this description evokes more emotion and sympathy in readers than the mere description of the torture of a slave might have. This association of Manzano with Christ also relates to Sweeney's point about the power of syncretism in the Cuban context where Catholic saints merge with African Orishas. On one level there is the literary moment in which Manzano and his mother are *like* Mary and Jesus of the Pieta; in a syncretic sense, in this moment they are these figures. What does it do to ideas of national identity, of humanity and belonging, if the slave is not a body, but rather is equated to the Messiah?

While much of the scholarship on Douglass includes reference to him as a prophetic figure, several readings of Frederick Douglass's *Narrative* include interpretations of Douglass's depiction vis-à-vis Christ. Although he emphasizes what he sees as Douglass's ambivalence toward religion, David Van Leer reads Douglass as placing himself in a "Christic" role similar to that occupied by Manzano, that of the suffering Christ on the cross; Van Leer mentions that during the Covey episode Douglass's initial beating takes place at 3 o'clock on a Friday, that he is torn by briars and thorns, and that he is likened to Daniel, who is a type for Christ.[50] Alternatively, Donald B. Gibson, who argues that to keep his faith Douglass had to create a distance between God and slavery, claims that the Douglass of the *Narrative* is "not the Christ suffering on the cross; he is the risen Christ who seizes . . . rather than lies subject to, the terms of the mythology."[51] Just as there are multiple readings of the metaphorical relationship between Douglass and Christ in the *Narrative*, Manzano's text also provides as nuanced and complex a depiction, which leads to more than one reading. Michael Stoneham provides an alternate reading from the metaphorical martyr suggested by Williams and Schulman. Stoneham starts with a single incident, one in which Manzano's godfather remarks that he will become worse than Rousseau and Voltaire.[52] While Stoneham admits that Manzano uses the passage explicitly to emphasize his piety as he determines not to be like these two demonized figures, he argues that the figures are key; for Stoneham, Manzano condemns slavery in Cuba "in a form worthy of Rousseau and a satire worthy of Voltaire."[53] When Stoneham examines the geranium leaf episode, he argues that Manzano mimics Voltaire's hyperbolic satire in *Candide*, and "configures himself, like the Christ in Michelangelo's marble Pieta, as both an artistic figure central to the battle for life and a static symbol of rebellion in a society that celebrated the Christian myth and relied upon it for its social structure."[54] Through the depiction of his torture and sufferings, Juan Francisco Manzano "both mocks his own slave society and exposes its hypocrisy."[55] He ultimately takes a similar tack to Douglass, seizing the terms of the mythology and transforming the suffering Christ into an anti-slavery rebel.

One might be tempted to look closely at the variety of the interpretations of the use of the figure of Christ by Manzano and Douglass and try to determine which is most convincing. Although some of these readings might seem contradictory, the use of Christ in these texts provides evidence as to how effective and successful these texts are; by drawing on the figure of Christ (and religious discourse in general) in the ways that they do, Douglass and Manzano allow a wide variety of readers, readers who may have differing interpretations or depth of knowledge of the Bible, to engage with these ideas in different ways. The common denominator is all of the interpretations of the comparison between the slave narrator and Christ end up concluding that such a comparison creates arguments that challenge slavery and the rhetoric used to support it. As William L. Andrews points out, during the period in which Manzano and Douglass were writing, as the slave narrative developed away from being a strict conversion narrative in the tradition of the spiritual autobiography, the focus turned from the salvation of the slave to the conversion of the reader to abolitionism.[56] Douglass and Manzano use religious discourse their audiences are familiar with and use it in such a way as to allow people from different backgrounds to understand their position as slaves and to get a view of the horrors of slavery. The power of these texts is their ability to harness the power of religious discourse and turn it into reverse discourse that undermines the justifications for slavery, *humanizes* both the experience of slavery and the slave narrator himself, and allows for the positing of alternate identities both for these individual narrators and for slaves in general. This reimaging and humanizing of the slave in the slave narrator's discourse of identity then implies a different nation and different ideas of citizenship based on a different kind of piety.

SECOND NARRATIVE THREAD: LITERACY

Paradigms of national identity are part of the official culture of a society, a culture which is fostered by, and which fosters, a certain kind of knowledge and a specific worldview. As Douglass and Manzano's texts demonstrate, literacy in the dominant language of the society is essential to participation in the official culture of the United States or of Cuba. Benedict Anderson cites the "central ideological and political importance" of "national-print languages" to successful national liberation movements in the Americas.[57] In *La ciudad letrada*, Angel Rama traces the importance of writing to the colonial period, calling writing a "kind of secondary religion" in the Americas and graphocentrism as one of the most important organizing metaphors.[58] Print media and the institutions that controlled them (including colonial officials, *tertulias*, publishers, journals, newspapers, presses, schools, and universities) played a vital role in the formation, preservation, transformation, and propagation of the nation. Henry Louis Gates Jr. eloquently summarizes European thinking about the lack of writing and the perceived cultural level, or "humanity," of a people in the following: "Without writing, there could exist no repeatable sign of the workings of reason, of mind; without memory or mind, there could exist no history; without history, there could exist no 'humanity' as defined consistently from Vico to Hegel."[59] The Western Man described by Weheliye was a man of letters and of reason and a perceived lack of these characteristics denigrated one to the status of nonhuman or not-quite-human.

The intellectual achievements and artistic abilities of slaves—including examples like Manzano's poems and Douglass's speeches as well as their narratives—challenged the dehumanizing force of slavery's rhetoric and justification. Lorna V. Williams writes that the mastery of written language in Manzano's text is reminiscent of Anglo-American slave narratives in that for Manzano, as for Douglass and many others, "the notion of existential possibility becomes inextricably linked to the idea of becoming literate."[60] Luis Jiménez sees both Douglass and Manzano as writing a "counterdiscourse" of the oppressed and emphasizes that their literacy is inherently political.[61] This is not to say that there are neither difficulties nor dangers involved with using the enslaver's language to critique him. According to Susana Draper, the most radical problem for the black body is having to write about slavery using the very language that marks the distinction between man and slave, a language which is implicated in the idea that slaves are bodies that must learn through punishment and torture.[62] Wendy Ryden points out the dangers of the "literacy myth," which she defines as "a culturally conservative belief in the unqualified developmental power of literacy"; she also emphasizes the danger that the slave narrator will become inscribed in the white word that he seizes.[63] Both Ryden and Nick Bromell emphasize that literacy itself is not enough to free Douglass; in and of itself, literacy is not his turning point; according to these critics, while literacy is important, the battle with Covey—including Douglass's physical resistance—is more important.[64] This is in line with the interpretation by Patterson that violence is the very basis of the power of slaveholders. Nonetheless, both Manzano and Douglass indicate the political import and the personal significance of literacy in the way they detail their relationships to language and to literacy in their discourses of identity. These depictions are further linked to the image each author creates of himself vis-à-vis ideas of citizenship.

Although both Douglass and Manzano achieve literacy and are ultimately able to write their autobiographies, their relationships with written language are complex and important to understanding their discourses of identity. Manzano presents his autobiography as being not merely the autobiography of a slave, but rather that of a poet who happens to be a slave, emphasizing his identity as an artist. This makes sense both since Manzano was already a published poet and was known as such and because it distinguished him from other slaves. In his narrative, Manzano carefully constructs an image of himself that, from the very beginning, undermines the idea that he is merely a body (and thus that he is naturally a slave). Sonia Labrador-Rodríguez sees him as not merely presenting himself as a poet, but as denouncing slavery from the point of view of a "creador/poeta esclavo"[65] [slave creator/poet]. Manzano describes himself in his autobiography as someone who always had the desire and ability to create and to narrate. He relates that by the age of twelve he had already composed many poems by memory.[66] Manzano clarifies that he composed the poems in his mind and committed them to memory because his godparents did not want him to learn to write, indicating that an injunction, rather than a lack of intelligence or ability, was the reason for his illiteracy. The slave poet makes clear that he recognizes the importance and permanence of the written word when he describes how he dictated his poems to a young morena named Serafina.[67] Manzano's choice of love as subject matter, as well as his association with the fairly powerless (although free) Serafina, works to create a nonthreatening image of a sensitive artist and may be strategically designed to align him with the values of the *delmontinos* in particular and with the elite *criollo* class of his day in general.

In discussing the education of the slave-intellectual, Sonia Labrador-Rodríguez notes that at every point in his development Manzano has both an individual who facilitates his learning and someone who seeks to repress or prohibit it.[68] In the case of his verses, Manzano's godparents play the role of the rhetorical watchdogs who try to limit the expressive capabilities of the young slave.[69] While describing the process by which he gained a sense of self as an artist, Manzano lays foundations of independence and merit which constitute the first step in his self-definition as a free man. The prohibitions, the controlling forces described by Labrador-Rodríguez, make every step a struggle. At one point, alarmed at his storytelling, his second mistress tells the other members of the household not to talk to him. While it is not clear the exact motivation for the fear of the mistress, what comes clearly into focus is Manzano's nature as an artist. He needs to create and to share his creations. Manzano is a consummate performer and storyteller, but one who is painfully aware of those who would silence him. Manzano's need to communicate is evident when he says that as a child he is purported to have talked to tables, paintings, and walls when there were no other auditors.[70] Manzano simultaneously describes the power of language and the way in which he created auditors out of the very furniture to affirm his authorship and his existence as a creator. However, Manzano is also careful where and when he shares his gifts because he has internalized the vigilance of his second mistress. Marilyn Miller emphasizes that when Manzano differentiates himself from the *bozales* [slaves, generally those who came directly from Africa], he is most significantly reacting out of fear of the *bozal* [literally, the muzzle].[71] Manzano fears being muzzled because in his mind control of language is related to his control—or even ownership—of himself. In writing about Douglass, Cynthia Nielsen provides a similar analysis that is relevant to most slave narrators when she points out "the master's continual obsession to render the slave mute, inarticulate, and docile," since "to *be* master required in some genuine sense an ongoing silencing of the slave."[72] Both Manzano and Douglass refuse to stay silent; they construct discourses of identity that challenge their dehumanization and take ownership of themselves as they make arguments for their humanity in an effort to force society to consider them as possible members. They are countering the radical negation of the slave as depicted in Douglass's 1842 speech.

Juan Francisco Manzano portrays himself in the *Autobiografía* as a man with the consciousness of the artist, presenting himself to his readers as more than a stereotypical brute. His propensity for performance and his awareness of the importance of the audience shape the discursive strategies he employs in his text. His text is not strictly chronological like most traditional autobiographies, but rather a careful construction of both story and protagonist. If Manzano's poetry "represents a step in the formation of national, autochthonous literature that borrows from the black vernacular to achieve freedom from the master grammar of urban, peninsular Spain,"[73] then his autobiography is another such step. Since the slave, as Manzano writes in a letter to del

Monte, is "un ser muerto ante su señor"[74] [a dead being in front of his master], the key is not merely writing, but rather learning to perform himself in language in such a way that he can overcome this social death and be seen as something other than a slave. On the national level, his performance also impacts the ideas of the emerging nation since his text existed among and influenced many of the texts created in Domingo del Monte's *tertulia*, texts that had as one of their goals the creation of a national literature in anticipation of the creation of a nation.

Manzano's artistic identity is not shared by Douglass, who focuses on learning to read as the process by which he acquired knowledge and the ability to define his identity independent of his enslavers. Like Manzano, Frederick Douglass lived in a slave society that made a concerted effort to keep slaves ignorant of reading and writing and he also faced a situation in which individuals attempted to repress or prohibit his learning. As readers of his *Narrative* know, even though Sophia Auld initially begins to teach him to read, it is not long before Mr. Auld forbids her to continue with the lessons, reminding her of the legal and social ramifications of such an act. John Sekora writes that slaveholders sought "even the words, the very language of their slaves" since the slaves' words were both personal forms of self-expression and politically charged "potent, lethal things;" he points out that "[b]y seeking to control language, masters sought to exact slave complicity in their own subjugation."[75] In a famous passage, Douglass quotes Mr. Auld as warning his wife that "If you give a nigger an inch, he will take an ell. A nigger should know nothing but to obey his master—to do as he is told to do" because "[l]earning would spoil the best nigger in the world. . . It would forever unfit him to be a slave."[76] According to the rhetoric believed and enforced by Mr. Auld, the educated slave, given that first inch, would be dangerous, "discontented and unhappy," and "of no value to his master," because he would at first opportunity "take an ell."[77] In an ironic confirmation of Mr. Auld's rhetoric, Douglass himself writes that, "Mistress, in teaching me the alphabet, had given me the *inch*, and no precaution could prevent me from taking the *ell*."[78] Mr. Auld's diatribe clearly demonstrates his attempts to maintain an artificial rhetoric of inferiority which defined the slave as a brute. In chastising his wife, Mr. Auld reveals the racializing assemblages working to enforce the line between human and non-human, reminding her that it is a crime to teach a slave to read. As Douglass deftly demonstrates, the vehemence with which enslavers guarded literacy proves not that blacks were intellectually inferior, but rather that the enslavers knew their slaves had the ability to learn. The masters wanted to keep control of the power of written language lest slaves realize a manner in which to break out of the monopoly on definition and meaning making held by those in power and be "spoiled." In order to keep their power, enslavers perpetuated the idea that because of the slave's nature, teaching him would cause him to be a danger to society, and would ruin him as an economic commodity.

Douglass represents himself as having understood instantly from Mr. Auld's reaction that literacy was of key importance in the maintenance of power over slaves. "Douglass learns to recognize and question the cultural constructs that dictate his behavior (and to a certain extent his thoughts) toward white people, white culture, and his own life and definitions of himself."[79] In no uncertain terms, Douglass links literacy and power and the ability to redefine and potentially free himself. He writes that Mr. Auld's words were "a new and special revelation, explaining dark and mysterious things," a revelation which allowed him to understand "what had been to me a most perplexing difficulty—to wit, the white man's power to enslave the black man. . . . From that moment, I understood the pathway from slavery to freedom."[80] Douglass comes to see the power inherent in the control of textual language in a graphocentric culture. Daniel Royer describes Douglass's literacy "not merely as a mastery of textuality, but as . . . an increasing awareness of and control over the social means by which people sustain discourse, knowledge, and reality."[81] One other interesting aspect of this point in Douglass's narrative is his use of religious discourse in the passage. Instead of someone who violently seizes the power of knowledge and language, he presents himself as someone who, like the Ethiopian taught and baptized by Philip in Acts 8:26–39, providentially receives the instruction he needs and is converted from ignorance to knowledge. This moment in his life is a moment of "special revelation," of coming from the darkness into the light. Once again, Douglass represents himself as a spiritual man, as a sensitive and perceptive person who had the humanity and temperament to struggle with "dark and mysterious things." While both authors are intellectuals, Douglass is a philosopher and prophet whereas Manzano is the artist.

Neither Douglass the philosopher nor Manzano the artist are content until they master written language. Both Manzano and Douglass present language in general, and written language in particular, as essential to their journey of self-definition.[82] For Douglass, as for other North American slave narrators, the power of the written word is paramount and twofold. First, written language held the power to define oneself; the authority that came from authorship allowed the individual to present an interpretation of his or her own identity and life. Second, and no less important, was the implicit argument in the slave's written testimony regarding the humanity of people of African descent. Slaves learned to read and write, producing evidence that challenged racist European ideas about race, reason, and humanity. Both Douglass and Manzano were self-taught slaves, figures who represented a particular danger to a slaveholding society, the danger of "un saber independiente, fuera del control de la elite"[83] [an independent knowledge, out of the control of the elite]. Having recognized this, Douglass the orator and Manzano the versifier appropriated the power of written language to construct their own discourses of identity in the form of the slave narrative.

As expressed in their texts, Manzano's desire for control of written language differs from Douglass's in that where Douglass emphasizes information (such as learning about abolitionism) and the mastery of the written word as a means of controlling ideas, Manzano emphasizes expression and artistry. Again and again, Marilyn Miller argues, Manzano demonstrates that he wants to be considered a man of letters, a writer, and a poet; she believes that his texts, including his autobiography, demonstrate that to Manzano, recognition of his artistic ability is as important to him as manumission and he considers them intrinsically related forms of freedom.[84] Douglass understands that because whites control literacy, they have the power to define and enforce social roles. Once he comes to associate reading and writing with the power of the enslavers, Douglass does everything he can to find opportunities to develop his reading skills and learn to write. He pursues literacy so that he can become an active participant in the conversation which defines his identity and status. Manzano also wanted to learn to write in order to break the enslavers' monopoly on meaning, but because he denounces slavery as a poet whose poetry began as an oral art form, his relationship to the written word differs from Douglass's. Manzano describes himself as learning to write in order to control his own creative production, to free his poetic expression from the mediation of others and the vigilance of an unwanted audience. The bottom line is that while Manzano and Douglass have different relationships to the written word, they are unified by the desire to break the monopoly on meaning held by whites by producing a black text. That the black text is double-voiced—that in a Bakhtinian sense the word (or utterance) resists them and is marked as they try to appropriate it—underscores the power negotiation in which these slave narrators are engaged.

In discussing race and the construction of the juridical subject, Julio Ramos emphasizes the *right to testify* as paramount to citizenship as writing is considered "uno de los derechos 'esenciales' constitutivos de la identidad y el poder del amo"[85] [one of the essentially constitutive rights of the identity and the power of the master]. Henry Louis Gates Jr. discusses the tendency in Western culture to connect both humanity and political rights with literacy.[86] Gates sees literacy as constitutive proof of the slave's humanity and further as a commodity traded for humanity and freedom.[87] Ramos emphasizes the fact that Manzano is constituted in the process of representing physical suffering and considers this pain as the commodity which he exchanges for the price of freedom.[88] Where Gates reads slaves as writing "not to demonstrate humane letters, but to demonstrate his or her own membership" in an *already defined* "human community,"[89] Ramos talks of the slave's testimony as a discourse that operates on the limits of definitions, effectively redefining humanity and citizenship.[90] Whether the focus is on the text as evidence of humanity, or the pain expressed in the text as currency allowing for the acquisition of freedom and the potential to challenge definitions, like human and nonhuman, in both cases, Douglass and Manzano must write to have this elusive *thing* that is supposedly the evidence of their humanity and which could become the basis for their claim to all of the other categories that had been denied to them, including freedom, manhood, Christianity, and citizenship.

To obtain this *thing*, Douglass and Manzano faced the problem of wanting to learn to read and write in a society that strictly controlled these skills and intentionally denied them to slaves. Manzano copies his young master Nicolas, reading his books and reproducing things he wrote. Manzano copies Nicolas to the extent that "hay sierta identidad entre su letra y la mia"[91] [there is a certain similarity between his handwriting and mine]. Douglass writes about the fact that he has to use clever means to learn to read in order to overcome legal and social restrictions similar to those faced by Manzano. He gets young boys on the street to teach him in exchange for bread, copies the letters written by carpenters on the timbers at a shipyard, and finally sneaks access to the copybooks used by his young Master Thomas, noting that he "continued to do this until I could write a hand very similar to that of Master Thomas. Thus, after a long, tedious effort for years, I finally succeeded in learning how to write."[92] During seven years at the Aulds', Douglass learns to read and write through "subterfuge, antagonism, direct imitation, and ultimately self-insertion in the margins of the 'authoritative discourse' of a southern ideology of literacy."[93] This is the apprenticeship necessary to gain a position in society from which Douglass and Manzano will be able to write and define themselves and to challenge the process of racialization that has excluded them from the categories of human and citizen.

The statements made by Douglass and Manzano as to the similarity between the slave and the master's hand are, themselves, strikingly similar.[94] Each man, in language, originally creates himself in the image of his master, in the image of the Western Man that Weheliye cites as the basis for definitions of who is human and who is not. Here it would be irresponsible to gloss over the fact that imitation of the enslaver is a problematic proposition. However, it is partly through the initial act of copying (to gain literacy) that Manzano and Douglass gain the power to enter into public discourse and contest the identities implied in the status of the master. Alma Dizon notes that while Manzano uses Don Nicolás' handwriting as his model, he refuses to stop writing even when this "father" figure tells him to do so.[95] Depicting him as someone who controls his own intellect, Dizon emphasizes that Manzano identifies with "the *means* through which he . . . will ultimately achieve his own identity" that is, reading and writing, rather than identifying with the master himself.[96] This is very similar to Douglass's contention that he came to understand literacy as the difference between slavery and freedom—as the path to freedom, one of the means to achieve personhood within a slave system. Ever a proponent of the transforming power of language, Julio Ramos argues that "la 'copia' de la letra del amo somete la jerarquía a una transformación intensa que rebasa la cuestión ontológica de la identificación, y que trastoca más bien las *posiciones* en esa escena de dominio"[97] [copying the letter of the master submits the hierarchy to an intense transformation that exceeds the ontological question of identification, and that also disrupts the positions in this site of power]. The act of writing, because it was associated with the enslaver and because language is occupied by the enslaver's intentions, implicated the slave in the power system that kept him in bondage. Sonia Labrador-Rodríguez explains this tension, arguing that for Manzano writing is simultaneously an act of freedom and subjugation, of vindication and submission.[98] She emphasizes the fact that Manzano may learn to write, and that he cannot fully express himself, but that his writing, even when it permits him to exercise freedom of thought and articulate his own ideas, is circumscribed within his social position as a slave and this is a difficult position because in Cuba no rules exist for a slave writer.[99] Manzano must recreate his past life and past identity in language as a normal autobiographer does, but in order to do this he has to recreate language itself to be able to write his future life and future (free) identity. Similarly, Douglass may have copied his master's hand when learning to write, but while he imitates that which is useful to him (the ability to read and to produce his master's hand), he does not do so in order to become his master. Douglass is not a reader, but a "radical misreader" of "everything Auld stands for and believes in."[100] Douglass imitates aspects of his master, gaining skills which will give him the power to defy his master's definition and write his own. For Douglass, part of the abolitionist movement in the United States, there were perhaps more rules for the slave writer, but even in his situation, as his relationship with William Lloyd Garrison indicates, the slave was always negotiating and even fighting to define himself in a rhetorical landscape that attempted to monopolize possible identities.

THIRD NARRATIVE THREAD: CONSTRUCTIONS OF FAMILY

If it was necessary for Manzano and Douglass to negotiate relationships with patrons, relationships which were as difficult as they were potentially beneficial, they had insight and strategies cultivated from their past experiences with their enslavers which helped them to negotiate relationships with those in power. One problematic aspect of the relationship between masters and slaves that becomes clear in the autobiographies of both Douglass and Manzano is that slavery in both Cuba and the United States complicated kinship relationships. Not only did the natal alienation inherent in slavery disrupt biological family relations, fictive kin bonds constructed to compel slave obedience further compromised slaves' ability to construct their own identities as autonomous, rational human beings. Slaves and enslavers were intimately related in ways that both reflected and undermined the inherent value these cultures placed on family. Manzano and Douglass draw on the complicated nature of their relationships vis-à-vis their masters—and particularly emphasize a narrative thread regarding kinship relationships—in order to make emotional appeals to their readers, to give themselves credibility, to provide a critique of slavery as an institution, and to make implicit arguments for their inclusion in the nation.

Both Juan Francisco Manzano and Frederick Douglass demonstrate the reality of natal alienation when they emphasize how slavery systematically destroyed biological family relationships. Manzano's *Autobiografía* contains the heartbreaking story of his nuclear family. Manzano includes several passages that emphasize his love for and connection to his biological family. At one point in the narrative, Manzano remarks that he has not seen his parents for years. He then speaks very fondly of a rare opportunity to see them, adding that this will allow him to meet siblings that had been born after he went away.[101] On other occasions, he mentions his mother and his brother waiting up to see him, remarking on his mother's grief over his sufferings and how close he was to his brother despite their separation. One of the most striking passages where we see the thread of violence once again woven into the narrative is that in which his mother tries to intervene in his punishment and is instead taken to the "sacrificial site" and whipped for trying to protect her son.[102] The pathos of this situation is obvious, and Manzano emphasizes it by reporting that when she is struck "lo sentí yo en mi corazón"[103] [I felt it in my heart]. This subtheme of the narrative thread of family consists of Manzano's depiction of the loving relationships he has with his biological family, as well as describing the ways in which slavery systematically undermines them, creating a classic critique of slavery as an institution.

Frederick Douglass's narrative puts even more emphasis on the destruction of family bonds under slavery. Early in the first chapter, Douglass laments, "I never saw my mother, to know her as such, more than four or five times in my life; and each of those times was very short in duration, and at night."[104] Douglass highlights the mental and emotional hardships faced by slaves when he describes his separation from his mother.[105] Moving once again from the personal to the political, Douglass tells his readers that the separation of mothers and infants was "common custom."[106] The few times they are together she has had to walk twelve miles each way to see him at night after a long day at work. For John Hansen, the "continuous use of the word 'night' in this passage exemplifies the kind of relationship that Douglass had with his mother" and "the word 'night' describes the relationship as nonexistent (or dead) from the time he was an infant."[107] Douglass is denied significant interaction with his mother; seven-year-old Douglass is even "not allowed to be present during her illness, at her death, or burial."[108] The mother-child relationship has been destroyed by slavery. While Douglass is not around his mother enough to see her tortured, the thread of violence appears early on when he includes a depiction of the whipping of his aunt in the first chapter of his narrative. Juan Francisco Manzano feels every blow his mother receives in his heart and is changed by it; similarly, Douglass reports that when he witnesses the barbarity with which his aunt is whipped it becomes "the blood-stained gate, the entrance to the hell of slavery, through which I was about to pass."[109] Both Douglass and Manzano depict emotional connections to their parents, but ultimately utilize the narrative threads of family and violence to emphasize the way slavery destroys familial bonds.

Although unlike many slaves Juan Francisco Manzano knew his biological parents and had more contact with them than Douglass was allowed, Lorna V. Williams points out that Manzano's account of his life story begins with his masters rather than his parents and further argues that his "genealogical link to Cuba's titled aristocracy" can be seen as connecting his work to the tradition of the Noble Negro which also "differentiates him from the common slave."[110] Manzano's depiction of Cuban slavery represents the relationship between enslaver and slave as metaphorically corresponding to the relationship between parent and child. The first quasi-filial tie between slave and master described in the narrative comes in Manzano's very first paragraph where he describes how his first mistress had the practice of taking the most beautiful of the light skinned slave girls as "criadas de *estimación,* de *distinción,* de *razón.*"[111] Schulman translates this final phrase as "maids of distinction, esteemed, or *singled out for training,*" adding in a footnote that Manzano underlined the final term (*razón*) in his manuscript "showing in this way, from the beginning, that he was born of a slave mother who possessed special qualities due in part to her training and education."[112] The choice of the word *razón* here is interesting as well in that it translates literally as reason, and can also be seen as having been used by Manzano to emphasize that his mother was recognized by the mistress as a rational, thinking (that is, human) being. Manzano reports that the Marchioness had the habit of freeing these women and caring for them "como a hijas propias"[113] [like her own daughters]. (Sadly, Manzano's mother is the last of these young women, so the mistress does not free her lest she be left without a maid.) This example establishes the pattern of the chosen slave being treated like a child with the master standing in as parent, a pattern repeated with Manzano. The case of Manzano's mother also indicates that while this kind of quasi-filial relation might appear to indicate an acknowledgment of the humanity of the slave and the possibility of freedom, it almost always does not.

Manzano describes two of his mistresses using the metaphor of motherhood. The first is the image of the good, loving, and just mother who never punishes without cause. Manzano, the child of a privileged slave, describes himself as having grown up among the mistress's grandchildren. He occupies a complicated and troubling position. On the one hand, Manzano writes that he was in the arms of his first mistress more than in his mother's arms, but on the other hand he says that the mistress took him as a type of amusement.[114] While the idea of the young Manzano as an amusement objectifies the slave child, Manzano's narrative also suggests that his mistress had affection for the boy she called the child of her old age.[115] He refers to her—likely at her insistence—as "*mamá mia.*"[116] According to Ivan Schulman, the mistress's treatment creates in Manzano a psychological complex that does not match his condition as a slave and that this treatment as son rather than slave challenges the readers' ideas by playing on their emotions.[117] However, Manzano is not the same as a real son; in another move that mirrors the idea of Manzano as the mistress's toy, he also describes himself as her "falderillo" or lapdog.[118] Despite the fact that the mistress's attitude belittles Manzano and disturbs his kinship relations, the overall effect of this description is that both Manzano and his mother had been chosen by the mistress and treated as children. They have been given a different status than other slaves and their treatment and identities trouble the distinctions wrought by racialization and potentially trouble the global color line that excludes them from humanity and citizenship.

Sonia Labrador-Rodríguez aptly remarks that although the first image of Manzano's experience as a slave is that of good treatment, the story contained in his *Autobiografía* is a story of cruelty and capriciousness.[119] The story is of his life of suffering *after* the fall, a narrative more in line with the themes and pathos of his poetry. The initial image of Manzano as the child of a Marquesa's old age stands in stark contrast to the treatment he receives at the hands of his second mistress. Alma Dizon demonstrates how Manzano uses the "abundance of mothers" in the *Autobiografía* to demonstrate "the perversion of the maternal image in the discourse of slavery."[120] Following the paradigm he has been taught, Manzano calls his second mistress "mama" and tells his readers that "amábala tanto como a madre"[121] [I loved her like a mother]. Although the metaphor remains, Manzano describes his second mistress as unpredictably capricious and inhuman. She punishes him for the slightest infraction, such as incarcerating and beating him repeatedly for "stealing" a leaf from a geranium plant.[122] The cruelty of the second mistress disturbs the reader since it contrasts with both Manzano's devotion and the image of the first mistress. In the depiction of the second mistress all of the critiques of slavery come together: the misplaced use of familial metaphors, violence, the systematic destruction of slave families, and the corrupting influence of slavery on masters. Toward the end of his narrative, Manzano's second mistress asks him if he remembers his *"mama mia"*; when he replies that he does, she pointedly tells him that she has taken her place.[123] The mistress's jealous insistence that he forget his former mother figure in deference to her shows the possessive nature of her attitude toward him: he is, after all, her slave. This is in stark contrast to his biological mother's willingness to sacrifice herself for Manzano. Ultimately it is the complex between the three mother figures that creates the strongest blurring of the way the rhetoric of family was used to justify slavery. Manzano's testimony demonstrates that although the legal expectation or the moral hope of fair, paternalistic/maternalistic treatment may have existed—including for Domingo del Monte—the reality was different. Dizon writes that, "Instead of an interceding spiritual mother [like in Marianism], we see one who claims complete authority over an adopted child. This tenuous double-talk, in which the devoted mother is at the same time omnipotent and abusive," ultimately reveals the corrupt nature of the system and destroys any illusion of "the slave owner's claim to moral superiority."[124] Manzano's text implicitly undermines the paternalistic narrative which was one of the ideas used to justify slavery. It also indicates that in negotiating national identity, former slaves like Manzano had to overcome the infantilization scripted onto them by society in order to be able to fully participate in the (then prospective) Cuban nation. They also had to carefully interrogate any metaphors of the national family.

While Frederick Douglass does not explicitly represent his relationship with a mistress as following the metaphor of motherhood, his interactions with Sophia Auld, both before and after she is tainted by "the fatal poison of irresponsible power,"[125] obliquely mirror the contrast Manzano establishes between his first and second mistress. If the "overabundance of mothers" in Manzano provides a strong argument against slavery, the transformation of Sophia Auld from angel to demon, from "a woman of the kindest heart and finest feeling" who initially treats Douglas like a child—one, for example, who needs to be taught his ABCs—to a woman who narrowly watches Douglass to make sure he does not learn to read as she believes that, as her husband teaches her, learning "would forever unfit him to be a slave,"[126] provides a similarly compelling argument. Douglass's nuanced argument regarding the fact that slavery degrades all who are involved is most poignantly and powerfully enacted in his depiction of Sophia Auld's transformation.

Manzano also reinforces his status as more than a slave by mentioning his quasi-filial relationship to Don Nicolas who "me quería no como a esclavo, sino como a hijo a pesar de su corta edad"[127] [loved me not as a slave, but as a son, in spite of his young age]. Here even a young boy, one not much older than Manzano himself, takes on not a brotherly role, but, following the logic of his time and the rhetoric of Cuban slavery, a paternal role. Dizon writes that one consequence of these depictions is that Manzano "appears to be trapped in a sort of eternal childhood in which everyone of consequence is an elder and superior despite actual ages."[128] If Manzano the soon to be former-slave truly wished to negotiate an equal place in the national family, he had to fight against the assumption that he would be forever in an inferior position vis-à-vis whites, an assumption emphasized in the master/slave relationship and even reflected in his relations with his patron Domingo del Monte who, as was pointed out in the previous chapter, was the younger of the two. According to Nwankwo, when Manzano emphasizes that he was a son and not a slave, or that he was treated by his first mistress like a (white) child, "[b]oth statements reinforce the same point—he wishes to be seen as a human being rather than a slave."[129] Dizon also astutely notes that in the case of Don Nicolás, Manzano "does not say that he loved the man as a father."[130] Perhaps Manzano's lack of expressed filial love may indicate his careful use of the metaphor. Ultimately, Manzano turns the paternalistic nature of the narrative back on the slave holders, emphasizing not their supposed right to have slaves, but his own humanity given that the prescribed role scripted him as a son.

Douglass never uses a familial metaphor to describe his relationship to any of the individuals to which he quite literally belonged. Even more than in Manzano's text, the account Douglass gives emphasizes that he was denied the connection to his biological family. In the case of his father, he is even denied explicit knowledge of his identity. After introducing his mother and lamenting her absence in his life, Douglass states simply that his "father was a white man" and that he knows this because his father "was admitted to be such by all I ever heard speak of my parentage"; the very carefully worded passage continues with Douglass attributing to others the whispers "that my master was my father," although he insists that "of the correctness of this opinion, I know nothing; the means of knowing was withheld from me."[131] Douglass does not dare to claim that his master was his father, except as held in the opinion of others. Although he states that he does not know the correctness of the opinion that his master was his father, Douglass shifts the blame to those who kept him from knowing. The fact that this passage "contains numerous negative expressions, such as 'no,' 'not,' and 'never,' all illustrating Douglass's lack of knowledge," is significant to John Hansen because it demonstrates the extent of Douglass's enforced ignorance and the fact that he does not have "even the most basic knowledge about his own personal life" and therefore, in some ways, lacks "a legal personal identity."[132] This sense of loss of identity is important to the text as one example of how Douglass invites readers to sympathize with, in this case, his very lack of knowledge about his parentage. Further, the reality that his father was likely his master is an indirect reference to the thread of violence running through the text. In addition, Douglass subtly constructs a discourse of paternity and legitimacy through his white blood. Although this was certainly not a sufficient discourse to disrupt the rhetoric of slavery since so many enslavers fathered children with their slaves, it reminded Douglass's audience that many gray areas existed, troubling the rhetoric that helped ensure the perpetuation of the institution of slavery and challenging his position outside of the national family.

FOURTH NARRATIVE THREAD: MISCEGENATION AND THE COMPLEXITY OF RACIAL IDENTITIES

Regarding family and legitimacy, one aspect that both Frederick Douglass and Juan Francisco Manzano include in their narratives is an indication that they are the products of miscegenation. Their narratives demonstrate the complexity of racial identities in both the United States and Cuba. The biological mixing of masters and slaves complicates the process of racialization and the maintenance of the global color line. The narrative thread regarding miscegenation and the complexities of racial identities is also tightly interwoven with the thread of violence in the texts even if the violence associated with these slaves' genetic makeup is implied rather than directly reported. In evoking the complexities of racial identities in their nations, Manzano and Douglass bring the thread of violence to a careful reader's consciousness once again, negotiate with the concept of whiteness as the standard for humanity and citizenship, and challenge the black/white nonhuman/human binaries used to exclude them from society.

Juan Francisco Manzano never explicitly talks about his specific genealogy, emphasizing instead his image as an adopted son of the masters, but he does make clear that he is not just one of the *negros*. According to Roberto Friol, in his day Manzano was identified as a *pardo*, the term found both on his marriage certificate and on the court documents related to the *La escalera* investigation.[133] A pardo is a term generally used to refer to a person of mixed race, often a mulato, and it can have a connotation of moral superiority over other mulatos.[134] Throughout the narrative, Manzano never refers to himself as a *negro* or a slave. References to Manzano's racial identity are generally reported in the *Autobiografía* as descriptions used by others rather than terms he uses to describe himself.[135] In the text, Manzano is first referred to as "un criollo."[136] This term was commonly used for slaves born in the New World, but it can also be tied to developing ideas of Cubanness. The distinction between *peninsulares* (those born in Spain) and *criollos* (those born in Cuba) was important to Domingo del Monte as he tried to foster the creation of a Cuban national identity and culture. In the text Manzano also reports that he is known as "el *Chinito* o el *Mulatico* de la Marquesa,"[137] a phrase which identifies him as belonging to the Marquesa, and emphasizes both his infantilization and miscegenation since it uses the diminutive form of two terms for mixed race individuals, *mulato* and *chino*.[138] Right before Manzano runs away at the end of the events of the narrative, he is asked by a free black why he puts up with his mistreatment since he is "un mulatico fino con tantas abilidades" [light-skinned mulato with so many talents] and Manzano finally describes himself as a "mulato entre negros" [mulato among blacks].[139] He intentionally positions himself outside of the general population of slaves, emphasizing his individuality, here in terms of his perceived racial identity, just as he does with his intellectual and artistic abilities. Although his narrative does not insist upon it, the first image remains—he is a child who deserves to be loved as a son, an individual apart from the masses. "What is evident is his sense of the availability of White privilege, and his insertion of self into that world of power."[140] When Manzano uses the metaphor of family, his mixed-race status is also relevant. He engages in a "strategic subjective identification with Whiteness" and a "skillful manipulation of the system of *padrinazgo* that characterized the patrician universe of the colonial plantation."[141] Manzano's negotiation of the metaphor of family is intricately connected to negotiations both with and for power, negotiations that, in this context, are also negotiations of identity that involve and revolve around the concept of whiteness and which relate to the association of whiteness with the proto-nation.

While Manzano finally refers to himself as a mulato among blacks after letting many others in the text comment upon his racial identity, Douglass does not make any direct references to his own race within his text. He does include one instance where he is identified by Betsy Freeland as a "yellow devil" and a "long-legged mulatto devil" when she is accusing him of having inspired two slaves to run away.[142] Two things stand out about this passage in this context: Douglass is clearly identified here as a mulato, and his readers are reminded of the perverse irony which led a white woman to consider a mulato as being fundamentally untrustworthy when in fact his complexion was evidence not of his own perfidy, but that of the white men who raped their slaves. Another interesting aspect of the fact that Douglass does not identify himself racially in the text is the fact that his title introduces him not as a black or negro slave, but as an *American* slave. In commenting on the famous chiasmus in Douglass's narrative—"you have seen how a man was made a slave; you shall see how a slave was made a man"[143]—Fionnghuala Sweeney notes that, "The cross-border, transformative quality of the chiastic structure is mirrored in the title of the *Narrative*, with the parallel tensions of the 'man/slave' of the one echoed in the 'American/slave' of the other."[144] Sweeney sees the "antithetical" juxtaposition of the terms American and slave in Douglass's title as "an early literary expression of the American 'house divided'"[145]—evidence of the conflict regarding national identity that would cause the Civil War. But Douglass's title does not just include the juxtaposition of American and slave; it also includes the phrase "*American Slave*," a phrase which simultaneously describes the slave's location, makes America culpable for slavery, differentiates him from slaves in other contexts, and makes a subtle yet powerful argument that he is both a slave *and an American*.

While there are many different critical approaches to Juan Francisco Manzano's depictions of his identity, the majority of them can be seen as relating to his desire to be seen as a human and potential citizen. Richard L. Jackson reads Manzano as preferring to obscure both the past and his blackness in favor of his Cubanness; Jackson's work emphasizes the points of commonality between Manzano and Morúa Delgado, both of whom, as shall become apparent in subsequent chapters, have what Jackson refers to as an "integrationist zeal."[146] That is, Jackson sees Manzano as making an argument for an integrated Cuba. While the focus on integration could imply the valuing of difference, Jerome Branche claims Manzano's "avoidance of blackness . . . and his espousal of the cultural markers of Whiteness . . . point to a conscious constitution of self as a racial subject, one that is in strict accordance with the dictates of the dominant ideology of Whitening."[147] Whether it is seen as espousing integration or identifying with the dominant ideology of Whiteness, Manzano is using racial categories and ideas in such a way as to intentionally and significantly negotiate with the racialization that has designated who is human and who is not. Even if his text does not imply human status for slaves in general, it makes an indirect argument for his own humanity which necessarily troubles the definitions constructed to exclude anyone of African descent from the category of human. Ivan Schulman clearly distinguishes between text and author when he describes Manzano's *text* as one that has assimilated the white perspective; however, since it is only the textual representation which has assimilated, the text itself is still able to express the hostility of Manzano as an alienated and marginalized self.[148] In focusing on the text as a construction which both is not the man and cannot fully represent the man, we can avoid seeing Manzano's narrative as evidence of his movement away from some inherent "black" self, and rather as a complex negotiation enacted by a mixed race individual who understood the power inherent in the idea of whiteness and the Western Man and who manipulated the narrative thread of whiteness in his text to best present himself as an individual worthy of freedom and citizenship. Further, as the references to Manzano in the text as *criollo, chinito, mulatico*, and *mulato* clearly indicate, merely discussing black and white does not fully encompass the racial realities within Plantation America and any conceptualization of the nation on the grounds of that binary is ultimately problematic.

As we have seen, in the opening to his *Narrative* Douglass is able to persuasively imply that his master was his father, without having to accuse his master of being his father. The image of the "white" or "whitened" slave introduces into the narrative the sexual violence perpetrated by white enslavers. The extent of the sexual abuse of female slaves by their masters indicates "the irrationality of the hegemonic, pro-slavery discourse and the self-deception in which its participants engaged."[149] Only through self-deception could many ignore the evidence of miscegenation. In addition, "as both the son and slave of his father-master, the mulatto Douglass deconstructs the fundamental opposition between white people and black animals on which much of the rationale for slavery was based. That separation between white and black cannot hold because it is culturally, not naturally, determined."[150] The birth of slaves who were children of their enslavers functionally disrupts the hierarchy that served as a basis for the justification of slavery and allowed for the maintenance of power by those who considered themselves white. Once again Douglass connects the personal to the political by taking a fact about his own life and creating a general critique of the institution of slavery. He moves from merely narrating his story as Garrison desired, to denouncing slavery on the basis of the realities he depicts. In this case, Douglass avoids painting himself as a helpless victim, adeptly manipulating ideas of race, family, and religion. In a famous passage, Douglass points out that "a very different-looking class of people are springing up at the south, and are now held in slavery, from those originally brought to this country from Africa;" based on this observation, Douglass notes that "if their increase will do no other good, it will do away the force of the argument, that God cursed Ham, and therefore American slavery is right."[151] Douglass brings his argument home when he speaks of the "thousands . . . ushered into the world" every year who, like him, "owe their existence to white fathers, and those fathers most frequently their own masters."[152] The biological and discursive "whiteness" established by Douglass in the narrative problematizes the myth of the curse of Ham. As Douglass explains, had the myth been true, it would have applied to Africans, not to those of mixed parentage. Douglass is not just a witness who narrates the conditions of slavery; he actively engages the religious and social discourses that enabled it, challenging the racializing assemblages that sought to delineate and enforce the global color line separating human from nonhuman, citizen from non-citizen. Douglass uses the ideology of family and legitimacy, complicated by the realities of miscegenation, coupled with religious rhetoric, to make a social commentary which challenges the rhetorical underpinnings of the institution his discourse intends to topple and ultimately paves the way for a reexamination of the fundamental categories of identity in the United States.

Both Juan Francisco Manzano and Frederick Douglass appear to reinforce a racial hierarchy based on skin color perpetuated by the ideology of whiteness. Manzano's attitude, the distance he establishes between himself and the darker field slaves, indicates both the hierarchy that exists within the slave community and the internalized racism of preferred slaves. In Douglass's case as well as Manzano's, the apparent racism in their self-identification as light-skinned may also be a necessary discursive move intended to align them more fully with their patrons and readers by aligning with conceptions of the citizen, who was always the western Man. Although it is certainly possible, and perhaps even likely, that Manzano and Douglass had internalized the racism of their societies, it is also likely that in order to argue for their freedom and to condemn slavery, both Manzano and Douglass had to leave some of the underpinnings of societal paradigms untouched. In other words, meeting their discursive ends (freedom and abolition) meant playing upon the values of their readers. In this case, they may have judged the fact of mixed blood to be something that would lend them credibility. It also was a fact that undermined the institution of slavery to the extent that the justification for that institution depended on a clear separation of the races. Whatever the racial politics, Manzano and Douglass both insinuated that they were the (figurative or literal) sons of masters because they hoped they could parlay both fictive and biological kinship relationships into inclusion in the national family.

FIFTH COMMON THREAD: RESISTANCE AND REBELLION

When Juan Francisco Manzano wrote in 1835, Cuba was more than fifty years from abolishing slavery and more than seventy years from becoming a nation. When Frederick Douglass wrote in 1845, the United States had been a nation for nearly seventy years, but was within twenty years of both a civil war that redefined the nation and the abolition of slavery. Despite these differences in context, both men experienced the ways in which racialization negated them and both fought to forge an identity in opposition to this negation. This can be clearly seen in the *Autobiografía* and *Narrative* themselves, and in the ways that Douglass and Manzano did not fully accede to the wishes of their patrons. They resisted being completely controlled and reserved to themselves both material and authority.

In 1845, Douglass was given an outlet for his story and imbued with the authority to tell it, but he was expected to play by the Garrisonian abolitionists' rules. The validation of Douglass and his narrative found in the paratext does not negate the limits placed upon Douglass by Garrison and other abolitionists. The Garrisonians imagined and allowed for a very specific and narrow role for Douglass within their movement, understanding his value as an eyewitness, but expecting Douglass to limit himself "to the received modes of discourse."[153] While in many ways writers like Douglass faced a "situation which seemed to force him to move to a public version of the self—one molded on the values of white America,"[154] a slave narrator who wrote as part of the antislavery movement had to perform, "subtly and simultaneously, literary acts of resistance *to* the antislavery movement" so that s/ he could remain "an independent entity, something more than a coopted organization man."[155] The fact that Douglass wrote two other autobiographies is a fairly good indication that the purpose and the context of the 1845 *Narrative* did not allow him to tell his whole story, or to tell it in the way he wanted to. It is also an indication of his ongoing negotiation of his relation to the republic. In his 1855 autobiography, *My Bondage and My Freedom*, Douglass writes about his relationship to the Garrisonian abolitionists from whom he had parted company in 1851.[156] He depicts his "then revered friend," William Lloyd Garrison, as whispering to him as he rose to speak, reminding him to merely tell his story. Douglass writes, "I could not always obey . . . . It did not entirely satisfy me to *narrate* wrongs; I felt like *denouncing* them."[157] Despite the picture painted by Garrison and Phillips, when it came down to it, the abolitionist who praised Douglass's wit and strength of reasoning did not trust him to articulate the philosophy of abolitionism. The use of the word narrate, emphasized by Douglass, reminds the reader of Douglass's *Narrative*, written while he still "revered" William Lloyd Garrison.

The contrast between the actions narrate and denounce in Douglass's statement implies that in the 1845 *Narrative* he was unable to be the philosopher who denounced instead of the body who narrated. In *Characters of Blood: Black Heroism in the Transatlantic Imagination*, Celeste-Marie Bernier aptly describes north American slavery "[a]s an institution and a national ideology" that supported "objectified categorizations of Black women, children, and men as they were repeatedly exploited as objects."[158] She adds that many anti-slavery discourses were problematic in that they "reimagined Black men and women as no more than spectacular commodities or bodies of evidence."[159] Several critics have pointed to ways in which Douglass successfully exceeded the limits Garrison desired to place on him.[160] Douglass is not merely the body (of testimony) desired by Garrison, not just the fugitive slave who is symbol rather than individual. He transforms from "the prosopopoeial subject speaking from the autobiography"—merely the narrator—to "an outsider who claims the right to comment upon and judge;"[161] he is an author, and thus an authority in his own right. Even more, for Bernier, his "acts and arts have resulted in the creation of a revisionist archive" in which Douglass is an icon of "living, breathing black . . . male humanity."[162] Douglass engages with narrative threads that were used by his patrons to invest him with authority, but his use of the narrative threads of violence, religion, literacy, family, and racial identities in the *Narrative* indicates the complexity of his relationship to these values; his text often implicitly, and sometimes explicitly, works to subvert, destabilize, or transform the assumptions and cultural values that served as the underpinning for both slavery and the exclusion of the negated *other* from the nation.

While Douglass shows his desire to exceed the limits placed on him by Garrison, a desire which will eventually lead to a split between the two, Juan Francisco Manzano shows resistance in another way. In terms of his relationship to del Monte, there is a part of himself that Manzano holds back. In a letter discussing his writing of the *Autobiografía*, Manzano writes to del Monte that he is prepared to write his life story, but that he will reserve the most interesting parts of the story in order to one day write a Cuban novel.[163] Molloy claims this as a definitive moment of resistance even though Manzano never wrote such a novel because "[f]rom the moment Manzano announces that there is a part of himself he will not cede—a part that is *ungiving*—that part informs, through its very defiant silence, the rest of the writing."[164] Roberto Friol finds it both extraordinary and important that Manzano planned to write a Cuban novel two years before Cirilo Villaverde began working on the "foundational" Cuban novel *Cecilia Valdés.*[165] It is incredibly striking that Manzano, in 1835, understands that his individual life story and experiences could be the proper content for a Cuban novel, particularly when we recall the desire within del Monte's *tertulia* to produce novels as part of the nation-building project. While Manzano's text was placed within one discourse of national identity—that defined by del Monte—another discourse of national identity with the Afro-Cuban man at the center was imagined but not produced. Manzano's resistance comes in claiming that the patron does not have the right to certain kinds of information, that there are certain things about which he cannot force even the slave to speak, that the narrator owns his own story as he owns himself. Perhaps Manzano's silence on the "most interesting" events of his life is a defiant silence he learned in response to having unwanted auditors sitting behind screens overhearing his stories. This defiance is similar to that of Douglass, who is not content to merely tell his story and let white men control abolitionist philosophy. Although Manzano and Douglass negotiate the paradigms of identity in such a way as to write free selves made to appeal to those in power, it is worth emphasizing the obvious: these constructs do not represent the entirety of who they are.

In both Cuba and the United States, the radical negation of the population of African descent was used to exclude them from citizenship. Even those like Manzano and Douglass who were invited by patrons to participate in the conversations about slavery and race in their homelands were circumscribed by the prejudices surrounding them. Recall that in Douglass's speeches one of the main themes is the problem of northern prejudice. Antonio Vera-León signals as the fundamental paradox of literary abolitionism "desear un sujeto blanco, pero tener que contar con el lenguaje del negro para la articulación del discurso literario nacional"[166] [the desire for a white subject, but the necessity of dealing with the language of the black man for the articulation of national literary discourse]. The race-based systems of slavery in the New World by necessity had to enact a radical alienation of the enslaved, organizing society and, through racialization, constructing the idea of humanity and citizenship with qualifications that excluded them. What Manzano and Douglass achieved in writing their discourses of identity was a Bakhtinian appropriation in which these Afro–New World men used a common set of symbols and narrative threads to identify themselves with a European paradigm of culture and manhood. Manzano and Douglass chose to define themselves by appropriating the tropes of family, religion, literacy, and the complexities of racial identity because these tropes spoke directly to the question of their humanity and to their intellectual and spiritual identities. Although neither Manzano nor Douglass explicitly sought or constructed an *alternative* definition of manhood or citizenship, choosing rather to seek inclusion on the terms set by society, the fact of their possible inclusion in a paradigm designed to exclude them could not help but weaken and potentially transform the paradigm. By inserting themselves into these definitions of freedom and citizenship, Douglass and Manzano disrupted the racializing assemblages of their societies by *overpopulating*, to continue with Bakhtin's analogy, the paradigms to the degree that the boundaries exploded. The common threads in their discourses of identity challenged the status quo, denying those in power the exclusive right to define citizenship and the very nature of the nation itself.

Douglass and Manzano continued to challenge the status quo in later works, two of which are worthy of note here. Seven years after writing his autobiography, Manzano published his longest work, the verse play *Zafira* (1842). *Zafira* is a work of historical fiction set in sixteenth-century Algiers that includes themes of tyranny, exile, rebellion, and slavery. The play was based on historic events and an earlier Spanish play of the same name.[167] Eight years after publishing his *Narrative*, Frederick Douglass published his only fictional work, the novella *The Heroic Slave* (1853). Douglass's novella is also historical fiction, based on the then much more recent past of the 1841 *Creole* Rebellion. These two works stand out in this context because they both represent a move by their authors from anti-slavery discourse based in their own experiences to an engagement with these themes in fictionalized historical material. Celeste-Marie Bernier describes Douglass's text as combining many different genres in a way that "testifies to Douglass's search for a new language and genre within which to dramatize competing constructions of black male heroism."[168] In these two works, both Manzano and Douglass experiment with a new genre and new language in the hope of achieving this end. Both texts include as a significant character a rebellious slave who can figure as a sort of Afro-Cuban or African American founding father and thus expand on the authors' discourses of identity by even more radically challenging the negation and exclusion of slaves and people of African descent from their nations.

On the surface, *Zafira* appears to have nothing to do with Cuba since it is set in sixteenth-century Africa. A number of critics have made a compelling case explaining the relevance of the play to Manzano's immediate context in mid-nineteenth-century Cuba, linking it with both slavery and colonial rule of the island. Olsen points out that "its performance of tyranny, exile, subjugation, slavery, and rebellion become charged with the weight of Spanish colonialism on the island,"[169] Miller believes that contemporary readers would have understood the play as at least partially an allegory of Cuba's colonial condition,[170] and Rodriguez Drissi considers the play as "important evidence on the ways in which the Moor, in its various guises, signifies for the individual and collective psyche of those who existed on the margins in Cuba under colonial rule."[171] As an anti-colonial text, the themes of the play clearly relate to discussions of emerging Cuban national identity. The plot of the play participates in the tragic mode that permeated Manzano's poetry: Selim, an exiled prince, returns to Mauritania years after his father was killed by the usurping tyrant Barbarroja. Barbarroja has just about convinced Zafira, the widow of the former king and Selim's mother, to marry him. Selim returns to claim the throne and, through a series of events, Zafira kills herself mistakenly thinking Selim has been killed when in fact it is Barbarroja who has died in a successful revolution.

While in the earlier Spanish play of the same name a Spanish hero arrives to save the day and unseat the tyrant, in Manzano's version the "true hero behind the scenes, standing in for the enslaved people of African descent in Cuba who will conspire with Selim . . . and act in rebellion when the moment is ripe" is the slave Noemí.[172] Manzano manipulates and subverts the Spanish text by "infusing it with echoes of revolutionary antislavery philosophy."[173] Noemí is described by Manzano as a "eunuco negro"[174] [black eunuch] and he conspires with Selim, the rightful heir to the throne, to overthrow the illegitimate ruler Barbarroja. The play, which is much more overtly political and transgressive than Manzano's *Autobiografía*, suggests that Cuban slaves would conspire with *criollo* leaders to fight against illegitimate Spanish rule, creating the possibility for Afro-Cubans to be agents of the emerging Cuban nationality. But the figure of a black slave rising up, even against a tyrant, is concerning in Cuba in 1842. With the fear of a Haitian-style revolution on the minds of the white *criollo* leaders and intellectuals, rebellious black masculinity is fraught with tensions, which may explain the choice to set the play in the sixteenth century and make Noemí a eunuch. On the other hand, while Noemí's emasculation can be seen as "a means by which Manzano diminishes the slave's dangerous *potential* for virility and the masculine act of revolt . . . Noemí is by no means a passive or submissive slave."[175] Noemí repeatedly saves the day with both "strategy and a song."[176] The use of songs by Noemí to warn and save both Selim and Zafira in the play points to the importance of artistic and intellectual contributions to the formation of national identity and links Manzano's work specifically to del Monte's nationalist project. More importantly, Manzano the former slave poet creates a slave character whose intellect and expressive capabilities are important both to his identity and to the establishment of legitimate rule in his homeland. Thus a version of manhood and citizenship emerges that is reflective of the kind of individual personhood Manzano put forth in his autobiography.[177]

The first time that Noemí helps Selim to escape from the tyrant's guards Selim offers him a purse. Noemí tells Selim to keep it to buy those that are being sold to the "infame interés"[178] [infamous business]. When Selim then asks Noemí if he is a slave, Noemí replies, "Soy superior en todo a la fortuna,/Mas tesoro no quiero, yo la canto/Según la encuentro, próspera, o adversa/Y así de sus caprichos nada extraño"[179] ["In all things I am above fortune,/but treasure I do not desire, I sing fortune/whether I find her favorable or adverse/thus her caprices surprise me not"].[180] This is a startling statement for the slave, particularly in light of Manzano's poetry in which there are repeated references to his own misfortune, terrible destiny, impious fortune, and unhappy birth. It is also, as Marilyn Miller reminds us, reminiscent of "Manzano's declaration that it was poetry that provided him with a means and a mode in which to recount situations that were 'ya próspera, ya adversa.' His status as a poet proved he had a soul and was more than the sum of the circumstances in which he found himself."[181] The figure of Noemí, despite being a slave, is a transformative agent who "sings" in a powerful and socially transformative way and who, a reader might imagine, will have a much different role in the society that will emerge now that Barbarroja has been defeated. Noemí may be a eunuch, but he is far from impotent when it comes to overthrowing the tyranny. In addition to his wit and song, he is shown in the play with a bow and arrow and a sword, and he is the one who appears on stage at the end of the play holding the severed head of Barbarroja. Noemí is a new kind of "Cuban national hero: a black slave who is permitted a bold act of bloody, violent retribution against an illegal imposition of power."[182] Manzano's radical play, made more circumspect, of course, by being set in sixteenth-century Africa, is very suggestive. He creates a model for an Afro-Cuban national hero and writes Afro-Cubans into the story of the resistance to Spanish colonial rule that was central to the emerging idea of Cuban national identity.

Frederick Douglass's *The Heroic Slave* is explicitly centered on a rebel slave, Madison Washington, the leader of the *Creole* rebellion. In the novella, Douglass works to write Washington into the canon of American national heroism and into American national identity. The introductory section of the novella does this by emphasizing the idea of Virginia as the mother of

American statesmen and heroes.[183] Douglass then indicates he will tell the unknown story of "*one* of the truest, manliest, and bravest of her children."[184] The choice of adjectives here is important. Madison Washington, the heroic slave of the title, is one of Virginia's—and America's—children, part of the national family and the nation. He is also a "true" American who stands as a model for manhood and bravery. Thus the radical negation of identity of slaves achieved through racialization is countered. Washington is a (hu)man and an American. By connecting Washington to a "motherland of white revolutionaries rather than a slave mother or father, Douglass supplants the slave's stigmatized racial identity with a glorified nationalistic identity, giving his Northern white readers a ready means of identifying or sympathizing with a black man."[185] Here the heroic slave follows the condition of his mother—the State of Virginia—a radical claim to national belonging for one born on American soil.

To reinforce Madison Washington's place as an American hero, Douglass specifically compares him to several important figures in the pantheon of American heroism; his love for liberty is equal to Patrick Henry's, his claim to freedom is as legitimate as Thomas Jefferson's, and his valor and strength in fighting against long odds for freedom are as laudable as George Washington's.[186] Douglass highlights American hypocrisy when he emphasizes that despite Madison Washington's characteristics, he is only recorded in chattel records.[187] "The oxymoronic nature of 'living' within 'chattel records,' surely a historical living death, bears witness to forces of black marginalization, alienation, and cultural erasure."[188] Douglass's "presentation of black slave heroism according to white revolutionary values countered the exclusivity of white rhetorical claims to an 'American' national identity."[189] By placing Madison Washington alongside Patrick Henry, Thomas Jefferson, and George Washington, Douglass creates a new portrait of the fathers of the country and presents a version of citizenship that radically reimagines the complexion of not just the national family, but the pantheon of national heroes.

Another aspect of *The Heroic Slave* that challenges the construction of slaves as not human, not free, not men, and not citizens is the depiction of Madison Washington himself within the text. The novella's narrator describes Washington as manly, but goes a long way to qualify that depiction. He is described as strong, possessing "Herculean strength; yet there was nothing savage or forbidding in his aspect" and he is reported to have a "good nature and kindness" and to be "intelligent and brave."[190] The focus here is beyond the physical and is in some ways reminiscent of the depiction of Douglass by William Lloyd Garrison as having true manliness of character. As Celeste-Marie Bernier has noted, the depiction of Washington in the novella does not focus exclusively on his body; Douglass also focuses on his use of language and eloquence and on his intellectual prowess.[191] All four of our rebellious slaves turned potential heroes—Manzano, Noemí, Douglass, and Madison Washington—have in common the insistence that they are rational beings, intellects, and *men* in the sense of the Western Man despite the fact that racialization would use their perceived racial identity as a means to disqualify them from that category. In the case of *The Heroic Slave*, while Krista Walker worries that Douglass uncritically adopts many nationalistic suppositions and "downplays the importance of racial or ethnic chauvinism as a key component of nationalism by rendering his black hero virtually raceless,"[192] the fact that Madison Washington is a slave only recorded in the chattel records whose story elevates him to the status of a heroic son of Virginia makes his physical description in the text less important. While Douglass toned down his depiction of Madison's racial characteristics in the novella as opposed to speeches he gave about the *Creole* revolt, if Madison metaphorically comes to be considered one of the great men of Virginia, a great patriot and American hero, it changes what it means to be an American.

While Manzano's Noemí is much more militant than his persona in the *Autobiografía*, Madison Washington is much more like Douglass. Early in the novella, Washington is overheard delivering a soliloquy that expresses his bravery, daring, and love of liberty. It ends with his steadfast resolution "*I shall be free.*"[193] Reflecting on this statement, the narrator declares "at that moment he was free, at least in spirit."[194] This statement ties to Frederick Douglass's determination, after the climactic battle with Covey, that he had reached "the turning-point in my career as a slave." [195] Douglass also makes the now-famous statement, "I now resolved that, however long I might remain a slave in form, the day had passed forever when I could be a slave in fact. "[196] Despite the fact that the paratext to Douglass's *Narrative* presents a nonthreatening manhood, in this passage Douglass promises violence against those who would try to whip him and ultimately implies violence to those who would keep him enslaved. Richard Yarborough reads the depiction of Madison Washington in *The Heroic Slave* as being the "epitome of militant slave resistance," while demonstrating how Douglass mitigates the fear of black violence by depicting him as "emotionally controlled, rational, and physically restrained."[197] Bernier highlights Douglass's "decision to dramatize the mutiny only in the margins of the text" as reflecting his desire to keep the focus on the white violence inherent in slavery and to allow for his audiences to "reimagine black heroism."[198] Madison Washington and Frederick Douglass have in common a determination that they will be free, the use of oratory and rhetoric, and a willingness to take up arms to physically resist their enslavement. While their manhood can be seen as being downplayed in many ways, ultimately the example, which is strongly linked to national identity, is of a strong black man who transforms society by both intellectually and physically resisting tyranny and slavery. While Manzano cannot be put in this list of black heroes who physically resist, his character Noemí is very much in line with Washington and Douglass and both he and Noemí present a prototype for a black Cuban hero.

NOTES

1. Henry Louis Gates Jr., *The Signifying Monkey: A Theory of African-American Literary Criticism* (New York: Oxford University Press, 1988), 64.

2. Mikhail Bakhtin, "Discourse in the Novel," 293–94.

3. Wendy Ryden, "Conflicted Literacy: Frederick Douglass's Critical Model," *Journal of Basic Writing* 24, no. 1 (Spring 2005): 17.

4. Pratt, qtd. in Ryden, "Conflicted Literacy," 18.

5. Ivan A. Schulman. "Introduction." In *Autobiography of a Slave/Autobiografía de un esclavo*, by Juan Francisco Manzano, trans. Evelyn Picon Garfield (Detroit: Wayne State University Press, 1996), 7.

6. For an annotated bibliography of Afro-American autobiographies written between 1760 and 1865, the majority of which are slave narratives, see William L. Andrews's *To Tell a Free Story: The First Century of Afro-American Autobiography, 1760–1865*.

7. Susan Willis, "Crushed Geraniums: Juan Francisco Manzano and the Language of Slavery," in *The Slave's Narrative*, ed. Charles T. Davis and Henry Louis Gates Jr. (Oxford: Oxford University Press, 1985), 202.

8. In "La intelectualidad negra en Cuba en el siglo XIX: El caso de Manzano," Sonia Labrador-Rodríguez addresses the problematic positionality of Manzano as both slave and intellectual.

9. Henry Louis Gates Jr. connects Douglass's narrative not only to other slave narratives, but through the slave narrative tradition to aspects of the confession, the picaresque, and the romance (see chapter 3 in *Figures in Black*). Frances Foster also notes Douglass's familiarity with the literary tradition, but she emphasizes the influence of oratory on his narrative.

10. Roberto Friol, *Suite para Juan Francisco Manzano*, 47.

11. DeCosta-Willis, "Self and Society," 7.

12. Edward J. Mullen, *Afro-Cuban Literature: Critical Junctures* (Westport, CT: Greenwood Press, 1998), 83.

13. Luis A. Jiménez, "Nineteenth Century Autobiography in the Afro-Americas: Frederick Douglass and Juan Francisco Manzano," *Afro Hispanic Review* 14, no. 2 (Fall 1995): 47, 49.

14. Ibid., 51.

15. Ifeoma Kiddoe Nwankwo, *Black Cosmopolitanism*, 200.

16. DeCosta-Willis, "Self and Society," 7–8.

17. What I mean to suggest with this shorthand of "whiteness" will be clarified later. In general, I am referring here to the tendency of these slave narrators to present a version of their racial and ethnic identity that complicates the easy association of slaves and blackness and often emphasizes their mixed-race identity or either literally or metaphorically associates the narrators with whiteness. The problematic aspects of this negotiation will be explored later in the chapter.

18. Orlando Patterson, *Slavery and Social Death*, 2.

19. Winthrop Jordan, qtd. in Berzon, *Neither White nor Black*, 20.

20. For a more comprehensive look at Christian paradigms on race and slavery in both Cuba and the United States, refer to part III of Klein's *Slavery in the Americas*, "Anglicanism, Catholicism, and the Negro Slave."

21. This is not an argument regarding either author's beliefs, but rather a discussion of how they use religious rhetoric in their texts.

22. Fionnghuala Sweeney, "Atlantic Countercultures and the Networked Text: Juan Francisco Manzano, R. R. Madden and the Cuban Slave Narrative," *Forum of Modern Language Studies* 40, no. 4 (2004): 404.

23. Ibid.

24. Ibid.

25. Ibid.

26. Ibid. While Sweeney makes these very important points regarding the extent to which and how texts from the Anglo-Protestant and Hispanic-Catholic traditions might be read, she does not engage in such a comparative reading in her essay, which has a different focus. Sweeney's point, which is a good one, is to make sure that her readers, who are more likely to be steeped in the Anglo-Protestant tradition, understand some of the nuances of Manzano's text.

27. Andrews, *To Tell a Free Story*, 123.

28. DeCosta-Willis, "Self and Society," 9.

29. Ilia Casanova-Marengo, "Desde el Jardín de bellísimas flores: Entre el silencio y la rupture en Autobiografía de Juan Francisco Manzano," *Monographic Review/Revista Monográfica* 16 (2000): 244.

30. Manzano, *Autobiografía del esclavo poeta*, 84.

31. Ibid., 85.

32. For a more detailed reading of Douglass as chosen by God, see Andrews's description of the *Narrative* as an American jeremiad (Andrews 123–27).

33. Douglass, *Narrative*, 36.

34. Ibid.

35. Ibid.

36. Cynthia R. Nielsen, "Resistance is Not Futile: Frederick Douglass on Panoptic Plantations and the Un-Making of Docile Bodies and Enslaved Souls," *Philosophy and Literature* 35, no. 2 (October 2011): 267.

37. Andrews, *To Tell a Free Story*, 123.

38. Lorna V. Williams, *The Representation of Slavery in Cuban Fiction* (Columbia: University of Missouri Press, 1985), 34. Ivan Schulman, "Introduction," in *Autobiography of a Slave/ Autobiografía de un esclavo*, by Juan Francisco Manzano, trans. Evelyn Picon Garfield (Detroit: Wayne State University Press, 1996), 21.

39. Manzano *Autobiografía del esclavo poeta*, 103.

40. Ramos, "La ley es otra," 308.

41. Ibid.

42. Andrews, *To Tell a Free Story*, 124.

43. Douglass, *Narrative*, 68, 56.

44. Ibid., 97.

45. There are several interesting alternate readings, particularly surrounding the appendix. Donald B. Gibson thinks Douglass feared accusations of apostasy so added the appendix to "sanitize the implications of the text"; Gibson feels the appendix is "logically nice . . . but in fact impossible" in that the distinction Douglass makes within it is not a meaningful one. Donald B. Gibson, "Faith, Doubt, and Apostasy: Evidence of Things Unseen in Frederick Douglass's *Narrative*," in *Frederick Douglass: New Literary and Historical Essays*, ed. Eric J. Sundquist (New York: Cambridge University Press, 1990), 87. Thomas Peyser argues that a "careful reading" of both the appendix and "crucial passages" suggest that behind the façade of placating Christian readers, Douglass's text indicates his suspicion that "slavery is not a perversion of Christian doctrine but rather its perfect embodiment." Thomas Peyser, "An Attack on Christianity in NARRATIVE OF THE LIFE OF FREDERICK DOUGLASS, AN AMERICAN SLAVE," *Explicator* 69, no. 2 (2011): 86. Zachary McLeod Hutchins goes further, claiming that Douglass is an atheist who "destabilizes the Bible and rejects Christianity proper," eliding the figures of Satan, Slavery, and Christ, all of which he firmly rejects despite the "lip service to Christianity" in the epilogue. Zachary McLeod Hutchins, "Rejecting the Root: The Liberating, Anti-Christ Theology of Douglass's *Narrative*," *Nineteenth Century Literature*, 16, no. 3 (2013): 292.

46. Nielsen, "Resistance is Not Futile," 252.

47. Manzano, *Autobiografía del esclavo poeta*, 94.

48. Molloy, "From Serf to Self," 46.

49. Michael Stoneham, "Juan Francisco Manzano and the Best of All Possible Worlds," *Journal of Caribbean Literature* 6, no. 1 (Summer 2009): 104.

50. David Van Leer, "Reading Slavery: The Anxiety of Ethnicity in Douglass's *Narrative*," in *Frederick Douglass: New Literary and Historical Essays*, ed. Eric J. Sundquist (New York: Cambridge University Press, 1990), 119.

51. Gibson, "Faith, Doubt, and Apostasy," 93.

52. Manzano, *Autobiografía del esclavo poeta*, 103.

53. Stoneham, "Juan Francisco Manzano," 93.

54. Ibid., 104.

55. Ibid.

56. Andrews, *To Tell a Free Story*, 99.

57. Anderson, *Imagined Communities*, 67.

58. Angel Rama, *La ciudad letrada* (Hanover: Ediciones del Norte, 1984), 33.

59. Henry Louis Gates Jr., *Figures in Black: Words, Signs, and the "Racial" Self* (New York: Oxford University Press, 1987), 21.

60. Williams, *Slavery in Cuban Fiction*, 39–40.

61. Jiménez, "Nineteenth Century Autobiography," 47, 49. In using the term "counterdiscourse" of the oppressed, Jiménez draws on the ideas from Roberto González Echevarría's *The Voice of the Masters: Writing and Authority in Modern Latin American Literature* and Richard Terdiman's *Discourse/Counter-Discourse: The Theory and Practice of Symbolic Resistance in Nineteenth Century France*.

62. Susana Draper, "Voluntad de intelectual: Juan Francisco Manzano entre las redes de un humanism sin derechos," *Chasqui: Revista de literatura latinoamericana* 30, no. 2 (November 2001): 106–7.

63. Ryden, "Conflicted Literacy," 4, 7.

64. Ryden, 16 and Nick Brommell, "A 'Voice from the Enslaved': The Origins of Frederick Douglass's Political Philosophy of Democracy," *American Literary History* 23, no. 4 (Winter 2011): 703.

65. Labrador-Rodriguez, "La intelectualidad negra," 14.

66. Manzano, *Autobiografía del esclavo poeta*, 87.

67. Ibid.

68. Labrador-Rodriguez, "La intelectualidad negra," 20.

69. Manzano, *Autobiografía del esclavo poeta*, 87.

70. Ibid.

71. Marilyn Miller, "Rebeldía narrativa, resistencia poética y expresión 'libre' en Juan Francisco Manzano." *Revista Iberoamericana* 71, no. 211 (April–June 2005): 422.

72. Nielsen, "Resistance is Not Futile," 258–59.

73. Mullen, *Afro-Cuban Literature*, 73–74.

74. Manzano, *Autobiografía, cartas y versos*, 84.

75. John Sekora, "Black Message/White Envelope: Genre, Authenticity, and Authority in the Antebellum Slave Narrative," *Callaloo* 10, no. 3 (Summer 1987): 485.

76. Douglass, *Narrative*, 39.

77. Ibid.

78. Ibid., 43.

79. Samantha Manchester Earley, "Dismantling Master Thought: Discourse and Race in Frederick Douglass's *Narrative*," *Atenea* 21, no. 1–2 (2001): 182.

80. Douglass, *Narrative*, 39.

81. Daniel J. Royer, "The Process of Literacy as Communal Involvement in the narratives of Frederick Douglass," *African American Review* 28, no. 3 (1994): n.p.

82. Douglass was not the only North American slave narrator to describe his development and desire for freedom as centered around the acquisition of literacy. Speaking of the texts of Douglass, Olaudah Equiano, and John Jea, Henry Louis Gates Jr. makes the generalization that "[t]hese representations of the mastery of letters (literally, the A B C's) are clearly transferences and displacements of the dream of freedom." Gates, *Signifying Monkey*, 166. The power to control written language, as Gates suggests, gave many slave narrators a sense of control over their futures. William L. Andrews writes, "The acquisition of literacy, the power to read books and discover one's place in the scheme of things, is treated in many slave narratives as a

matter equal in importance to the achievement of physical freedom." Andrews, *To Tell a Free Story*, 13.

83. Labrador-Rodríguez, "La intelectualidad negra," 16.
84. Miller, "Rebeldía narrativa," 420.
85. Ramos, "La ley es otra," 308, 317.
86. Gates, *Figures in Black*, 17.
87. Ibid.
88. Ramos, "Cuerpo, Lengua, Subjetividad." *Revista de Crítica Literaria Latinoamericana* 19, no. 28 (1993): 227.
89. Gates, *Signifying Monkey*, 128.
90. Ramos, "La ley es otra," 326.
91. Manzano, *Autobiografía del esclavo poeta*, 104.
92. Douglass, *Narrative*, 43, 46–47.
93. Lisa Sisco, "'Writing in the Spaces Left': Literacy as a Process of Becoming in the Narratives of Frederick Douglass," *ATQ* 9, no. 3 (1995): 201.
94. Manzano's text, translated into English, was presented at the General Anti-Slavery Convention in London in 1840 (Molloy, 38), five years before Douglass's narrative was published, but there is no direct evidence that Douglass ever read it. The similarity in their accounts of learning to write has been previously mentioned by Jiménez (Jiménez, 50).
95. Dizon, "Mothers, Morals and Power in the Autobiography of Juan Francisco Manzano," *Revista de estudios hispánicos* 21 (1994): 116.
96. Molloy, qtd. in Ibid.
97. Ramos, "La ley es otra," 319.
98. Labrador-Rodríguez, "La intelectualidad negra," 15.
99. Ibid.
100. Andrews, *To Tell a Free Story*, 13.
101. Manzano, *Autobiografía del esclavo poeta*, 88.
102. Ibid., 93.
103. Ibid.
104. Douglass, *Narrative*, 18.
105. John Hansen, "Frederick Douglass's Journey from Slave to Freeman: An Acquisition and Mastery of Language, Rhetoric, and Power Via the *Narrative*," *The Griot* 31, no. 2 (2012): 16.
106. Douglass, *Narrative*, 18.
107. Hansen, "Frederick Douglass's Journey," 16.
108. Douglass, *Narrative*, 19.
109. Ibid., 21.
110. Williams, *Slavery in Cuban Fiction*, 40–41.
111. Manzano, *Autobiografía del esclavo poeta*, 83.
112. Juan Francisco Manzano, *The Autobiography of a Slave*, ed. Ivan Schulman trans. Evelyn Picon Garfield (Detroit: Wayne State University Press, 1996), 45n2.
113. Manzano, *Autobiografía del esclavo poeta*, 83.
114. Ibid., 84.
115. Ibid.
116. Ibid.
117. Ivan Schulman, "Invención y disfraz: el discurso cubano de la *Autobiografía* de Juan Francisco Manzano," in *Discursos sobre la 'invención' de América*, ed. Iris M. Zavala (Amsterdam, Netherlands: Rodopi, 1992), 177.
118. Manzano, *Autobiografía del esclavo poeta*, 93.
119. Labrador-Rodríguez, "La intelectualidad negra," 17.
120. Dizon, "Mothers, Morals and Power," 109.
121. Manzano, *Autobiografía del esclavo poeta*, 112.
122. Ibid., 94.
123. Ibid., 107.
124. Dizon, "Mothers, Morals and Power," 109, 113.
125. Douglass, *Narrative*, 38.

126. Ibid.
127. Manzano, *Autobiografía del esclavo poeta*, 104.
128. Dizon, "Mothers, Morals and Power," 110.
129. Nwankwo, *Black Cosmopolitanism,* 201.
130. Dizon, "Mothers, Morals and Power," 111.
131. Douglass, *Narrative*, 15.
132. Hansen, "Frederick Douglass's Journey," 15.
133. Friol, *Suite para Juan Francisco Manzano,* 153.
134. Stephens, *Dictionary of Latin American Racial and Ethnic Terminology*, 341.
135. Nwankwo, *Black Cosmopolitanism*, 200.
136. Manzano, *Autobiografía del esclavo poeta*, 84.
137. Ibid., 108.
138. A chino, as the name implies, is the term that was generally used to indicate the "off-spring of a mulatto and a black who had skin the color of the Malays and who were mistaken for Chinese" (Stephens, *Dictionary of Latin American Racial and Ethnic Terminology*, 67).
139. Manzano, *Autobiografía del esclavo poeta*, 114, 115.
140. Branche, "*Mulato entre negros* (y blancos)," 83.
141. Ibid.
142. Douglass, *Narrative*, 91.
143. Ibid.
144. Fionghuala Sweeney, "An American Slave: Representing the Creole Self," in *Frederick Douglass and the Atlantic World* (Liverpool: Liverpool University Press, 2007), 56.
145. Ibid.
146. Richard L. Jackson, "Slavery, Racism and Autobiography in Two Early Black Writers: Juan Francisco Manzano and Martin Morúa Delgado," in *Voices from Under: Black Narrative in Latin America and the Caribbean*, ed. William Luis (Westport, CT: Greenwood Press, 1984), 59, 60.
147. Branche, "'*Mulato entre negros*' (y blancos)," 81.
148. Schulman, "Invención y disfraz," 178.
149. Nielsen, "Resistance is Not Futile," 252.
150. Andrews, *To Tell a Free Story*, 131. Andrews believes that although Douglass begins with this argument, "[b]y the time we finish the last chapter of the *Narrative*, however, it becomes evident that Douglass is not bent on the same kind of critique of the binary oppositions that govern and validate the symbol of America" (131). While Douglass does destabilize binaries in the narrative, I agree that the overall effect is one that values inclusion within the system over the destruction of the system.
151. Ibid., 17–18.
152. Ibid., 18.
153. Selby, "The Limits of Accommodation," 53, 64.
154. Houston A. Baker Jr., "Autobiographical Acts and the Voice of the Southern Slave," in *The Journey Back: Issues in Black Literature and Criticism* (Chicago: University of Chicago Press, 1980), 251.
155. Andrews, *To Tell a Free Story*, 105.
156. Gary Selby effectively outlines the divergent interests and ideas held by Douglass and the Garrisonians all along and convincingly argues that where Garrison was idealistic, Douglass was pragmatic and political. Selby, "The Limits of Accommodation," 62.
157. Ibid.
158. Celeste-Marie Bernier, *Characters of Blood: Black Heroism in the Transatlantic Imagination* (Charlottesville: University of Virginia Press, 2012), Introduction, EPUB, EBSCOhost.
159. Ibid.
160. For John Sekora, the fact that the main text ends with Douglass depicting his address to the Nantucket convention in 1841 brings the narrative "full circle" to Garrison's preface; since Douglass does not make mention of Garrison he reverses the "persistent abolitionist tactic" that made former slaves "minor characters in *their* [abolitionists'] great antislavery story" and "deftly ensures" that Garrison and Phillips are shown as "minor characters in *his* story." Sekora finishes this analysis by claiming that it is Douglass who authenticates Garrison in this case.

Sekora, "Black Message/White Envelope," 168. In her work on the paratext, McCoy demonstrates that it is a space "through which white supremacy could be channeled," but also a space that offers "possibilities for resistance." McCoy, "Race and the (Para)Textual Condition," 159. Rachel Blumenthal looks to the appendix, another paratextual aspect of Douglass's narrative, as being important not for its content per se, but rather for the fact that "Douglass disembodies himself in the appendix by inhabiting the role of literary critic." Rachel A. Blumenthal, "Canonicity, Genre, and the Politics of Writing: How We Read Frederick Douglass," *Callaloo* 36, no. 1 (Winter 2013): 181.

161. Blumenthal, "Canonicity, Genre, and the Politics of Writing," 181.

162. Bernier, *Characters of Blood*, Introduction.

163. Molloy, "From Serf to Self," 43.

164. Ibid., 43–44.

165. Friol, *Suite para Juan Francisco Manzano*, 30.

166. Antonio Vera-León, "Juan Francisco Manzano," 22.

167. Marilyn Grace Miller, "Imitation and Improvisation in Juan Francisco Manzano's *Zafira*," *Colonial Latin American Review* 17, no. 1 (June 2008): 54.

168. Bernier, *Characters of Blood*, chap. 5.

169. Margaret M. Olsen, "Manzano's *Zafira* and the Performance of Cuban Nationhood," *Hispanic Review* 75, no. 2 (spring 2007): 139.

170. Miller, "Imitation and Improvisation," 53.

171. Susannah Rodríguez Drissi, "Between Orientalism and Affective Identification: A Paradigm and Four Case Studies Towards the Inclusion of the Moor in Cuban Literary and Cultural Studies" (PhD Dissertation, UCLA, 2012), 8, http://escholarship.org/uc/item/5ps5d43t.

172. Olsen, "Manzano's *Zafira*," 145.

173. Ibid., 155.

174. Manzano, *Zafira*, 10.

175. Olsen, "Manzano's Zafira," 147–48.

176. Miller, "Imitation and Improvisation," 60.

177. Abdelsam Azougarh sees Noemí as a mouthpiece for Manzano, claiming that some of his lines in the play seem like a continuation of "*Trienta años*." He makes this argument in the context of a larger claim that all of Manzano's works are autobiographical. (Azougarh, 59–60).

178. Manzano, *Zafira*, 28.

179. Ibid.

180. Matthew Feshkens, email message to author, August 23, 2017.

181. Miller, "Imitation and Improvisation," 60.

182. Olsen, "Manzano's *Zafira*," 155–56.

183. Douglass, *The Heroic Slave*, 3.

184. Ibid., 4.

185. Krista Walter, "Trappings of Nationalism in Frederick Douglass's *The Heroic Slave*," *African American Review* 24, no. 2 (2000): 237.

186. Ibid.

187. Ibid.

188. Bernier, *Characters of Blood*, chap. 5.

189. Celeste-Marie Bernier, "From Fugitive Slave to Fugitive Abolitionist," *Atlantic Studies* 3, no. 2 (2006): 203–4. Bernier emphasizes that Douglass downplays the role of Washington's wife as "Black female slave heroism was at best only a secondary consideration and, if included at all, always embedded in constructions of black masculinity" (204).

190. Douglass, *The Heroic Slave*, 7.

191. Bernier, "Arms Like Polished Iron," 94–95.

192. Walter, "Trappings of Nationalism," 237.

193. Douglass, *The Heroic Slave*, 6.

194. Ibid., 7.

195. Douglass, *Narrative*, 68.

196. Ibid.

197. Richard Yarborough, "Race, Violence, and Manhood: The Masculine Ideal in Frederick Douglass's 'The Heroic Slave,'" in *Frederick Douglass: New Literary and Historical Essays*, ed. Eric J. Sundquist (New York: Cambridge University Press, 1990): 172.

198. Bernier, *Characters of Blood*, chap. 5.

Chapter Four

The Discourse of the Future Citizen in the Nonfiction of Martín Morúa Delgado and Charles W. Chesnutt

When Juan Francisco Manzano and Frederick Douglass emphasize their status as mulatos, differentiating themselves from blacks, they demonstrate the rhetorical power of whiteness as an institution and a performance; in their insistence on their mixed-race identities they also highlight their own liminality and the reality of miscegenation in their homelands. Manzano and Douglass used their slave narratives as discourses of identity in which they could manipulate the symbolic language of national identity to recast themselves as subjects rather than objects, free men rather than slaves, and as potential citizens. Their rhetorical struggles to undermine the power of slavery and to identify with and transform the body politic represent only one of the stages of the negotiation of people of African descent to be accepted within their New World homelands. Their continuation on these themes in their fictional works on black heroism presented even more radical approaches to these topics. Once slavery ended, the conflict continued and while the terms changed, Afro-Cuban and African American authors continued to fight against the negations that excluded them from society and citizenship.

While the citizens of the United States struggled through reconstruction and various attempts to incorporate and reconcile the differences so starkly put into relief through the violence of the Civil War, after the abolition of slavery in Cuba, those fighting for independence from Spain also struggled to forge a unified national identity in light of the diversity of the Cuban population. While many visions of national identity were based on racial and ethnic chauvinism, some individuals in Cuba and the United States dedicated themselves to imagining a more truly unified national identity. In 1890 Manuel de la Cruz, author of *Episodios de la revolución cubana*, wrote that Martín Morúa Delgado "representa una bandera: la aspiración de fundir en una sola y levantada acción a todos los elementos de la sociedad cubana"[1] [represents a flag: the hope of forging together all of the elements of Cuban society with one unique and elevated action]. In the United States, Charles W. Chesnutt also engaged in the type of project Manuel de la Cruz associates with Martín Morúa Delgado: he imagined a forging that would bring together and elevate all the disparate aspects of society into a common national identity. However, there were also many whose vision of their nation was based on the association of humanity and citizenship with the Western Man, a vision that excluded all those below the global color line from full participation in the polity in order to maintain the power of the free, white, (hu)man elite. Members of the second group demonstrated a racist fear of the "dark"—what they considered as the nonhuman or not-quite-human elements of their nations. This amounted to anxiety about the racial and ethnic makeup of *the people*, so that their concerns and desire to control went beyond images of the *ethos* of the people and intruded into the bedroom and the bloodstream. As Morúa and Chesnutt presented their visions for future national identities that would eliminate the line between human and nonhuman, black and white, citizen and subject, they had to negotiate this irrational "fear of the dark."

RACIALIZATION IN THE SECOND HALF OF THE NINETEENTH CENTURY

As the nineteenth century wore on, Cuba remained a colony long after other former New World colonies had achieved their independence. The simultaneous condition of being subjects of a foreign empire and being a vastly outnumbered ruling population created a Cuban *criollo* elite particularly jealous of its status and believed superiority. As they sought to imagine an independent Cuban nation, Cuban *criollo* elites both on the island and abroad worried about the biological makeup of the island. Some members of the Cuban elite believed that as part of the process of national formation Cuba needed to undergo a process of *blanqueamiento* [whitening].[2] Cuban sociologist, historian, journalist, and proto nationalist José Antonio Saco was a member of del Monte's group; he was anti-slavery and anti-annexationist, but wrote passionately that, "The only remedy for making us respectable is whitening, whitening."[3] Whitening was believed necessary to create an appropriate Cuban citizenry that could break free from Spanish rule and have good standing in the international arena. While many Cubans hoped that increased European immigration would improve the island's pedigree by lightening the future nation's complexion, others proposed that the "stain" of

African blood be removed through miscegenation.[4] Ironically, the proposal of *blanqueamiento* as a nation-building project reflected the ongoing process of miscegenation in Cuba. Mulato children were born in large numbers before anyone proposed whitening as the solution to Cuba's social woes. Franklin W. Knight cites census records indicating that in 1791, for example, there were 33,886 free "persons of color" who had at least one white ancestor and an additional 12,135 mulato slaves.[5] By 1841 the number of free mulatos had risen to 88,054 and mulato slaves to 10,974.[6] It is important to bear in mind, as Richard L. Jackson emphasizes, that the proposed *blanqueamiento* of the Cuban population through race mixture did not reflect "*mestizaje positivo*," a desire for "a blending of cultures in which there is equal respect for both," but rather "*mestizaje negativo*," the process by which "a minority culture is absorbed as an inferior culture."[7] Emphasis on *blanqueamiento* through biological means, and particularly the reality that it involved unofficially sanctioning the *criollo* elite to father children with black women, obviously reinforced both racist stereotypes of the superiority of white blood and the feminization of the black race through a discourse based on a patriarchal, and often misogynistic, culture. It also facilitated and worked to hide, if not technically sanctioning, sexual violence against black women.

The process of *blanqueamiento* in Cuba required the production of whitened offspring without sanctioning interracial relationships. At times the emphasis on women engendering children whiter than themselves was so strong that promiscuity and secrecy were implicitly accepted. The project encouraged illicit sexual relationships between the races and since the power of whiteness also meant that often paternity was unknown or at least unspoken, more fundamental social institutions and mores were threatened. In some cases, white male privilege and the project of whitening replaced a more explicit emphasis on traditional values like marriage and paternal responsibility. This reality only reinforced and legitimized the sexual abuse and violence done to black women in Cuba. In the more extreme cases this protection of white male sexual privilege enabled sexual violence, and could lead to situations in which individuals lacked the knowledge of kinship necessary to avoid extremes such as incest. Incest was only the most extreme case of a set of anxieties about social position that arose from miscegenation. Julio Ramos suggests that hybridity itself is the most important threat of miscegenation because it problematizes hierarchy, ruining notions of purity and separation.[8] By his/her very existence, the nineteenth-century mulato/a violated the boundary between categories and threatened social hierarchies.

The "whitened" proto-citizens *blanqueamiento* was to produce would always be, by definition, illegitimate. The project of whitening gave Cuban male elites the justification they needed to enjoy the sexual and social privileges afforded them outside marriage while maintaining the ability to produce legitimate white heirs through the convention of marriage. However, the production of both legitimate heirs and illegitimate offspring as part of nation-building constituted a conundrum: how could Cuba escape colonialism and create a unified modern nation while maintaining the system of white privilege they had learned from the European colonizers from whom the ruling elite descended? Vera Kutzinski reminds us that as part of the mythology of the emerging nation, *mestizaje*, which can be translated miscegenation and whitening, among other things, was held in tension with the idea of racial mixing as a destroyer of hierarchies. This tension increased in the second half of the nineteenth century when José Martí made *mestizaje* "perhaps the principal signifier of Cuba's national cultural identity."[9] Despite the seemingly utopian nature of Martí's emphasis on *mestizaje* which implied an embracing of Afro-Cuban culture, in reality, at the end of the nineteenth century, the Cuban independence movement and the concepts of national identity it proposed continued to reflect cultural anxieties about people of African descent and their effect on the face and fate of Cuba.

In the post–Civil War United States, and particularly after the failure of reconstruction, race also remained an essential marker in the negotiation of identity, place, and privilege. Miscegenation complicated a system that was constructed on a strict binary—an inflexible view of race as black and white. By denying the humanity as well as the freedom of Africans and their descendants, chattel slavery necessitated strict divisions between the races; it caused complicated identity issues due to the inevitable interaction and mixing of slaves, masters, and all of their various descendants. Historian Eugene Genovese estimates that by 1860 13 to 20 percent of the black population of the United States had at least one white ancestor.[10] The legacy of slavery and the legal structures used to support it, such as the legal ban and social taboo placed on intermarriage, created a system that engendered a neurotic consciousness about race, identity, and legitimacy. Carol Allen argues that the way in which American culture polices racial categories forces individuals to understand themselves and their place in society only in terms of their skin color rather than by virtue of what she calls their "own intrinsic qualities"; Allen adds that the effect of this is that any individual, regardless of race, "absorbs social messages when they look in the mirror, messages which affect what the subject will construct as reality."[11] Skin color is only one marker of social status or of racial categorization, and social messages about a whole variety of aspects of perceived racial identity occupy language and inscribe themselves on individuals. As Allen implies, these messages are often internalized and even enforced by the individual him/herself. While clearly "[i]n and of itself, color has no meaning," through racialization, Eurocentric societies that privilege whiteness, like the United States and Cuba, have imbued the idea of whiteness with "political, social, economic, historical, physiological and philosophical" meanings which translate into placement in a hierarchical order.[12] In fine, social messages about race affect what the subject will construct as reality, as well as the way that society reads and reacts to each individual.

The process of miscegenation was well underway in the United States by the late nineteenth century. As products of miscegenation, mulatos/as did not fit; they were marginalized as members of the subjected race, but simultaneously liminal in that they embodied a vast borderland between the races. In both aspects, the mulato/a existed necessarily outside of a system set up to rigorously segregate white from black, "human" from "non-human." It was a system that made them into a discursive object "already as it were overlain with qualifications, open to dispute, charged with value, already enveloped in an obscuring mist—or, on the contrary, by the 'light' of alien words that have already been spoken about it."[13] In systems of slavery based on racial difference and the societies that obtained after emancipation, the child of a black mother and a white father had no place, but s/he was, paradoxically, distinctly marked by society. Society marked the mulato/a because his/her very conception represented a threat to the effectiveness of the racializing assemblages working to protect the status of the "white" masters. While many wanted to remove the perceived "stain" of black blood from the American body politic, there were no serious proposals by those in power for miscegenation to be the method by which this took place. Miscegenation was increasingly viewed as detrimental to society, particularly after emancipation. The fear of miscegenation in the general population gave new life to racist stereotypes of the mulato/a as "degenerate, sterile, and short-lived."[14] The American Freedman's Inquiry Commission appointed by Abraham Lincoln in 1863 was led by Dr. Samuel Gridley Howe, a physician, philanthropist, and reformer who felt that "mulatto-ism" represented "one of the chief evils of the slave system he was striving to abolish."[15] However, since mixed-race individuals were not degenerate, sterile, or short lived, their growing presence complicated a society in which the social and economic roles of people of color continued to be at issue.

Long after the Thirteenth Amendment was made law in 1865, whites worked to maintain the power and privilege they held under slavery. The social messages coming out of the American consciousness of race and legitimacy were a part of a symbolic system meant to reinforce the power and legitimacy of what they understood as whiteness. Frances Richardson Keller explains that whites in power after the Civil War feared that it would become impossible to distinguish between blacks and whites, and since the ability to distinguish was linked to the ability to reserve human status for a particular group and keep others in an inferior social position, "white leaders began to plan how the races could be physically separated to a greater extent than had appeared necessary under the slave system."[16] Jim Crow laws, laws forbidding intermarriage, laws and practices designed to disenfranchise African Americans, and the terror campaign of lynching were among the many methods used by whites to try to maintain power and privilege after the end of slavery. These and other methods worked, among other things, to regulate interracial interaction and to measure and mark identity.

In Cuban society where certain portions of the white elite attempted to "solve" the race problem by incorporating blacks into the lower classes of white society through miscegenation, in the United States various efforts to "repatriate" African Americans to Africa, movements which implied that separation, not integration, was the way to solve the problem of racial difference, were more common. These movements never had a large enough impact to significantly affect the complex racial makeup of the United States, so custom and law worked to keep the races separated. Jim Crow laws and segregation were the offspring of the culture's neurotic race consciousness. The system was designed to keep the races separate but *unequal,* which reinforced the idea that the products of miscegenation were to be considered anathema. The mulato/a was neither white nor black, but also both white and black. The mulato/a destabilized the hierarchy because, despite the rhetorical distinction between black and white, his/her doubly alienated or doubly included status challenged the artificially constructed binary system of racial identity and privilege.

One peculiar aspect of the North American system that warrants emphasis here, particularly as it is distinct from the Cuban context, is the so-called one-drop rule. Samira Kawash refers to the one drop as "an empty mark" which the "arbitrary, contingent character of the law of race" transforms into "the sign of difference."[17] In addition to marking all individuals black who were determined to have one drop of black blood, in the United States (as opposed to Cuba and other Latin American countries) the term mulato/a quickly came to be applied to any mixed race person rather than solely to the half black, half white individual.[18] For the most part, the North American system ignored variations of mixed ancestry, dropping terms such as quadroon and octoroon from official language. The absolute ideological privileging of whiteness to the extent of excluding an individual because of one drop of black blood trapped mulatos in the United States in what Berzon refers to as "an indeterminate area between the boundaries of the American caste system."[19] That the mulato is forced to occupy this liminal space challenges the very categories into which society is formed, a point highlighted by Barbara Johnson when she describes the mulato as an "allegory" for a society divided on racial lines, "simultaneously un-American and an image of America as such."[20] The mulato/a is in the exact space of the color line—which is neither narrow nor well-defined—and his/her presence challenges the racializing assemblages working to reinforce the line between those considered human and those non- or not-quite-human.

Martín Morúa Delgado and Charles W. Chesnutt shared the common experiences of being mixed-race individuals who, during the final two decades of the nineteenth century, wrote both nonfiction and fiction works about race and national identity in their homelands. Both authors wrote revisions of the tragic mulata novel, revisions which engaged many of the themes and ideas from their nonfiction. One major common thread is the fact that both authors presented visions of racial integration as part of their view of the future of their societies. Interestingly in relation to reading these authors' works as a continuation of the arguments about race and nation in the previous chapter, both authors looked back to slavery and to figures who resisted slavery, and incorporated figures from this past into their body of works. Their interest in black heroism echoes that of Manzano and Douglass. Morúa translated both a biography and autobiography of Toussaint L'Ouverture around 1892 and Chesnutt wrote a biography of Frederick Douglass, published in 1899. Morúa's fiction, although intended as a response and corrective to the major abolitionist novel *Cecilia Valdés*, was influenced both by Juan Francisco Manzano's autobiography and by Gertrudis Gómez de Avellaneda's abolitionist novel *Sab*. Likewise Chesnutt thought of himself as continuing on in the tradition of abolitionist writers including slave narrators like Douglass, but also novelists like William Wells Brown and Harriet Jacobs.

The political nonfiction of Martín Morúa Delgado and Charles W. Chesnutt in the period leading up to their production of the novels *Sofía* (1891) and *The House Behind the Cedars* (1900) shows a complex engagement with issues of miscegenation, race, and national identity. As will become clear in the following discussion, there are problematic aspects to the ideas of racial integration presented in Morúa and Chesnutt's works; both authors express complicated and controversial ideas about how to get a unified national identity beyond the quagmires of race. Examining the nonfiction is important because, as Matthew Wilson argues, there is a "complicated cross-fertilization" between the nonfiction and fiction written by Chesnutt. [21] The same can be said for Morúa and so this examination will both lay the foundation for the reading of their novels in the next chapter and play an important role in our understanding of the ideas of Morúa and Chesnutt, and also in our understanding of the complexities of race and national identity in late-nineteenth-century Cuba and the United States.

MARTÍN MORÚA DELGADO'S INTEGRATED CUBAN FAMILY

Martín Morúa Delgado was born on November 11, 1856 in Matanzas, Cuba, to a Spanish father and a free Cuban-born black mother. Morúa, then, was the first entirely Cuban born generation of his family, a mulato son of a *peninsular* and a *negra criolla*.[22] While neither Morúa nor his mother were enslaved, his political formation was based on opposition to both slavery and Spanish colonial rule. After early work as a journalist and publisher, he was imprisoned in 1879 for working against the colonial power. Like Emilia Margarita Tuerbe Tolón y Otero and the other progenitors of the Cuban flag, political exile was a part of Morúa's experience. He spent 1882 to 1886 in the United States where he was involved with other expatriate Cubans working for Cuban independence. During the early years of his exile, Morúa wrote an essay that he titled "Ensayo político o Cuba y la raza de color" (1882) ["Political Essay, or Cuba and the Colored Race"]. This essay represents his political thinking on integration and the problem of race in Cuba couched in such a way as to help support the cause for Cuban independence. Morúa is writing in the same era as José Martí, whose vision of nationalism is crucial to Cuba's identity. Martí desired to see a free, independent, democratic Cuban nation that was able to avoid the mistakes of its northern neighbor. His was a moral vision centered around republican ideals including self-sacrificial patriotism. While there is some debate regarding the extent to which Martí's vision for Cuba was truly inclusive, he famously worked with Afro-Cuban independence leader Antonio Maceo with whom he shared a vision of mutual love and forgiveness between the races for the good of the emerging nation. Morúa had a similar vision of moving beyond the divisions of race for the good of the desired nation. In Aleyda T. Portuondo's study of Morúa's political and literary prowess, she explains that, "Morúa se vio mulato, se reconoció negro y entendió que a la vez era hombre y que ésta era su condición *básica*"[23] [Morúa saw himself as a mulato, recognized that he was black, and understood that at the same time he was a man and that that was his *essential* condition]. This quotation echoes Manuel de la Cruz's characterization of Morúa and indicates Portuondo's assessment that Morúa understood the extent to which racial identity was socially constructed; the fact that she emphasizes how he saw himself versus what he recognized about himself indicates the difference between a self-constructed and a socially imposed identity. Having understood that social and political identities were constructed rather than essential, Morúa used his nonfiction writings to try to influence the way that ideas of Cuban national identity were constructed. Morúa's vision of Cuban identity as described in his "Political Essay" might better be represented by the idea that Morúa saw himself as a mulato, recognized that he was *considered* black, but insisted that he was a *Cuban* man, and that was his most essential identity. In emphasizing not just his manhood, but his *cubanidad*, Morúa projected a future that moved beyond race to incorporate all the aspects of the Cuban populace in the project of liberation and into the imagined future nation.

In writing about "la raza de color" in Cuba in order to advance the larger project of Cuban independence, Morúa first addresses the idea propagated by Spanish thinkers that Cuban independence would lead to a massacre of white

Cubans by the black majority. Just as Manzano and Douglass had to be careful in their constructions of black heroism in light of Haiti, Morúa helps readers distance themselves from the misunderstandings and negative connotations associated with Haiti and the Haitian revolution. In the essay, Morúa explains how Spanish intellectuals use a version of the Haitian revolution to play on the emotions of Cubans, works to combat unjustified race fear so that he can project his vision of an integrated anti-colonial Cuban nationality, and explains that Spanish intellectuals are trying to divide and conquer Cubans by making ridiculous charges against Cuban blacks so that they can more effectively keep all Cubans under control.[24] Morúa understands that by reinforcing fears of the Africanization—and potential black domination—of Cuba, Spanish historians (whom he addresses directly in the essay) and other Spanish officials make possible the continued exploitation of the island. By directly addressing the Cuban "fear of the dark," Morúa hopes to replace an ephemeral specter (that of black domination) with a vision of a unified Cuban populace who can defeat the very real enemy, their Spanish colonial rulers, and establish an independent Cuban nation.

Morúa discusses the Revolution of Santo Domingo because addressing the specter of Haiti is critical to his project of diffusing the fear of Africanization in his "white" Cuban brothers. He quickly points out that the cause of the revolution on this neighboring island was essentially the same as their cause: the sacred principles of liberty and independence.[25] However, he spends a great deal of time making sure that this is the only similarity his readers see between their projected struggle and the image of the Haitian Revolution that was being put forth by historians at the time. He calls on ideals of freedom and self-determination and implies similarities between the experiences of the Haitians and the oppression experienced by Cubans as colonial subjects. Morúa provides an alternate version of the story of the Revolution of Santo Domingo, focusing on the social conditions in the colony preceding the revolution and particularly on the experience of mulatos in Haiti.[26] Morúa knows that mulatos were the group most vilified in the aftermath of the violence in Haiti. His twofold purpose in this discussion is to demonstrate that historians have given an inaccurate picture of what happened, and also to argue that what happened in Haiti could never happen in Cuba. In addressing the myth of the desire of blacks to murder whites, Morúa also brings to light his version of the Aponte conspiracy, an 1811 rebellion in Cuba led by a free black and involving free blacks, slaves, and whites in which many lives were lost. Spanish historians claimed that the Aponte conspiracy was proof that blacks wanted to exterminate all whites, but Morúa argues that these are Spanish lies and that the true motivation behind the rebellion was the desire for freedom.[27] Morúa works hard to remove all of the historical specters that might haunt the minds of his white countrymen and that could limit their willingness to work for the freedom and independence of all Cubans, regardless of color. He continually reinforces the point that the fear of blacks is a fiction manufactured by the Spanish in order to keep Cubans under their power, arguing that this fear needs to be expelled in light of the true history of the island (and the region) for the sake of the creation of an independent and inclusive Cuban nation.

When Morúa emphasizes in his "Political Essay" that the Spanish are the common enemy of all Cubans, he hopes that his readers can move beyond their preoccupations with racial identity for the good of the independence of Cuba. Morúa explains that his purpose in revisiting both the history of blacks in Cuba and the history of the Haitian Revolution is to contribute "a la major marcha possible de nuestra raza y de nuestro país hacia la vida de la liber-tad"[28] [to the greatest possible advancement of our race and our country toward the life of liberty]. Here Morúa identifies himself both as a member of a collective race signified by the use of the first person plural possessive term "nuestra" [our], which might be taken by his readers to be the "raza de color" [colored race] about whom he writes the essay, but simultaneously identifies himself as a member of "nuestro país" [our country], in which term the use of the first person plural possessive "our" creates a common connection with all Cubans working toward the goal of independence and implies the establish-ment of a *Cuban* race. He later refers to other Cubans as "our" brothers and asks them to remember the long history of degrading oppression of blacks in Cuba.[29] Having linguistically identified himself as part of both groups, the "raza de color" and the larger "país," Morúa becomes a symbolic bridge, a figure who in and of himself represents the commonality and common inter-ests of these two groups. Having eliminated the gap between the "raza de color" and *cubanidad*, Morúa explains that his purpose for discussing the history of oppression is so that all Cubans can avoid the mistakes of their ancestors. In Morúa's version of history, race hatred and strife are imputed to the colonial system; they are attributes of the Spanish system that must be overthrown, or inventions of Spanish intellectuals that must be purged, in order to establish an independent Cuban nation. It is important to note here that it is Spanish greed and autocratic rule that Morúa implies are the most significant problems Cubans face. In his text, Morúa insists that race simply is not the central issue.

In "Ensayo politico," Morúa discusses other political realities that arise out of the fear of Africanization or that are associated with plans to create a whitened Cuban national identity. Morúa, himself a mulato, does not address, nor does he seem to fear, miscegenation or whitening. He cogently demon-strates the absurdity of plans to "repatriate" Afro-Cubans to Africa,[30] and his vision encompasses all elements in Cuban society. Morúa further explains that despite Spain's offers of autonomy as a solution to the Cuban desire for freedom, autonomy is not an option since "La libertad no admite términos medios"[31] [Freedom does not allow for half measures]. Morúa rejects the idea of annexation to the United States for similar reasons.[32] Again and again he emphasizes that true freedom, true independence, and true progress can only be found when Cuba is an independent nation that embraces all of the disparate elements of which it is composed.

This second part of Morúa's argument is most important to understanding his views on integration and the Cuban nation he envisions. To present his readers with a vision of a unified Cuban identity he employs the idea of Cuban brotherhood, evoking the Grito de Yara of 1868, the proclamation of the institution of a Cuban Republic, which began the ultimately unsuccessful Ten Years War for Cuban Independence. Morúa also engages the symbolic language of Cuban independence through reference to the Cuban flag sewn by Emilia Margarita Tuerbe Tolón y Otero. Morúa writes, "La bandera tricolor que ondeó en Yara ostenta rojo triángulo, símbolo de la idea republicana, cuyos tres grandes principios son, Libertad, Igualdad y Fraternidad"[33] [The tricolor flag that waved at Yara boasts a red triangle, symbol of the republican ideal, whose three great principles are Liberty, Equality, and Fraternity]. He adopts and adapts the symbolic language, here emphasizing the republican ideals that are most important to his vision of Cuban national identity. With the use of the principles of liberty, equality, and fraternity, Morúa downplays the United States as a republican model, likely because he is not a proponent of annexation, and instead evokes the motto that ties his ideas to the French and Haitian revolutions. The significance of his previous arguments about Haiti becomes apparent here. Most importantly, the principles themselves—liberty, equality, and fraternity—encapsulate the kind of society he hopes Cuba will become.

Immediately after his statement about the flag, Morúa continues, describing an independent Cuba that "no reconocerá diferencias entre sus ciudadanos, que gozarán de los mismos derechos, libres todos, todos iguales y hermanos como hijos de la misma madre, la patria, Cuba"[34] [will not recognize differences among its citizens, who will enjoy the same rights, all free, all equal, all brothers as sons of the same mother, the homeland, Cuba]. The emphasis on not recognizing differences among citizens is crucial because even positive examples of revolutionary movements that Morúa cites—like the American Revolution—did not lead to the kind of egalitarian society that he describes in this essay. The thread of family is important to note as well. Morúa uses the statement cited above to explain what it means to have a nation that represents the republican ideals—liberty, equality, fraternity—he associates with the flag. He insists that for Cubans to be free and equal, differences must not be recognized and rights must be universal. Further, Morúa justifies this on the basis of the ideal of Republican brotherhood, but he does not just write that all Cubans are brothers. He emphasizes that they are brothers because they have the same mother, and then lest his readers miss the point as to the source of their familial connection, he uses two appositives to clarify that their common mother is their homeland, Cuba. The equation of Cuba, common mother, and homeland is a strong foundation for his project of equality and the basis for his program of integration. As with slave narratives and similar to Douglass's use of Virginia as the mother of national heroes, in Morúa's writing the reality and metaphor of familial relations between blacks and whites is an important cornerstone to the creation of a unified Cuban nationality that was understood beyond the terms of black and white. While slave narrators like Manzano and Douglass used the rhetoric of family through relation to or resemblance to a variety of white parental figures, here it might be said that Morúa argues that all sons of the island *follow the condition of their mother—they are Cuban.*[35]

There was another consequence of Morúa's vision that must be mentioned. The idea of not recognizing differences stated in the above passage is also one of the underlying principles that formed Morúa into the politician who would, in later years, propose the amendment that bore his name. The Morúa amendment of 1910 banned the organization of political parties based on race. While this law was consistent with Morúa's integrationist politics, sadly and ironically given Morúa's own beliefs about brotherhood and integration, the amendment played a central role in the justifications for the 1912 Race War in Cuba. The Morúa amendment was a move to unity and while it may have been used to justify the race war, it was not the cause of the war; Morúa's idealistic amendment and the racially motivated violence were two opposite responses to the Cuban "fear of the dark."[36] Those who spawned the violence of those bloody days, particularly those who armed white Cubans and who killed Afro-Cubans without discovering their political affiliations, certainly never read some of the other passages of Morúa's "Ensayo politico," for they clearly did not understand the vision behind his amendment. In "Ensayo politico," Morúa imagines a future in which "crea el blanco en el amor del negro; crea el negro en la sinceridad del blanco, y la union que resulte de esta franca exposición y práctica de ambos sentimientos, nos traerá la independencia de la isla"[37] [whites are nourished in the love of blacks; blacks are nourished in the sincerity of whites, and the union that results from this open-hearted manifestation of both sentiments will lead us to the independence of the island]. What is most striking about his vision is the fact that Morúa simultaneously recognizes the difference in power held by each group—the blacks give love while the whites must exercise the sincerity to share power—and emphasizes the necessary contributions of both, albeit in a metaphorical way. This passage is almost a love story between the races, an extension of the family metaphor, love and sincerity and even *union* leading to an independence which contains both blacks and whites and is, at least metaphorically, a union creating a nation as mulato as Morúa is himself. In fact, he claims that in Cuba, unlike in the United States, white *criollo* and *peninsular* fathers claim and value their mulato sons.[38] As Aleyda T. Portuondo describes it, Morúa grew up in a home characterized by love and tenderness shared by two people who loved each other despite their differences in race, class, and status.[39] This home is in many ways the prototype for Morúa's vision of the nation. Because of his experience as son of a *peninsular* (white, male, and Spanish—the paragon of status and power colonial Cuba) and a *negra criolla* (black, female, and born on the island—an embodiment of objectification and powerlessness) who loved each other and who loved him, he imagines a Cuban nation that embraces everyone regardless of color.[40] Here, then, is a metaphorical love story in which the white Cuban males who are most significantly Morúa's intended readers can overcome their "fear of the dark"—fear of the fictitious threat of *lo negro* in Cuba—and see themselves as the proud fathers of an independent and integrated Cuban motherland. In this way, eventually everyone will be a son of the same mother, the homeland, Cuba.

CHARLES W. CHESNUTT'S AMALGAMATED FUTURE AMERICAN

In 1858, two years after Martín Morúa Delgado was born in Cuba, Charles W. Chesnutt was born in Cleveland, Ohio, to free black parents. Technically one-eighth black, Chesnutt would likely have been able to pass for white but chose to identify himself with the black part of his heritage and accept society's definition according to the one-drop rule that he was a black man. Chesnutt was an intellectual, novelist, educator, and businessman who, as Matthew Wilson astutely emphasizes, firmly believed that "fiction can effect social change," particularly change in the way that the general American population understood ideas of race.[41] Fiction was not the only genre employed by Chesnutt in his campaign to effect change in the ways in which Americans understood the idea of race and also of national identity. A series of essays and speeches written and delivered between 1882 and the publication of *The House Behind the Cedars* in 1900 demonstrate the development of his thinking related to ideas of race, discrimination, justice, and national identity. These essays were written in the post-Reconstruction period during which the African American press and social commentary by African American authors played an important role in renegotiations of American national identity as they fought for a society that would allow for greater inclusion for all. In the 1890s, Ida B. Wells argued for women's rights and documented and protested lynching, Pauline Hopkins addressed miscegenation and the absurdity of racial prejudice in her works, and W. E. B. DuBois began his powerful critiques of the material injustices in America. As white supremacy was becoming even more entrenched and powerful through lynching and Jim Crow laws, Chesnutt's voice joined these writers and others to combat the racializing assemblages at work in the nation.

In an 1882 speech titled "The Future of the Negro," Chesnutt addressed his audience as "friends and fellow-citizens," putting an emphasis on the common citizenship of all Americans regardless of color. The speech was given in honor of the anniversary of the Emancipation Proclamation and begins by paying homage to Lincoln, as well as John Brown, Charles Sumner, William Lloyd Garrison, Wendell Phillips, Elijah P. Lovejoy, and "our own Douglass."[42] Chesnutt first emphasizes that *all* of the South was emancipated by the proclamation, an argument that can be seen as a post–Civil War corollary to Frederick Douglass's assertion that all of society was degraded by slavery.[43] Chesnutt then turns to the subject of the future and writes that while national laws may technically provide "civil liberty, and political equality . . . it is still within the power of the States individually to make many unjust discriminations."[44] The two specific types of unjust discriminations Chesnutt mentions are "laws which require the white and colored people to be kept apart" and those "which forbid them to intermarry."[45] The early emphasis on both segregation and on the laws forbidding intermarriage are important ideas to Chesnutt's developing stance on race in the United States and what he sees for the nation's future identity because that future identity, as we shall see, is based on miscegenation. In this early speech, he writes that what he "hope[s] and pray[s] for is the time when a man's social position and success in life will not depend upon his race or complexion."[46]

In 1889 Chesnutt wrote two pieces that demonstrate his continuing engagement with these ideas. In the first essay, "An Inside View of the Negro Question," he directly addresses the American "fear of the dark," as embodied in white denial that racism, discrimination, and racial violence persist in the United States. In one part of the essay he specifically addresses violent reactions to miscegenation. Chesnutt starts by pointing out the hypocrisy inherent in the fact that miscegenation is "much-dreaded" when it was "so freely condoned by a former generation of white people when it was the result of unbridled license," license which, Chesnutt implies without explicitly stating it, often excused and facilitated miscegenation in the form of sexual violence.[47] His critique of the hypocrisy of white attitudes toward miscegenation continues by focusing on the fact that attitudes have changed to condemnation by the "present generation" only now that "there is a possibility that it may someday receive the sanction of law,"[48] implying that power rather than an absolute moral principle is at stake. His final point is that miscegenation "never was and never will be possible without the consent of the white people."[49] This statement is a reminder to Chesnutt's audience that most miscegenation initially took place through the exercise of illegitimate and unconscionable power by whites. It is also a subtle rebuttal of the racist belief that mulatos were likely to rape white women. Chesnutt understands how deeply and neurotically engrained the desire for white purity is following the Civil War, particularly in the south, and in addressing "The Negro Question" he points to miscegenation—and attitudes toward miscegenation—as a central issue.

A second Chesnutt article from 1889 asks the titular question, "What is a White Man?" According to William L. Andrews, in "What is a White Man?" Chesnutt continues developing his ideas on the social construction of racial identities, arguing that racial categories are "man-made" and "counterfeit" rather than innate, and that the laws, such as those against intermarriage, which are intended to preserve these counterfeit categories are "obnoxious to people of color and impossible to enforce."[50] Chesnutt's understanding of the social construction of race was fundamental to his ideas regarding American society. As Matthew Wilson points out "[a]t this point in his thinking, Chesnutt hoped that the third term—the mulatto, the white negro—would be able to split apart the binary of black and white, forcing the American racial imaginary to stop insisting on the rigid demarcation of the color line."[51] In Chesnutt's own words, "the human intellect long ago revolted at the manifest absurdity of classifying men fifteen-sixteenths white as black men."[52] Here once again Chesnutt presents race as a social construction and explores some of the consequences of such an idea, including the absurdity of ignoring the complexities of the American racial landscape and the problem of laws against intermarriage which "make mixed blood a *prima-facie* proof of illegitimacy."[53] As in "An Inside View of the Negro Question," in "What is a White Man?" Chesnutt argues against those who would deny, outlaw, or vilify miscegenation.

In 1900 Chesnutt wrote a series of three articles under the general title "The Future American" which appeared in *The Boston Evening Transcript*. In these articles Chesnutt addressed very real anxieties about the future of the American nationality in a time of great population growth brought about by reproduction, immigration, and imperialism. Most whites desired to maintain their status as those above the color line who monopolized human and citizen with all the rights and privileges thereto appertaining. Chesnutt's purpose in addressing these anxieties was to project his vision of what the "future American race" was going to become. In these articles, Chesnutt looked past the paradigms of racial identity handed to him by society, understanding before most that the identity of peoples of African descent in the United States was determined as much by a national concept of whiteness as by anything else. Chesnutt sought to empower non-whites by continuing to expose white identity as, in Stephen P. Knadler's terms, a "rhetorical performance" designed "to stand (as if naturally so) as the norm, the core, the point of reference against which every other people are measured."[54] Chesnutt hoped that through his writings—both fiction and nonfiction—he could persuade white readers to see racial identity as more complicated than the black/white paradigm held by many Americans, a paradigm created through racialization which valued and included whiteness and devalued and sought to exclude that which was considered black.

The first of the "Future American" articles is subtitled, "What the Race is Likely to Become in the Process of Time." The choice of the term race here is key: Chesnutt's definition of the "Future American" directly equates race and nationality just as Morúa implies that there is a *Cuban* race. But where Morúa's Cuban race is more metaphorical, Chesnutt's vision as presented in these essays appears to propose a biological solution to racial difference. In his essay Chesnutt is defining and prophesizing a future American race outside of the either/or, black/white paradigm of his day. He points out that the "popular theory is that the future American race will consist of a harmonious fusion of the various European elements which now make up our heterogeneous population."[55] Chesnutt might be thinking here of the section from the chapter "True Americanism" in Theodore Roosevelt's *American Ideals* (1897) in which Roosevelt talks about Americans as "a people of mixed blood," but mentions only Europeans as being included in the mix.[56] Roosevelt curiously sidesteps the issue of race when he states that "Americanism is a question of spirit, conviction, and purpose, not of creed or birthplace."[57] In his first "Future American" article, Chesnutt seems to combine the two when he explains that he uses the word race "in its popular sense—that of a people who look substantially alike, and are molded by the same culture and dominated by the same ideals."[58] Here he adds similarity of appearance to Roosevelt's focus on culture and ideals. While Chesnutt claims to use the popular sense of the word race, the ideas he posits are quite different from those which divide American society along the color line. Chesnutt makes it clear in these essays, and elsewhere in his writings, that racial categories are artificial constructs controlled by legal means, societal mores, and social pressures. Like Martín Morúa Delgado, Chesnutt believes that the focus must be on the commonality of the whole in order to eliminate the strife between the parts. In "The Future American" articles, Chesnutt works to counteract false assumptions held by his readers, presents the idea of a future American race that is the amalgamation of what he holds to be the three main components of American society (black, white, and Native American), and discusses both the progress of and the barriers to the process by which the future American race is coming about.

In his attempts to undermine and eradicate the false assumptions held by his readers regarding race, Chesnutt begins by attacking the assumption that the Anglo-Saxon race has been scientifically proven superior. Morúa argued against a vision of black Cubans as a violent threat to the Cuban nation and Chesnutt begins by arguing against the idea of white superiority in order to chip away at the "fear of the dark" in the United States. The important thing is the manner in which Chesnutt addresses the body of thought of his time. Chesnutt cites scientific advances made at the end of the nineteenth century that he believed served to replace "many hoary anthropological fallacies" on which racism had been based, including the very idea that there is a European race.[59] He explains that according to scientists, "European races, as a whole, show signs of secondary or derived origin" and are most likely an "intermediate between the extreme primary types of the Asiatic and Negro races."[60] This sets up the argument that there is no purity of race even among Europeans, since the European race is merely the confluence of other races. Chesnutt argues against the "popular theory" that the future American race will come about through the "fusion" of "European elements" by pointing out that Europeans are not racially pure *and* the "various racial varieties" within the population of the United States, including non-Europeans, have already been mixing.[61]

In order to further his project of the construction of a future American race, Chesnutt emphasizes the fallacy of the belief that racial purity exists. Chesnutt clearly states that, "Any dream of a pure white race, of the Anglo-Saxon type, for the United States, may as well be abandoned as impossible, even if desirable."[62] He continues by explaining that his future American "will be predominantly white" and that it will likely "call itself white" as well since "it will conform closely to the white type;" what he emphasizes as well is that this so-called white race "will have absorbed and assimilated the blood of the other two races mentioned."[63] Chesnutt considers this process of absorption as being "as certain as the operation of any law well can be that deals with so uncertain a quantity as the human race."[64] This acceptance of the rhetorical and social power of whiteness on the part of Chesnutt is troubling and complicated. Matthew Wilson refers to these essays as presenting "more complicated and more audacious" thinking about race than in Chesnutt's previous works, particularly since Chesnutt presents "miscegenation as a kind of utopian solution to a problem that seemed otherwise intractable."[65] In terms of the emphasis on the erasure of difference through miscegenation, Chesnutt's articles resonate with the plans of the Cuban *criollo* elite to counteract the Africanization of the island through biological *blanqueamiento*, plans which were based on a fundamental belief in the superiority of white blood.

A modern reader might be tempted to consider Chesnutt's position as illustrating a large degree of shame or race hatred—particularly if such a reader accepted *Plessy v. Ferguson*'s one-drop rule and simply considered Chesnutt black;[66] certainly Chesnutt is an interesting case since he chose to be socially defined as black despite the fact that he is of predominantly European heritage, yet he imagines a future American race that would consider itself white in spite of its lack of racial purity. However, Chesnutt's future American race cannot be considered white according to the *Plessy v.*

Ferguson ruling. Arlene Elder argues that Chesnutt's "advocacy of racial amalgamation as the ultimate solution to America's social ills . . . would result in an invisibility guaranteed to strike terror" into the hearts of those who valued the fiction of racial purity.[67] Chesnutt tries to allay these fears, noting the accomplishments of the current mulato population of the United States. Perhaps Chesnutt is best seen not as a black man whose self-hatred leads him to support amalgamation, but rather as a man who hopes that "[p]hysical differences between the races will gradually disappear, and with them, the marks upon which racial discrimination have been based."[68] Despite the problematic aspects of his "utopian illusion," Chesnutt is exceptional because he directly addresses the ongoing process of miscegenation, attempts to allay white fears about race mixing, and challenges essentialist conceptions of race. As Dean McWilliams summarizes, "the Future American" posited by Chesnutt "is the mulatto."[69] The Future American it seems will look a lot like Chesnutt himself. Just as Morúa's vision of an integrated Cuban family can be seen as rising from his own family and experiences, Chesnutt's life and very being may be the model for his future American. This is, of course, assuming that Chesnutt is really, literally proposing such a solution. Keith Byerman argues that Chesnutt's focus is on the absurdity of the ideas of his time regarding race and that his proposed solution in these essays are "calculated acts of provocation designed to discomfort the audience rather than persuade it," noting the essays should be seen "not as an actual proposal for social change . . . but rather as a hypothesis that carries science and social practice to a logical end."[70] I think that either way the essays are provocative in that they force readers to confront both the reality of miscegenation and the difficult project of imagining a unified American society.

Whether taken literally or not, in his "Future American" essays, Chesnutt indicates that it is in this mixing of "the three broad types—white, black, and Indian—that the future American race will find the material for its formation."[71] It is regrettable that Chesnutt does not acknowledge the fact that American society in 1900 was made up of more than these three groups. Clearly Chesnutt's main focus is on trying to change both the de jure and de facto means by which African Americans are excluded from full participation in American society—from full entrance into the American race—and due to this focus he downplays the importance of this process for groups other than the three he mentions. This is not to say that Chesnutt did not want full participation for all, merely that his singularity of purpose appears to belie the complexities of the process he describes. In the case of Native Americans, a group which he discusses in detail, Chesnutt's ideas are oversimplified and, at times, problematic. Chesnutt emphasizes their small numbers, argues that "there is no prejudice against Indian blood, in solution," and claims that if Native Americans in the United States "be not speedily amalgamated with the white population" it will be their fault.[72] Chesnutt's emphasis was on his "awareness of the legal and social power inherent in assimilation rather than to suggest any value to ethnic diversity, an understandable, if unfortunate, position for a mulato writer living during the racially turbulent turn-of-the-century."[73] As Morúa Delgado insists on amalgamation and unity to the detriment of the rights of groups united by race, Chesnutt insists on assimilation rather than differentiation. For both thinkers, hope lay in the ability to move beyond distinctions and to view everyone as equally entitled to citizenship.

Chesnutt ends his first installment regarding the "Future American" by explaining that the "real problem" will be the incorporation of the "Negro element" of the population since there will be a slow social struggle involved; anticipating his next article, he emphasizes that the process of amalgamation has already begun.[74] He insists that the "mixture" of the races needs to take place because in his utopian future: "[t]here would be no inferior race to domineer over; there would be no superior race to oppress those who differed from them in racial externals."[75] For Matthew Wilson, given an "unparalleled outburst of racist speculation on the impending disappearance of the American Negro" in the 1890s, "Chesnutt's proposals . . . are quite stunning, as if he had taken the assumptions of the racist imaginary and turned them inside out."[76] Wilson thinks the kind of amalgamation predicted by Chesnutt is striking because it replaces a society radically segregated along the color line for one in which African Americans are integrated "not only into the body politic but also into the bodies of white folks" turning black blood from "a kind of infectious agent" to an antidote to "the incessantly racialized American imagination."[77] Chesnutt's ideas move from the political integration of the previously dehumanized black body as a citizen in the nation to the biological incorporation of blackness into the American race.

In his "The Future American" articles, Chesnutt works to demonstrate that the process of amalgamation is both natural and desirable, and that it can occur relatively easily. Part of Chesnutt's argument is that so much miscegenation has already gone on in the United States that the process was inevitable. In order to emphasize this idea of the inertia of amalgamation, the second of Chesnutt's articles presents anecdotal evidence of the "Stream of Dark Blood in the Veins of Southern Whites," including examples of miscegenation and passing to emphasize that the process of "amalgamation" is already well underway.[78] Here one might remember Douglass's claim that he was the blood-kin of his white audience. For Chesnutt, the laws made to limit miscegenation and to categorize individuals according to race were "certain proof of the fact that Negro blood is widely distributed among the white people."[79] Chesnutt may have had decisions like *Plessy v. Ferguson* from four years earlier or anti-miscegenation laws in mind when he made this argument. He argues that laws are not made for individual cases; they are only made when there are enough instances of something to require a general rule.[80] Dean McWilliams points out another problematic aspect of Chesnutt's vision when he notes that as much as Chesnutt insists that the process of assimilation is well under way and inevitable, his metaphor of amalgamation as a "bitter pill" that must be swallowed "acknowledges, and then minimizes" the fact that people must cooperate in order for his vision to come about, a move that also minimizes "the obstructive power of white prejudice" to his project and "undervalues black pride and underestimates black resistance to assimilation."[81] Chesnutt is trying to project a desired future, and in doing so minimizes the strength of the cultural resistance to his ideas. His vision is utopian, which implies that it may also be impossible. The same could be said for Morúa's vision of a unified Cuban family.

The third "The Future American" article, in Chesnutt's prophetic fashion, is subtitled, "A Complete Race-Amalgamation Likely to Occur" and provides a discussion of those things which Chesnutt emphasizes will either "retard" or "promote" this amalgamation.[82] Those things that Chesnutt condemns both in principle and because he feels they will retard the amalgamation process are not hard to guess after reading the first two essays; he mentions prejudice, laws against intermarriage, lynching, and segregation.[83] Those things that will promote amalgamation include the power of money and status, for "the possession of a million dollars . . . would throw such a golden glow over a dark complexion as to override" the American "fear of the dark."[84] Chesnutt also predicts that change will come about through a growing understanding of the fact that the color line includes a lot of "social fiction" including that which "makes of a person seven-eighths white a Negro; he is really much more a white man."[85] Chesnutt imagines a world free of the racializing assemblages that create and enforce ideas of difference.

At the end of his third installment of "The Future American," Chesnutt writes that the "formation of this future American race . . . . must come . . . as the result of natural law . . . a hard pill, but one which must be swallowed" since "homogeneity of type, at least in externals, is a necessary condition of harmonious social progress."[86] At least one aspect of Chesnutt's ideas has changed from earlier essays in switching his focus from rights to the constitution of a new American national identity. Although the 1889 essay "An Inside View of the Negro Question" included the emphatic statement that "The Negro believes that *now* is the time to settle" the question of the place of the "negro" in society,[87] the three "The Future American" articles posit a long, slow process which, while utopian on the one hand, demonstrates an inherent pessimism on Chesnutt's part regarding the ability of American society to accept difference. Chesnutt's theory of amalgamation necessitates the elimination of difference, a position not entirely comfortable to those who value diversity. Chesnutt's choice to focus on the idea of a unified American race in order to posit a future in which racial strife and inequality will not, indeed *cannot*, exist represents a radical rejection of a culture which valorized whiteness and demonized blackness, creating a stark distinction between those who were accepted as full citizens and those who were excluded from that category because they were also excluded from whiteness, manhood, and full humanity.

MORÚA AND CHESNUTT AND THE
FUTURE OF NATIONAL IDENTITY

Chesnutt's idea of amalgamation to create future Americans and Morúa's vision of integration of all of mother Cuba's sons are projections they hope their readers will see as inevitable, but they only represent possible futures for their homelands. The visions created by Chesnutt and Morúa create unified national identities by subsuming difference in the cause of nationalism and equality. Chesnutt's vision of a literal subsuming of difference through an eventual biological amalgamation that will erase visible difference is contrasted to Morúa's use of a metaphorical figuration of kinship that assumes that difference need not be emphasized. While neither Chesnutt nor Morúa's visions came true, the Cuban Race War of 1912 may be an indication that Chesnutt was, sadly, more realistic in his assumption that turn of the twentieth century racism demanded that difference must literally be erased from the face of a post-plantation New World nation, even at the cost of making blackness invisible.

Chesnutt and Morúa were both very much concerned with the kind of societies that would come about as their nations continued to struggle with issues related to race and national identity. Through the writing of "Ensayo político" and "The Future American" they hoped to help create desired futures that would reflect their ideals of full humanity and citizenship for all. One way in which these two authors engaged some of the main ideas discussed in these essays was through their appropriation and transformation of the trope of the tragic mulata. The novels that contain these transformations reflect some of the ideas in the essays discussed earlier in this chapter, but it would be an exaggeration to suggest that they reproduce the exact arguments developed in their essays. The following chapter contains an examination of Morúa's *Sofía* and Chesnutt's *The House Behind the Cedars* to see how the novels represent the authors' further engagement with the issues addressed in these essays.

NOTES

1. De la Cruz qtd. in Rufino Pérez Landa, *Vida Pública de Martín Morúa Delgado* (Havana: Academia de la historia, 1957), 131.

2. Franklin W. Knight, *Slave Society in Cuba During the Nineteenth Century* (Madison: University of Wisconsin Press, 1970), 99–100.

3. Saco, qtd. and trans. Richard L. Jackson, *The Black Image in Latin American Literature* (Albuquerque: University of New Mexico Press, 1976), 3

4. Kutzinski, *Sugar's Secrets*, 31.

5. Knight, *Slave Society in Cuba*, 93.

6. Ibid. Knight does not provide numbers for later in the nineteenth century because, as he explains, the 1860 census the authorities had changed the system of classification to one in which there were no distinctions between blacks and mulatos, but rather only one category called the gente de color [people of color]. Knight suggests that the change "might have been a significant index of deteriorating social and racial relations" (93).

7. Richard L. Jackson, *Black Writers in Latin America* (Albuquerque: University of New Mexico Press, 1979), 14.

8. Ramos, "Cuerpo, Lengua, Subjetividad," 233.

9. Kutzinski, *Sugar's Secrets*, 5.

10. Berzon, *Neither White nor Black*, 11.

11. Carol Allen, *Black Woman Intellectuals: Strategies of Nation, Family, and Neighborhood in the Works of Pauline Hopkins, Jessie Fauset, and Marita Bonner* (New York: Garland Publishing, 1998), 67.

12. H. Rap Brown, qtd. in Berzon, *Neither White nor Black*, 3.

13. Bakhtin, "Discourse in the Novel," 276.

14. Berzon, *Neither White nor Black*, 19.

15. Ibid., 26.

16. Frances Richardson Keller, *An American Crusade: The Life of Charles Waddell Chesnutt* (Provo, UT: Brigham Young University Press, 1978), 42.

17. Samira Kawash, *Dislocating the Color Line: Identity, Hybridity, and Singularity in African-American Narrative* (Stanford: Stanford University Press, 1997), 157.

18. Berzon, *Neither White nor Black*, 5.

19. Ibid.

20. Barbara Johnson, "The Quicksands of the Self: Nella Larsen and Heinz Kohut," in *Female Subjects in Black and White: Race, Psychoanalysis, Feminism*, ed. Elizabeth Abel, Barbara Christian, and Helene Moglen (Berkeley: University of California Press, 1997), 52–3.

21. Matthew Wilson, *Whiteness in the Novels of Charles W. Chesnutt* (Jackson: University Press of Mississippi, 2004), 3.

22. Aleyda T. Portuondo, *Vigencia política y literaria de Martín Morúa Delgado* (Miami: Ediciones Universales, 1978), 5.

23. Ibid., 6.

24. Martín Morúa Delgado, "Ensayo Político o Cuba y la Raza de Color" in *Obras completas de Martín Morúa Delgado*, vol. 3 (Havana, Cuba: Comisión Nacional del Centenario de Martín Morúa Delgado, 1957), 47.

25. Ibid., 49.

26. Ibid., 50–51.

27. Ibid., 70.

28. Ibid., 48.

29. Ibid., 48–49.

30. Ibid., 85–87.

31. Ibid., 97.

32. Ibid., 101–2.

33. Ibid., 52.

34. Ibid.

35. The use of a female figure as a symbol rather than an agent is problematic in many ways, particularly considering that the language of republican bourgeois nationalism is distinctly male. The state or nation may be the unifying mother of all the national sons, but what about the nation's daughters?

36. For a contemporary Cuban interpretation of Morúa and the race war of 1912, see Dimas Castellanos's 2007 article "Morúa y la matanza de 1912" in *Revista Digital Consenso*.

37. Morúa Delgado, "Ensayo Político," 63.

38. Ibid., 88.

39. Portuondo, *Vigencia política y literaria,* 5.

40. Different sources give differing versions of Morúa's mother's identity; all sources indicate that she was born in Cuba, while some identify her as having been born a slave (for example Richard L. Jackson in "Slavery, Racism and Autobiography"), while others identify her as a free-born *negra criolla* (*The Africana Encyclopedia* and George B. Handley, among others). If she had been born a slave, then the argument concerning Morúa's childhood home being a utopian space in which the two extremes of identity (Spanish, white, male, citizen/free versus Cuban-born, black, female (ex-)slave) is even more pronounced. The ambiguity of Morúa's mother's identity is also a reminder of the issue raised by Frederick Douglass concerning the inability for the black under slavery (particularly when enslaved) to know his/her parentage or the date/conditions of his/her birth.

41. Matthew Wilson, "Who Has the Right to Say? Charles W. Chesnutt, Whiteness, and the Public Sphere," *College Literature* 26, no. 2 (Spring 1999): 19.

42. Chesnutt, *Essays*, 25.

43. Ibid., 28.

44. Ibid., 29.

45. Ibid.

46. Ibid.

47. Ibid., 59.

48. Ibid.

49. Ibid.

50. William L. Andrews, *The Literary Career of Charles W. Chesnutt* (Baton Rouge: Louisiana State University Press, 1980), 140.

51. Wilson, *Whiteness in the Novels*, 5.

52. Chesnutt, *Essays*, 68.

53. Ibid., 72.

54. Stephen P. Knadler, "Untragic Mulatto: Charles Chesnutt and the Discourse of Whiteness," *American Literary History* 8, no. 3 (Fall 1996): 427.

55. Chesnutt, *Essays*, 121.

56. Theodore Roosevelt, *American Ideals* (New York: G.P. Putnam's Sons, 1897), 47.

57. Ibid., 48.

58. Chesnutt, *Essays,* 97.

59. Ibid., 122.

60. Ibid.

61. Ibid., 121–22.

62. Ibid., 123.

63. Ibid.

64. Ibid.

65. Wilson, *Whiteness in the Novels*, 11.

66. See Anne Fleischmann for a fruitful discussion of the problematic tendency in Chesnutt studies to over-simplify his racial identity by accepting America's two-race system. Anne Fleischmann, "Neither Fish, Flesh, Nor Fowl: Race and Region in the Writings of Charles W. Chesnutt," *African American Review* 34, no. 3 (Autumn 2000): 461–473.

67. Arlene A. Elder, "MELUS Forum: 'The Future American Race': Charles W. Chesnutt's Utopian Illusion," *MELUS* 15, no. 3 (Fall 1988): 123.

68. McWilliams, Dean, *Charles W. Chesnutt and the Fictions of Race* (Athens: University of Georgia Press, 2002), 45.

69. Ibid., 51.

70. Keith Byerman, "Performing Race: Mixed-Race Characters in the Novels of Charles Chesnutt," in *Passing in the Works of Charles W. Chesnutt.* 86. Byerman imagines Chesnutt as having wondered, "What if, then, instead of resisting this natural and inevitable process, Americans embraced it? The outcome, in Chesnutt's view, would be the resolution of an otherwise intractable problem. The article offers little indication that the society will actually do something so reasonable" (86).

71. Chesnutt, *Essays*, 123.

72. Ibid. Chesnutt sounds sympathetic when he argues that Native Americans should not be "treated as wards of the Government" but rather "given their rights once for all, and placed upon the footing of other citizens" (*Essays* 131). However, Chesnutt does worry about the fact that the "wilder Indians" still need to be "educated and by the development of the country brought into closer contact with civilization" (*Essays* 131). Nor does he consider the possibility that they might not want to be amalgamated. Chesnutt writes that "there is no evidence of any such strong race instinct or organization as will make the Indians of the future wish to perpetuate themselves as a small but insignificant class in a great population, thus emphasizing distinctions which would be overlooked in the case of the individual" (*Essays* 131). He assumes that Native Americans want to "fade into the white population" and "leave no trace discoverable by anyone but the anthopological [*sic*] expert" (*Essays* 131).

73. Elder, "MELUS Forum," 123.

74. Chesnutt, *Essays*, 125.

75. Ibid.

76. Wilson, *Whiteness in the Novels*, 12.

77. Ibid.

78. Chesnutt, *Essays*, 126.

79. Ibid., 129.

80. Ibid., 129–30.

81. McWilliams, *The Fictions of Race*, 46, 55.

82. Chesnutt, *Essays*, 131.

83. Ibid., 132–3.

84. Ibid., 133.

85. Ibid., 134.

86. Ibid., 135.

87. Ibid., 60.

Chapter Five

Generating the Future Citizen in Morúa Delgado's *Sofía* and Chesnutt's *The House Behind the Cedars*

Miriam DeCosta-Willis argues that Juan Francisco Manzano is "the archetypical tragic mulato" since he was "the miscegenated victim of a slave owning society" who "prefigured the Romantic stereotype" of the mulato seen in nineteenth-century Cuban anti-slavery novels like Gertrudis Gómez de Avellaneda's *Sab* and Cirilo Villaverde's *Cecilia Valdés*.[1] As DeCosta-Willis points out, nineteenth-century Cuban anti-slavery novels used the conflicted figure of the mulato/a to illustrate the complexity of race relations in Cuba; these novels also brought to light the double horror of the rape of slave women and the rejection of the children born out of this violence by their white, slave-owning fathers.[2] Like the tragic mulato, Manzano is a victim of the caprices of a racist slave society and while he did not try to pass for white in a literal sense, Julio Ramos argues that a slave like Manzano who learned to write with the same handwriting as his master is just like a mulato/a who passes for white.[3] As I argued in chapter 3, both Manzano and Frederick Douglass performed a type of literary passing in their discourses of identity as they appropriated rhetorical whiteness in order to write themselves into the nation. Unlike Manzano, Douglass may not have been the prototypical tragic mulato in the United States, but his slave narrative is a foundational text in the anti-slavery literary tradition that included novels like Harriet Beecher Stowe's *Uncle Tom's Cabin*, William Wells Brown's *Clotel*, and Frances Ellen Watkins Harper's *Iola Leroy*. Like Douglass and Manzano's narratives, mulato novels often participated in the negotiation of ideas of national identity.

Novelistic representations of the mulato/a in Cuba and the United States during the nineteenth century could have two opposite functions: they could either reinforce or challenge existing social boundaries. That many of these representations are female followed from the preoccupation, noted by Kutzinski, regarding the ways in which race, gender, and sexuality affected power relations.[4] Some depictions of the tragic mulata attempted to reinforce the existing power structure through the maintenance of social categories. The tragic mulata is a figure of mixed heritage who appears white, but whose fate is "darkened" by the accident of mixed parentage. The most common plot of the tragic mulata story is one in which a beautiful, apparently white young woman falls in love with a white man (usually of a high social station) and yet cannot marry him because the repressed evidence of blackness and social negation becomes known. The tragic mulata often pays for the perceived discrepancy between appearance and racial "reality" with her life. These stories trouble the boundaries of how individuals are identified and placed within society by exploring themes like legitimacy, incest, whitening, and passing.[5] The figure of the tragic mulata in nineteenth-century Cuban and American literature, and particularly the way in which her tragic fate embodied how the punishment by society for the crime of miscegenation was enacted on the product/victim rather than the perpetrator, reinforced racialization and highlighted the importance of the supposed purity of the white race to constructions of national identity.

Post-emancipation novelists Martín Morúa Delgado and Charles W. Chesnutt adapted the trope of the mulato/a to challenge the racist underpinnings of their societies. Stephen P. Knadler argues that in late nineteenth-, early twentieth-century American fiction the mulato/a figure is an "abject figure who would . . . expose the arbitrariness of society's racial classifications."[6] In Bakhtin's terms, the figure of the mulato was a trope that writers made use of despite the fact that it was "already populated with the social intentions of others"; writers could appropriate such figures and, as Bakhtin writes, force them to "serve a second master."[7] Although the figure of the mulato/a was a populated term—one that came laden with connotations and interpretations—a variety of Cuban and North American authors used this figure as part of the negotiation of social hierarchies and ideas of national identity. As Margaret Toth explains, the use of the mulata in this context was often a "politico-aesthetic strategy whereby African American authors worked not only to deconstruct racist visual iconography but also to engage forcefully in contemporary arguments about race."[8] Certain fictional representations of the mulato/a served to blur the boundaries between racial categories as they challenged the characters', and by extension the readers', ability to identify, place, and control individuals. This, in turn, worked to undermine the social power of racialization.

This work is an extension of and conversation with George B. Handley's *Postslavery Literatures in the Americas*, and particularly his chapter "Reading behind the Face: Martín Morúa Delgado, Charles W. Chesnutt, and Frances E. W. Harper." Handley examines the narrative strategies used by these three authors in their "attempt to loosen white culture's grip over the categories of racial difference" and the ways in which they "criticize the genealogical claims of the white family on the national patrimony."[9] We have already seen how Morúa's "Ensayo político" and Chesnutt's "The Future American" participate in this critique, a critique furthered in their novels. Handley is also important to this study in his emphasis on the "uncanny parallels" and "deep and hidden forces across postslavery American nations" which he finds evidenced in novels such as those by Chesnutt and Morúa.[10] Whereas Handley examines both *Sofía* and Morúa's later novel *La familia Unzuázu* in relation to Chesnutt's *The Marrow of Tradition* with a focus on genealogy and perception, this chapter reads *Sofía* with Chesnutt's *The House Behind the Cedars* since *Sofía* is a direct conversation with the iconic Cuban tragic mulata novel *Cecilia Valdés*, and *The House Behind the Cedars* more closely relates to the traditional tragic mulata trope in the United States. In addition, while many critics show preference to Chesnutt's *The Marrow of Tradition*, William L. Andrews claims *The House Behind the Cedars*, "more than any single work of Chesnutt's, reflects his peculiar knowledge of the distinct problems of people of mixed blood as they negotiated the South's color line after the Civil War."[11] It is precisely the complex realities and implications of miscegenation which are at issue in both *Sofía* and *The House Behind the Cedars*.

Both Handley and Doris Sommer before him have explored the idea of nation as family, an idea that is very much present in my analysis as well. In *Foundational Fictions*, Sommer writes about "national romances," and her analysis indicates the hostile nature of the rhetoric of national identity created in these romances to the racial other. She writes that "the pretty lies of national romance are similar strategies to contain the racial, regional, economic, and gender conflicts that threatened the development of the Latin American nations," emphasizing that the novels helped to further "a general bourgeois project to hegemonize a culture in formation."[12] Sommer identifies these cultures as being set up to deal with the complexities of identity in their societies, but through the creation of "a cozy, almost airless culture that bridged public and private spheres in a way that made a place for everyone, as long as everyone knew his or her place."[13] Pre-emancipation tragic mulata fictions like *Cecilia Valdés* can be seen as this type of romance. However, as Werner Sollors argues, many works present the mulato/a figure as "a living challenge to the central contradiction of the New World" because "the anti-aristocratic promise of abandoning hereditary systems in favor of self-made men clashed with slavery and segregation which reinstated a particularly sharp focus on the question of a character's ancestry."[14] Morúa and Chesnutt's versions of the genre challenge the very categories into which individuals might be "placed" within the nation, providing a counter-romance that reimagined the national family in new, if sometimes troubling, ways.

Martín Morúa Delgado's 1891 novel *Sofía* and Charles W. Chesnutt's 1900 novel *The House Behind the Cedars* are discourses of identity which use the trope of the mulato/a to serve counter-cultural political and social purposes, challenging their cultures' oversimplistic notions of race and identity. Although published nine years apart, the two novels were written in an overlapping period; *Sofía* was written between 1888 and 1890, and *The House Behind the Cedars* was a longer adaptation of the story "Rena Walden," which Chesnutt began writing in 1890. Morúa Delgado's novel serves as a revision of Cirilo Villaverde's *Cecilia Valdés* and centers on what readers begin the novel assuming is a tragic mulata character, the titular Sofía. Chesnutt's novel also adapts and transforms the tragic mulata trope, appearing at first to similarly highlight a single tragic mulata character, Rena Walden. In both cases, however, the trope of the tragic mulata is transformed and complicated, in part through the inclusion of a number of other characters whose presence and attributes help the authors to challenge aspects of the caste systems within their homelands. In *Sofía*, Morúa Delgado employs a number of other characters to help expand his critique of slavery and colonialism, including Sofía's half-siblings, brother-in-law, and family friend Eladislao Gonzaga. These characters allow for a discussion of various topics surrounding the figure of the mulata, including questions of legitimacy, sexual abuse, and the engendering of the national family. In *The House Behind the Cedars*, Chesnutt focuses on four mixed-race figures—Molly Walden, her two children John and Rena Walden/Warwick, and John Warwick's young son Alfred. By including multiple mulato/a characters across three generations, Chesnutt is able to suggest generational distinctions in the experiences of these mixed-race individuals. In addition, while the male mulato and the female mulata both represent a similar challenge to caste systems based on a black/white binary, each figure also represents gender-specific concerns regarding social erotics, libidinality, reproduction, and legitimacy.

The similarity in *Sofía* and *The House Behind the Cedars* lies in the fact that both Chesnutt and Morúa Delgado use the mulata trope as a vehicle to challenge racialization in their respective lands and to represent their ideas regarding citizenship and national identity beyond the global color line. The post-emancipation discourses of identity created by Chesnutt and Morúa in *The House Behind the Cedars* and *Sofía* present their ideas regarding the national family written in order to trouble existing notions of national identity and to engender a new future citizen. The authors engage the legacy of slavery in order to demonstrate the possibility of changing cultural constructions of racial identity and national identity. Chesnutt and Morúa engage the legacy of slavery and set their novels in the past; however, their concern is not really with the past. They are with trying to lead their readers *through* the past in order to obtain a desired future. Their fictional works emphasize the social construction of identities in order to project futures in which the fictions of racial identity held by society are removed so that all citizens will have the rights and opportunities to which they are entitled. An examination of these two novels within the context of the reading of Morúa Delgado and Chesnutt's nonfiction in the previous chapter will allow for a fuller understanding of how *The House Behind the Cedars* and *Sofía* serve as discourses of identity depicting part of the process by which these two authors worked out their visions of racial equality and national identity.

TRANSFORMING THE TROPE IN *SOFÍA*: THE TRAGEDY IS SHE IS NOT A MULATA

In his note to the reader at the beginning of his novel, Martín Morúa Delgado claims that it is the first in a series of social portraits that would be copied from everyday Cuban life.[15] The action of the novel takes place around the time of the Guerra Chiquita of 1879–1880, an attempt by Cubans to gain their independence from Spain. Setting the novel during a time of anticolonial conflict makes natural its engagement with ideas of emerging Cuban national identity. It is also significant that while the novel was written after slavery was abolished, it is set during slavery, engaging both the experience and legacy of slavery as it relates to the construction of national identity. Perhaps Morúa's choice to set the novel during slavery relates to the fact that he intended his novel as a corrective of Cirilo Villaverde's *Cecilia Valdés*, the canonical Cuban tragic mulata novel he strongly criticized for its unrealistic portrayal of blacks.[16] Or perhaps Morúa feared that setting his social critique in the present would open it up to more intense criticism. In either case, the choice to go back in time is consistent with his emphasis in "Ensayo politico" on the need to revisit and revise notions of history in order to contribute to the advancement of Cuba's independence movement. In *Sofía*, Morúa presents a revised vision of a particular time in history; he also reworks the dominant novelistic representation of that time. By rewriting *Cecilia Valdés*, Morúa desires to rewrite the ways in which Cubans understand race and power relations under slavery and beyond. Further, by taking his readers back into slavery and addressing issues of power and ideas of race in that system, Morúa is able to emphasize one of the practical aspects of his social project for creating the conditions for full participation by all Cubans—an emphasis on both independence from Spain and on education in order to allow former slaves to be productively incorporated into Cuban society. Pedro Barreda sees these aspects of Morúa's work as similar to, and perhaps even an extension of, Manzano's attitudes: namely, that it is "useless" to insist on differences; that slaves are characterized by slavery, not blackness; and that after slavery all will rise through education to full participation in the nation.[17] For Barreda, both Manzano and Morúa have "a desire to become integrated into Cuban life, to be Cuban, without any further adjectival or ethnic classification."[18] *Sofía* contains the seeds of a new approach to the nation, one in line with Morúa's vision in "Ensayo Político" of a nation that includes all.

The story of Morúa's protagonist, the titular character Sofía, incorporates many of the aspects of the tragic mulata trope, but Morúa also transforms the trope to serve his purposes. Sofía is a beautiful slave who finds herself the object of desire of one of her young masters, Federico Unzuázu, who corners her and rapes her in her own room despite her innocence and purity. Although she tries to hide her pregnancy, the master of the house, Acebaldo Nudoso del Tronco, discovers her secret and beats her to the point that she miscarries. In this weakened state, the revelation that her rapist is, in fact, her half-brother, leads to Sofía's untimely and tragic demise. Morúa repeats the incest theme from *Cecilia Valdés* but makes it even more radical. Federico and Sofía are half-siblings living in the same house. Sofía is a slave in the household and there is no fiction of consent in the novel; Federico rapes her. Both Federico and Nudoso demonstrate the illegitimate power of white men over the bodies of non-white women who they assume are not-human due to both their perceived racial identities and their sex. In the example of a female slave we see a negation with one more aspect than that suffered by Manzano and Douglass: as a slave, Sofía is considered not human, not free, not white, and definitely not a man. Racialization works to exclude her from the national family despite the irony that she is biologically related to the white family in the novel.

Sofía could have been and even would be a tragic mulata had Morúa not transformed the trope by making Sofía white. Indeed, as the reader eventually learns, Federico and Sofía share the same father and Sofía's mother was a white woman. It turns out that after her father's death, his son-in-law Acebaldo had taken charge of the household and assumed that Sofía was a slave although it is later revealed that he has no proof that she is one. Aleyda T. Portuondo argues that Morúa decided to make Sofía white in order that her mistreatment and death would have a more potent emotional impact on his white male readers.[19] Sofía's whiteness and the horror that arises from the revelation of her kinship with the Unzuázus demonstrates that Morúa's novel is not intended to reify racial castes, but rather to highlight the fact that miscegenation makes it impossible to identify who's who according to that caste system. This, in turn, further emphasizes that the racial categories which constitute this caste system are fictional. As George B. Handley explains, Morúa's fiction "suggests that racial difference is an invention of the colonial overseer."[20] Pedro Barreda emphasizes the importance of Sofía as a "symbolic victim" of slavery, arguing that the fact that she is white helps to emphasize that slavery is based on a system of "social determinism" that illegitimately "denies [slaves] the freedom to direct their lives."[21] Sofía is the symbolic victim of slavery and the Spanish colonial system of which slavery is a part. By making Sofía white, Morúa demonstrates the ways in which the irresponsible power of colonialism denies Cubans the freedom to direct their lives. Sofía's whiteness, then, allows for his critique of Spanish colonial rule. Further, the critique is not just of Spanish rule, but of the effect of colonialism and slavery on all of society, since the novel also depicts the degradation of an educated white elite family.

The revelation of Sofía's kinship to the Unzuázu family and her whiteness are a shock to both Sofía and the family. Morúa foreshadows the revelation several times throughout the novel's early chapters by focusing on the ways in which Sofía never easily fits within the ready-made categories of the Cuban slave system. By emphasizing the difficulties other characters have in placing Sofía, Morúa is able to undermine the assumption that people can be easily identified and kept in their place. The first example of the problem of placing Sofía occurs when the readers are first introduced to her. Sofía is in a group of slave women and she is described as "una trigueña que se distinguía de sus demás compañeras por el caracter reposado y los dulces modales que realizaban su belleza natural"[22] [a *trigueña* who was distinguished from the rest of her companions by her quiet character and sweet manners that arose from her natural beauty]. It is interesting that in addition to the use of the somewhat ambivalent racial term *trigueña*, Sofía is described as being set apart by her beauty, character, and manners. While these characteristics are inventions of the author, it is important to his purposes here that he create a character along the lines of the trope of the tragic mulata, and this figure traditionally must have light skin, and the beauty, character, and manners that make her passable and potentially tragic. In addition, Vera Kutzinski has noted that the term *trigueña* is an "unreliable appellation," particularly since "in Sofía's case, white skin alone does not guarantee a privileged identity,"[23] a fact which destroys the stability of a caste system based on race. One way in which the term *trigueña* is unreliable is that while it literally means "wheat-colored" or "light brown," it does not indicate a particular race-mixture and has been used to designate everything from a "black person" to a "person whose skin color is somewhat darkened."[24] Another way in which the term is unreliable is that it does not clearly indicate Sofía's status because she is not a part of any group. She is the only *trigueña* among the ranks of the slaves promenading in the Plaza de Armas in the first scenes of the novel. She is the exception that challenges the rule.

Morúa mentions that everyone who meets Sofía feels sorry for her due to her position and that "Las negritas, y las mulaticas atrasadas de color, la miraban con cierto recelo al principio, obedeciendo inconscientes a las arraigadas preocupaciones de toda sociedad esclavista, considerándose inferiores a Sofía, porque la veían blanca"[25] [The blacks and mulatas who were darker in color looked at her with certain misgivings at first, unconsciously obeying the customary preoccupations of all of slave society, as they considered themselves inferior to Sofía because she looked white]. The reaction of her fellow slaves places an important focus on the extent to which Cuban society is preoccupied with issues of color and the extent to which these preoccupations are reproduced within the psyche of enslaver and slave alike, to the detriment, in this as in all cases, of those marked by racial heritage as other. Sofía is problematic because she *looks* white, but it is assumed that she must *be* black since she is a slave. In his initial introduction of his main character, Morúa also foreshadows his choice to make Sofía other than she appears when he places Sofía in a less common and ambiguous racial category outside of the most prevalent categories of black, mulato, and white. Kutzinski explains that the whiteness of Sofía's skin coupled with the fact that she is a slave destroys the stability of a caste system based on race.[26] Pedro Barreda believes that the fact that Sofía is white but conditioned to be a slave helps demonstrate two of Morúa's main ideas: first "that society and heredity— ethnic heredity is not implied here—condition the individual, and second, that racial differences do not exist" since whites placed in the same position as blacks (i.e., slavery) react just as blacks do.[27] Sofía's apparent whiteness alone could have undermined the caste system if she had been the stereotypical tragic mulata; the fact that she does not merely appear white but literally is white by the definition of her society is an even stronger blow to the assumptions of Cuban readers. By undermining these assumptions, in *Sofía* as in the "Ensayo politico," Martín Morúa Delgado underscores his belief that stable individual—and national—identities cannot be based on the singular criterion of race as understood under the Cuban caste system.

There are other important moments in which Sofía's identity is problematized or complicated in the novel. Sofía is twice compared in appearance to white women. When she is sent to the sugar mill as a young girl, one of the slaves there makes the mistake of saying that Sofía looks like the daughter of the mill keeper.[28] This infuriates the mill keeper's wife, who punishes the slave who says this, wounds Sofía, cuts her hair, and makes her wear a kerchief in order to emphasize that she is a slave.[29] Vera Kutzinski explains that the punishment is important for Sofía has to be physically marked as other so that her status is visibly etched on her.[30] Here is a visceral presentation of racializing assemblages in action as Sofía's blackness is constructed to maintain the color line. The reaction by the mill keeper's wife is swift and extreme because the slave must be kept in her place. These lower-class whites are perhaps even more jealous than the Unzuázus of their difference in status from slaves.

The second white woman to whom Sofía is compared is Magdalena Unzuázu. We learn that Magdalena enjoys hearing about the whispers that go around town regarding the fact that "más que señora y esclava . . . parecían hermanas"[31] [more than mistress and slave they look like sisters]. That Magdalena enjoys the whispers is an indication of her privilege. She knows the slave is considered beautiful, and the idea that they look like sisters makes her seem like a very magnanimous mistress. Here is another iteration of the fictive kinship ties established under slavery. Like Douglass, Sofía has been denied the right to know her parentage; her identity is defined by her masters, and she is constructed in part by them but also by others as if she is a member of the family. By emphasizing Sofía's similarity to Magdalena, Morúa may be foreshadowing the revelation that Sofía is white and also *is* Magdalena's half-sister. He may also be suggesting that his readers' ability to differentiate between mistress and slave is as precarious as their ability to read an individual's status by their skin color or to identify kinship within a system that defends male sexual privilege and takes away the power of consent from slaves.

Morúa reveals that as a child Sofía was adopted by a white woman, Doña Bríjida. This apparent blessing becomes a curse. After Ana-María, Magdalena, and Federico's father dies, Ana-María's husband Acebaldo Nudoso del Tronco becomes the head of the household. It is partly because one day Sofía calls Doña Bríjida mother in front of Acebaldo that she is sent to the sugar mill. Acebaldo asks Sofía why she calls Doña Bríjida mother and further asks if she can see that she is a mulata and Doña Bríjida is a white woman. After asking these questions, Acebaldo invokes the idea of fictive kinship and, as Manzano's second mistress did, declares that she has no one besides her masters.[32] It is telling that Acebaldo, one of the two antagonists in the novel, is a Spaniard. He objectifies Sofía in part because of his hatred for Doña Bríjida, who is referred to in the novel as an "isleña"—an islander, that is, someone both from and associated with Cuba. If Doña Bríjida represents Cuba, Sofía's childhood becomes the story of how mother Cuba tried to claim and nurture her, but father Spain rejected and enslaved her. This is consistent with Morúa's vision in "Ensayo político" of Cuba as both homeland and maternal figure and with his critique of the Spanish.

Sofía is punished by Acebaldo for "misreading the signs of her identity."[33] Acebaldo speaks with the power to define Sofía as a slave despite her color because she does not know her mother or her father. George B. Handley adds that in Morúa's novel, "[t]he absent or unnamed father . . . becomes . . . a space that is usurped by the ideological needs of the white plantation family to create the fictions of racial difference and slavery."[34] Vera Kutzinski further highlights the fact that when Acebaldo defines Sofía, he in effect changes her from *trigueña* to mulata; he takes advantage of her unknown parentage because while it is assumed that Sofía's father was a white man, the unknown mother is "read not as blank but as black."[35] Sofía's identity is determined by the perceptions, desires, and power of the white man. The identities and power relations produced by racialization are further emphasized because, unlike other mulata fictions, in Morúa's novel when the hidden evidence of the mother is revealed, it turns out that the mother is white.

Sofía may be the tragic (non) mulata around whom the novel's questioning of the caste system and slavery is focused, but many other characters are central to Morúa Delgado's social critique. Acebaldo Nudoso del Tronco is an important figure for several reasons. First, Acebaldo is the one who declares Sofía a mulata and a slave. As a white man and the head of the household he has the power to do so and his motive is fairly clear as well—he is protecting his economic interests. Aside from the fact that enslaving Sofía increases the wealth of his household by one slave, Acebaldo is also protecting his capital in another way. His deceased father in law, Don Sebastían Unzuázu, had left a behest of 10,000 pesos to an unspecified person, a behest that had never been claimed. Acebaldo thinks it is likely that this money was left to an illegitimate child, and more specifically wonders if that child might be Sofía since he has no papers proving that she is a slave.[36] Since Acebaldo assumes that Sofía is the child of Don Sebastían and a black woman, it being a common occurrence for enslavers to father children with slaves, his insistence that Sofía is mulata might be considered justified. Acebaldo knows that he cannot prove that she is a slave and the fact that he sends Sofía to the sugar mill shortly after he names her as a slave is an indication that he is intentionally having her broken so that he can construct her as his property. Part of Morúa's purpose in having his main character sent to the sugar plantation is to provide him a further opportunity to depict the physical and psychological horrors of slavery. However, there are other aspects to this decision. When he discusses Morúa's novel, William Luis demonstrates how through Sofía's experiences both in the city and on the sugar plantation, "Morúa questions the racial nature of slavery. The concept of destiny as a consequence of race becomes an important issue when Sofía, as a white, is subjected to the same conditions as blacks."[37] Here again we see one of the ideas from "Ensayo politico," the questioning of easily determined and understood ideas of racial identity. Lorna V. Williams's analysis also challenges us to understand the extent to which Morúa critiques the master's phallic and violent power under slavery when she links Nudoso's verbal violence, Sofía's experiences at the sugar mill, one of her nightmares, and Federico's rape.[38] Here again the thread of violence is used to demonstrate the way that the type of power involved in slavery and colonialism corrupts society.

Martín Morúa Delgado's critique within the novel is not merely a critique of slavery, but of the Spanish colonial system as a whole. William Luis explains that Sofía's tragedy arises from the nature of the Cuban slave system; he writes that in the novel, "[h]er innocence is juxtaposed to the selfish interests of her white owners; the contrast underscores her moral superiority over those considered to be more powerful than she."[39] Sofía is a symbolic victim of slavery; her objectification and the contrast between her selflessness and her owners' selfish interests form yet another condemnation of the Spanish colonial rule responsible for slavery. Vera Kutzinski argues that in addition to the fact that Morúa "mocks and ultimately explodes his fellow countrymen's continued belief in the reliability of appearances" he ultimately does more than "simply turn the tables on his readers in order to prove racial prejudice a logical absurdity."[40] Kutzinski summarizes Morúa's point to his readers as being that Cuban society is sick with a "colonial disease."[41] Morúa's project is to create a unified Cuban polity that can break free from colonial rule, but his writings demonstrate his understanding that there are many ways in which the aftermath of slavery and the realities of colonialism hamper this process. "[L]ike Sofía," Kutzinski writes, "all Cubans are caught up in a web of power relations and conflicting impulses from which there is no easy escape."[42] Nudoso is an embodiment of the worst attitudes of enslavers, and through his character Morúa includes a critique of the greed and irresponsible power of the Spanish colonial system, a system which creates and fosters the "fear of the dark" in white Cubans and which exploits not only individual slaves, but the island as a whole.

Acebaldo Nudoso del Tronco is not the only member of the Unzuázu household whose attitude toward Sofía serves to objectify her and define her as slave. Vera Kutzinski's compelling reading demonstrates the way in which Morúa depicts Sofía as constructed by the gazes of both Nudoso and Federico. Kutzinski writes that she is "doubly objectified [. . .] constituted at the intersection of desire for wealth with sexual pleasure" as she is literally made into an object first by Nudoso and later by Federico. [43] Kutzinski notes that Morúa has Sofía dressed in gold in the rape scene, a detail which underscores her status as a commodity.[44] In his attempts to seduce Sofía, Federico reveals the complex nature of her position. At one point, after threats have not worked, Federico tries to entice her to be with him by offering her another life. While the reader, like Sofía, would be foolish to take what Federico says at face value, the language he uses to try to seduce her is very significant. As he protests the purity of his intentions, Federico tells Sofía "tu natural delicadeza, tu condición moral, tu color, todo se opone á tu triste posición social. Tú estás destinada a ser la esposa de un hombre capaz de labrar tu felicidad"[45] [your natural tenderness, your moral fiber, your color, all these are contrary to your unfortunate social position. You are destined to be the wife of a man capable of cultivating your happiness]. The list of attributes employed by Federico serves as a reminder that skin color is not the only marker of racial identity within the Cuban caste system, but it is significant and extremely ironic that he does list her white appearance as one of the factors making her enslavement seem improper. It is also significant that this son of a slave trader whose own wealth is based on both the slave trade and the slave system studiously avoids a direct reference to her enslavement, mentioning instead her unfortunate social position. Where Manzano used similar euphemisms for his status as slave to more effectively appeal to the emotions of his readers, Federico uses the phrase to manipulate Sofía as he attempts to seduce her.

The pathos of Sofía's position comes from the fact that she is unjustly enslaved and all enslavement is unjust, particularly that based on the empty sign of race. It also comes from the fact that her enslavement causes her body to be misread and puts her at the mercy of her master and half-brother. Before Federico rapes Sofía, he attempts to seduce her. Ironically, in his attempt to make Sofía his slave concubine Federico invokes the image of Sofía as wife—as a woman *destined* to be a wife, a status at the opposite end of the social spectrum from a slave concubine. His choice of enticements responds to her own musings; right before Federico emerges from where he has been hiding in her room, Sofía had been pondering how lucky white women are because they can marry.[46] It is not surprising that Federico's image shifts the focus back from an image of Sofía as wife to the idea of a man who is capable of changing her fate from a sad one to a happy one. Federico continues by promising to take her to the United States where they can marry. Although his promises are most likely empty, he wants her to believe that he will be the man who can rescue her from her bondage so that she will give herself to him. As the dénouement of the scene indicates, her status as slave and possession makes Sofía's consent ultimately irrelevant, and Federico can easily take what he wants by force. The rape of Sofía—the image of purity and beauty—would be critique enough, but the ultimate revelation of both her whiteness and her kinship with her rapist serves to shock Morúa's readers into the understanding that they must find new ways to understand identity and social relations in the process of forming a strong independent Cuba.

The need to unite and throw off the history of slavery and its aftereffects for the betterment of all Cubans is one of Morúa's most important emphases both in the "Ensayo politico" and in the novel *Sofía*. We see this in the use of the retelling of Sofía's childhood ordeal at the mill which echoes the experiences of Cecilia Valdés at the ingenio, and which Morúa uses to criticize the system of racialization as a whole. We also see Morúa's larger social critique in the attitude of the narrator who, in an extended passage after Sofía's death, ponders the many sins of his society including the fact that the powerless are judged by their supposed social betters. He describes Cuban society as a "carnaval perpetuo" [perpetual carnival] in which the ones who are most lauded by society are those who are most accomplished in the arts "del cinismo y de la hipocresía mas refinada" [of cynicism and the most refined hypocrisy]; in an outburst of *fin de siècle* angst, Morúa's narrator explains that "así anda éllo, y andará. ¿Hasta cuándo?" [so things go, and will continue going. For how long?].[47] The fact that the narrator's final question is followed in the text by more than a line of periods as if the author were including a much-extended ellipsis leaves the reader to stop and ponder the decadence of Cuban society. The reader may also be challenged to consider whether or not things can and have changed in the time between the setting of the novel and the present tense of its publication. Furthermore, the extended ellipsis makes the question of how long things can go on as they are become an ominous portent of what will come if the powerful continue punishing the powerless for violating the very standards they themselves so flagrantly flaunt. These conclusions reinforce another sub-theme in Morúa's novel, namely the inhumanity and barbarity of slavery versus the need for education and civilization.

One of the more sympathetic characters in the novel, Sofía's half-sister Magdalena, is described as being "cubana de corazón, y no alimentaba el odio de raza"[48] [Cuban at heart, and does not cultivate race hatred]. Here Morúa directly links essential Cuban identity with a lack of race hatred. Magdalena has been sent to the United States for a Quaker education and seems to represent a version of Cuban national identity that is influenced by the more magnanimous aspects of the United States. During the party scene in chapter 6, Eladislao praises her necklace, asking if it was made abroad. Magdalena replies that it was made entirely in Cuba according to her own design. When Eladislao asks her whether it is an American symbol, she replies "no he querido colgarle un águila en la punta vacante para no completer la idea norteamericana"[49] [I did not want to put an eagle in the empty part so that it does not complete the North American idea]. Magdalena's design for her necklace is reminiscent of the creation of the Cuban flag using North American symbols and ideals, but adapted to symbolize an imagined Cuban nation. Echoing the connection between American and Cuban symbolism, Eladislao exclaims that the only thing missing to make it genuinely Cuban is to put a parrot where the eagle would be.[50] This implies that in some ways Cubans can follow the American example of achieving freedom from their colonizers, but in other ways they must construct their own unique form of national identity.

Magdalena is a complicated character. She is drawn to Eladislao for his ideals, but is also attracted to him and, as he is married, this is problematic.[51] She initially blames Sofía when she learns the slave is pregnant, feeling betrayed by her ingratitude, especially because in Magdalena's mind she has treated Sofía "como si fuse su hermana"[52] [as if she were her sister]. Magdalena betrays Sofía's trust when she falls back into the trap of believing in the moral instability of slaves/blacks and blames the victim, stating "¡No podia negar que era negra, aunque su piel fuse casi blanca!"[53] [It was impossible to deny that she was black, although her skin was almost white!]. Magdalena takes an ironic stand on the moral high ground because it is in fact a white man, her own brother Federico, who has violently violated Sofía, and the rape is possible because the system of slavery has been set up to protect white male privilege and victimize "black" female bodies. Although Magdalena does think better of her actions later, especially after Nudoso beats Sofía causing her to lose the baby, her initial reaction belies her investment in and formation by a system based on the valuing of the Western Man to the exclusion of all others.

Once Nudoso is murdered and is no longer present to define identities, Morúa introduces the character of Manuela Corrales who shows up to claim the 10,000 pesos on behalf of her child, Juana Sofía, who she thinks is a deceased child of Don Unzuázu. At this point, Magdalena begins to wonder whether Sofía could be their sister.[54] Magdalena's suspicions are partially confirmed when Eladislao informs her that an unknown woman has claimed Sofía was her daughter by Don Unzuázu. Magdalena then falls into the trap of thinking she can trust appearances, searching Sofía's face for "los rasgos familiares que confirmasen [sus] vehementes sospechas"[55] [familiar features that would confirm her strong suspicions]. Magdalena, too naïve to be truly helpful, thinks that she can make up for things by telling Sofía they may be sisters; besides, she reasons, since Sofía is white, her lover will have to marry her.[56] Here we see Morúa's appeals to pathos in full swing through the use of dramatic irony. Readers know that her half-brother has raped Sofía and is the father of her now-dead child, facts which both heighten the effect of Magdalena's ignorance and the emptiness of her intentions, intentions made empty by a system which objectifies slaves and protects white male privilege.

The most important character introduced in *Sofía* by Martín Morúa Delgado to support his emphasis on the drive towards integration, unity, and a particular vision of civilization may very well be the Unzuázu family friend Eladislao Gonzaga. If the trope of the tragic mulata is the vehicle that Morúa Delgado transforms to introduce his ideas on race, identity, and nation, one of the most important aspects of his transformation is the inclusion of this character. Gonzaga is a friend of the Unzuázu family and one of the characters most sympathetic to Sofía. When Sofía's pregnancy is discovered and she is given papers and sent out by Nudoso to look for a buyer, Gonzaga is the one who takes her in. The narrator tells the tale of Gonzaga's fall from riches, through failed insurrection, to the modest means he finds himself in during the novel. He is described as an honorable man whose anti-colonial patriotism is increased by his loss of riches.[57] Perhaps the greatest recommendation for this character is the fact that both Acebaldo Nudoso del Tronco and Federico Unzuázu dislike him. Indeed, Gonzaga's ideas often stand in stark contrast to those of Nudoso.

Martín Morúa Delgado must have hoped that his late nineteenth-century readers would understand the need for healing and education in order for Afro-Cubans to take their rightful place in Cuban society. Rufino Pérez Landa sees the character of Eladislao Gonzaga as representative of Morúa's idea that, as Gonzaga says in the novel, the slave of yesterday is the citizen of tomorrow.[58] In a conversation where a friend mentions newspapers written by and for former slaves, Nudoso shows his racism and avarice when he gets angry, sneers at these efforts, and reasserts that he "no transijía con *éso* de la intelectualidad del negro"[59] [does not hold with *that idea* of the intellectual ability of blacks]. In a continuation on this theme, Morúa reintroduces Gonzaga as "un hombre de arraigados principios de libertad, de justicia, de amor humano . . . demócrata por convicción"[60] [a man of inveterate principles of liberty, justice, and the love of others . . . a true democrat]. Gonzaga is the mouthpiece through which Morúa's ideas on education and betterment for blacks can be presented directly in the novel. When faced with the vicious disdain of masters like Acebaldo who belittle former slaves, Gonzaga exclaims that the problem is that the former slaves were not made ready, that they need help in order for there to be established "una era de gloriosa fraternidad"[61] [an era of glorious brotherhood] in which the natural rights of all are respected. This era of glorious brotherhood is reminiscent of Morúa's vision in his "Ensayo Político." One interesting aspect of Gonzaga's argument is that he talks of the "great human destiny" of Cuba in achieving true civilization. Morúa also assigns to the journalist an important role in the process of rehabilitating former slaves. It is perhaps not that surprising that Morúa's novel includes the idea that writing can bring about the social change he hopes to see in his nation. This also ties Morúa to Manzano in that both emphasize the importance of literacy in the construction of free, affirmed identities for non-whites in Cuba. Both authors imply that the ability for non-whites to define themselves in language is an important part of the process by which they can overcome their radical negation and forge identities as (hu)man citizens. After all, that was Morúa's goal in writing both the "Ensayo político" and *Sofía*.

TOO MANY MULATOS? OVERPOPULATING THE COLOR LINE IN *THE HOUSE BEHIND THE CEDARS*

Like Martín Morúa Delgado, Charles W. Chesnutt's political ideas are reflected in both his nonfiction and his fiction. Chesnutt's exploration of the idea of racial amalgamation as an American reality and as a potential solution to America's racial strife can be seen in his first novel, *The House Behind the Cedars*, published in 1900, the very same year his "Future American" articles appeared. The novel engages the issue of postslavery anxieties surrounding the figure of the mulato/a, but Chesnutt's take on the genre is more complex than the popular versions that served to reify a black/white caste system by punishing (indeed often destroying) the body of the mulato/a. Stephen P. Knadler highlights the importance of Chesnutt's fiction as an alternative to popular depictions of a pure white American identity and future.[62] *The House Behind the Cedars* can be read as a discourse which challenges the rhetoric of national identity constructed through racialization. This idea of national identity is based on keeping human and not-quite-human separate and unequal. It is a version of national identity that stereotypes the other in order to exclude. As Chesnutt's white doctor, Dr. Green, states, "All negroes are alike, except that now and then there's a pretty woman along the borderline."[63] Indeed, "all negroes are alike" to those in power in that they have been stereotypically associated with certain qualities, and are excluded from white society. Chesnutt engages this idea of stereotypical identities and uses the trope of the tragic mulata to challenge it.

As a color line novel, *The House Behind the Cedars* centers on individuals of mixed-race heritage challenging the line between the two social castes as they either more or less successfully pass for white. Where Morúa transforms the trope by making the mulata white, Chesnutt does so by including several passable mulato/a characters to intentionally address a variety of issues regarding racial and national identities. For Ryan Simmons, Chesnutt's novel fulfilled the author's two main goals, goals which are very akin to those pursued by Morúa: a "creative troubling of racial categories" and an "acute analysis of the tangled, pernicious, and confoundingly durable conventions of race in American society."[64] For Chesnutt, in a society where "not-white" meant *other*, excluded, and not-quite-human, the fact that those who appeared white despite their mixed racial heritage would be tempted and even willing to pass into the white world is no surprise because they are by their very nature outside of the dominant paradigm. Chesnutt does not merely concern himself with condoning or condemning passing. Anne Fleischmann explains that "Chesnutt's mixed society functions as a metaphor for the rejection of a two-race culture; as such it also indicts segregation's color-coded '*placing.*'"[65] *The House Behind the Cedars* and "The Future American" are both part of a project focused on a broad challenge to the basis and perpetuation of the system of white privilege in post-emancipation America by challenging the exclusively binary definitions of racial identity constructed through racialization on which segregation was based.[66] What the novel does not challenge, as critics such as Kerstin Rudolph and Melissa Ryan have recently explored, is the exclusively male construction of national identity.[67]

When *The House Behind the Cedars* begins, John Walden is returning to the home of his mother, Molly Walden, a free quadroon, and his sister, Rena, after a ten-year absence. John and Rena are the children of Molly and an unnamed white man, who is already deceased at the start of the novel. Ten years earlier, wanting to forge his own way in the world, John changed his last name to Warwick (after Warwick, the king-maker), moved to Clarence, South Carolina, and passed for white. Trained as a lawyer, in the chaos following the Civil War John created a new identity for himself, married the daughter of a rich southern planter, and had a son. John returns to his mother's house in part because his wife has died and he wants to see if his sister will be able (in terms of her looks and culture) and willing to come and care for her nephew and take advantage of the chance to pass into the white world as he did. The majority of the novel focuses on Rena and her ill-fated attempt to pass into white society.

The crux of a passing novel is the social valuation of whiteness and the desire to regulate and exclude those marked through racialization as nonhuman and not-quite human from all of the advantages that are believed to be the due of the Western Man/citizen. Matthew Wilson discusses the discomfort of racists who thought they could "infallibly" identify any amount of black blood and the anxiety that arose from their inability to do so; he particularly mentions that "[t]he sexual transgressions of the fathers, then, haunted their sons in the nightmare of the simulacrum, the white negro."[68] Although it often stemmed from white male privilege which the system protected, interracial reproduction was considered an anathema; the products of interracial unions became themselves anathema—necessarily illegitimate. Illegitimacy was not the only characteristic unjustly ascribed to mulatos. Just as Juan Francisco Manzano and Frederick Douglass had to negotiate the plethora of negative stereotypes associated with those of African descent in the New World, since the mulato and the "white negro" disrupted white society's sense of security, racialization wrote upon the mulato a series of negative connotations, including, but not limited to, implications of feeble-mindedness, criminality, degeneracy, and—as the term mulato implies—sterility. Chesnutt wrote about mulato characters knowing that they were considered *particularly* non-white and nonhuman.

While it might appear that Chesnutt merely reproduces the tragic mulata stereotype in Rena's character,[69] the novel represents a more complex negotiation of the identities of his mulato/a characters as part of a larger project that concerned the very nature of American national identity. It is an example of what Susan Gillman has redefined as "race melodrama," a genre that "focuses broadly on the situation of the black family—almost always of an interracial genealogy—and specifically on the issue of 'race mixture' as a means of negotiating the social tensions surrounding the formation of racial, national, and sexual identity."[70] Martín Morúa Delgado's *Sofia* can be seen as a race melodrama from a slightly different angle, a novel that focuses broadly on the situation of a Cuban family that is only apparently of an interracial genealogy and focuses on race to engage with ideas of racial, national, and sexual identity. Similarly, *The House Behind the Cedars* is not merely a tragic mulato/a story, but rather a discourse of identity in the form of a novel of racial melodrama. In this novel, Chesnutt includes several examples of the symbolically overpopulated figure of the mulato/a, and uses them to destabilize the color line. In doing this, Chesnutt reminds his readers of one of his main points in the "Future American" articles: that the color line has long been crossed—a reality which undermines the very distinction implied by a rhetoric of racial identity consisting of only two fundamental terms and also challenging a paradigm of national identity that is exclusive and based on assumptions of white purity.

Although the majority of *The House Behind the Cedars* focuses on Rena and her generation, Chesnutt includes an account of the life of Molly Walden, the mother of Rena and John. The author describes Molly Walden as having had a complexion "of an old ivory tint" in her youth.[71] While the narrator indicates that her complexion has "darkened measurably" over time, and admits that "[t]radition gave her to the negro race," the narrator clearly indicates that she is quite light skinned when he explains "[d]oubtless she had a strain of each [black and Native American blood], with white blood very visibly predominating over both."[72] Chesnutt uses his description of Molly to indicate the fact that miscegenation has long been taking place and racial categories are social constructions. He mentions that tradition considers her black despite the complex reality of her heritage, but he also mentions that different societies would have read and defined her differently. He writes that in other places, "like Louisiana or the West Indies she would have been called a quadroon, or more loosely, a creole"; but "[i]n North Carolina, where fine distinctions were not the rule in matters of color, she was sufficiently differentiated when described as a bright mulatto."[73] The discussion of the different ways in which this one body of this one woman could and would be viewed in different places is a clear indication both of the ways in which miscegenation undermined social hierarchies based on the ability to distinguish black and white and the fact that the racial identities on which such hierarchies were based were socially constructed fictions, not biological facts.

As a youth, Molly, who was free but whose family was under economic hardship, became the kept woman of a prominent white man. Chesnutt's narrator describes Molly's story as "the old story."[74] That it is an old story is evidence of the reality of miscegenation, evidence of, as Chesnutt puts it in "The Future American" articles, the "stream of dark blood in the veins of Southern Whites" and the stream of white blood in the veins of Southern blacks.[75] As Chesnutt's paragraph-long description of her racial identity indicates, Molly is not simply black; she represents at least two generations of miscegenation and the fact that miscegenation—contrary to the wishful thinking of many Southern whites defining things in terms of black and white—was a fait accompli. Making this argument was an important part of

Chesnutt's project as outlined in the "Future American" articles. Sally Ann Ferguson explains that *The House Behind the Cedars* represents "a fictional version of his non-fictional theory" by introducing Molly Walden's children, Rena and John, "who are supposed to continue the author's racial evolution with marriage to and children by whites."[76] For Chesnutt, Molly is a representation of past miscegenation, and a link in the chain of miscegenation that has continued and will continue.

Since the fiction of race was devoutly and stridently protected by those in power, Molly lived a marginalized existence, hidden behind the titular cedars in a liminal area of town because of her "choice" to live as the mistress of a white man. Her social marginalization was based on the taboo associated with miscegenation. "In fact, so tabooed did the racist ideologues wish the mixing of racial blood to appear to be that miscegenation was often imagined as analogous to incest."[77] In the southern United States, miscegenation was considered as horrifying by many as the incestuous rape of Sofía by Federico. In fact, both miscegenation and incest often occurred because of the way white male power and sexual privilege were protected in Cuba and the United States. One interesting note provided by Wilson's analysis is that in metaphorically comparing miscegenation to incest whites really were "acknowledging not the inevitable difference in races but their metaphorical consanguinity: the incest taboo is in place to keep apart people who are *related* rather than separated by blood."[78] Molly's story, then, does not merely highlight miscegenation as an ongoing and established reality. It also invites readers to examine the contradictions in a system that vilified miscegenation and its products, kept hidden the culpability and involvement of white males (including the thread of violence that runs through all these stories), and denied the inherent human *relation* between blacks and whites by denying the full humanity of blacks.

While Molly's social position was clearly set in her position behind the cedars, things are more complicated for her children. The story of Rena Walden/Warwick closely follows the rise and fall of a tragic mulata tale. As with Morúa's introduction of Sofía, Rena's racial identity is not clearly defined when Chesnutt first describes her. Generally, the first and most crucial description of a character in a race-conscious society would include a description of his race, or of the features that would identify her racial identity. In the opening of *The House Behind the Cedars* the reader follows John Warwick—whose racial identity is likewise obscured at the start of the novel—as he walks through Patesville. John sees and then follows a young woman walking through town. The narrative, following his point of view, describes her as "strikingly handsome, with a stately beauty seldom encountered."[79] Like Morúa Delgado's Sofía and following the tragic mulata trope, Rena is depicted as good-looking, intelligent, capable and morally upright, not flawed, nor degenerate in the way that society would often stereotypically consider mulatos to be. Through John's eyes, the reader sees a woman with "abundant hair, of a dark and glossy brown" and "ivory" skin.[80] John's description is echoed later on by Rena's suitor, George Tryon, whose "heart had thrilled at first sight of this tall girl, with the ivory complexion, the rippling brown hair, and the inscrutable eyes."[81] Tryon considers that "To win this beautiful girl for his wife would be a worthy task."[82] As these two descriptions suggest, nothing about Rena's physical appearance indicated that she was of mixed heritage.

Rena does not merely function as an example of the fact that a distinct black/white divide was as fictional as Chesnutt's novel. Chesnutt employs the figure of the mulata not to reinforce social ideas and stereotypes, but rather as, in Margaret Toth's terms, "a politico-aesthetic strategy whereby African American authors worked not only to deconstruct racist visual iconography but also to engage forcefully in contemporary arguments about race."[83] In the novel, Chesnutt includes a series of images that indicate Rena's precarious status, conspicuously linking her to the tragic mulata trope. He plays with the fact that she is both an "overembodied noncitizen"[84] and an example of how unreliable the body is as evidence of "race."[85] When Rena makes her entrance into high society in Clarence, South Carolina, we see the timocracy described by Patterson at work; Patterson attributes to this "chivalric cult . . . an excessively developed sense of honor and pride, militarism, the idealization and seclusion of women, and regional nationalism."[86] All of these aspects are evident in the series of events at the end of which Rena is crowned the "Queen of Love and Beauty" at a ball following the mock chivalric tournament won by John's friend George Tryon. The inherent irony of an elite Southern society unknowingly—for how could it be otherwise—enthroning and adoring a mulata woman is a reminder of how likely it is that Chesnutt is right to insist in the "Future American" articles that there is a significant amount of black blood running through the veins of Southern whites.

After the ball, Rena states that she feels like "Cinderella before the clock has struck."[87] Rena is never secure because of the hidden evidence of her heritage, and she worries that George will discover her secret; if he were to discover her secret, "The Prince would never try on the glass slipper."[88] His sense of honor and pride, pride based in part in his status as the Western Man in a timocratic society, would not allow him to accept her. While the reference to Cinderella might seem a bit overdone, the fairy tale does revolve around a character who has two identities—that which should be assigned to her by birth and that which is she is forced to perform by her wicked stepmother. Similarly, much of Chesnutt's novel revolves around identity as social construction or performance rather than biological fact. Margaret Toth provides a compelling reading of *The House Behind the Cedars* in which she emphasizes the "Theater of the South" and the performance of identities in the novel, including but not limited to the tournament and the masquerade ball. The most interesting thing about Toth's argument is that she concludes that in this theater it is the *whites* who are passing, that "Chesnutt has put evident work into contextualizing Rena's passing" within a system of performances by white characters.[89] According to Toth, Chesnutt "invites us to compare these characters' performances, asking us to consider which are more disingenuous, which more hypocritical, and, certainly in the case of George," who turns out to be neither a prince nor knight in shining armor, "which more destructive."[90] Aaron Ritzenberg offers another, related reading of the tendency of white southerners to relate to fantasy rather than reality. He considers the tournament and ball (and much of supposedly chivalric white Southern culture) not as theater, but as Freudian fantasy. In his reading, "the white fantasy is that its culture adheres to the natural order of things" rather than being "a fictional copy of a fictional copy" and "communal wish-fulfillment for a culture of nobility and honor."[91] Both Toth and Ritzenberg emphasize through their readings the extent to which Chesnutt's asserts the unnaturalness of the social order both in terms of and significantly beyond questions of racial identity.

The House Behind the Cedars continually pushes readers to consider performance versus being, appearance versus reality. At one point Rena stands in front of a mirror brought to America from France by one of John's wife's ancestors. There in front of the European mirror, in the plantation home of the prominent white Southern family into which her brother John has married, Rena scrutinizes her appearance, looking to see if there is any "mark upon her brow to brand her as less pure, less innocent, less desirable, less worthy to be loved, than these proud women of the past who had admired themselves in this old mirror."[92] Rena finds no such mark—she cannot be distinguished from the "real thing"—and it is indeed her beauty, purity, innocence, and desirability that make the tragic mulata tragic, because she is worthy of a better end than her seemingly inevitable death. "To be old or ugly for a woman in a sexist society was a tragedy that compelled little sympathy. To be black in a racist society likewise compelled little sympathy, but to be young, beautiful, ladylike, and only technically black was truly pathetic."[93] Because part of Charles W. Chesnutt's project was the transformation of the attitudes and ideas of his readers, effectively portraying the true pathos of Rena's position and fate played an important part in the novel.

Indeed, as a beautiful and *passable* mulata, how could Rena end up being, in 1900, anything *but* tragic? Chesnutt sacrifices Rena to the expected end of dying even as her suitor decides he will overlook her background and marry her. Despite his insistence in "The Future American" articles that miscegenation can and will (and depending on your reading of his tone, even should) continue, Chesnutt does not redeem the major plot structure of the tragic mulata tale. However, like Morúa who transformed the Cuban tragic mulata trope by making the mulata white, Chesnutt transforms it more covertly. He may have believed, as Matthew Wilson conjectures, that what would "act as an antidote was what was most tabooed: love and marriage between men and women of different races."[94] This idea is present in the novel, but the main focus of the denouement is the death of the heroine. With Rena's death can come George Tryon's remorse; Wilson argues that Chesnutt hoped Tryon's "agon" would ideally change his readers views about Rena and about race, that like George, with Rena's death the reader would "plumb the depths of his sin."[95] He concludes that, "The children, Tryon and Rena, pay for the sins of their fathers, and only through sentiment can white readers fully realize, in the words of Hopkins, that 'the sin is the nation's.'"[96] Rena's character is forced through the paces of the old tragic mulata trope, and Chesnutt uses the trope to challenge his readers to question the reality of racial identities and the nature and sins of the nation.

Although the majority of the narrative follows Rena's tragic course, this dominant plot partially masks the ultimate fate of John Warwick. Chesnutt uses John's story, which happens around and behind Rena's story, to explore his ideas of national identity. And it is in John's story that readers see a strong reflection of the ideas Chesnutt posited in his nonfiction regarding racial amalgamation. Despite what Dr. Green says in the novel regarding the only exception to the monolithic nature of "negroes" being the occasional "pretty woman on the borderline," not all mixed-race children were female. In the second of his "Future American" articles, Chesnutt writes that the mulata is well known both in life and fiction, but "it is more than likely that she had brothers of the same complexion, though curiously enough the male octoroon has cut no figure in fiction."[97] Chesnutt implies a correspondence between the invisibility of the "male octoroon" in literature with his signifi-cant invisibility—or at least the invisibility of his blackness—in society. Ferguson explains that John "follows the pattern" of Chesnutt's project of amalgamation "so perfectly" that he is the embodiment of Chesnutt's "Future American."[98] Chesnutt includes John Warwick's story in his novel, a move which could potentially trouble the complacency of the parts of society which were ignorant of the realities that the "male octoroon" represented. John's character is carefully obscured by the second part of the novel which focuses on Rena's drawn out tragic end. He is able to pass out of sight. Rena is, significantly, the "overembodied noncitizen"—black and female—who is to be excluded from ideas of national identity.[99] At the very end of the novel when a repentant Tryon arrives too late and asks, "Who's dead?" he receives the answer, "A young cullud 'oman, suh."[100] The last words of the novel emphasize that the other—the black female—has been identified and safely excluded from white society following the trope of the tragic mulata. Rena is sacrificed so that on the surface of the novel it appears that the abstract ideal of citizenship is not being contaminated. In this context, it is particularly significant that John Walden/Warwick is not the protagonist of Chesnutt's novel. Since he is not the main focus, he can pass into the white world. It is also interesting to consider that Sofía, despite being white, is also destroyed. This implies that concepts of national identity based on maintaining the global color line are not only fictions created to maintain the power of the few, they are also inherently destructive even to some they are supposedly set up to protect.

The main narrative of *The House Behind the Cedars* may follow Rena's tragic course, but the novel begins with John arriving back in Patesville and registering at the hotel under his assumed name. While the novel ends with Rena's death, it begins with an inscription that bears witness to John's successful story of passing. According to the logic of Chesnutt's day, in John, the preponderance of white blood has masked the evidence of his mixed heritage. The narrator describes John as "tall, dark, with straight, black, lustrous hair and very clean-cut, high-bred features," and the clerk of the hotel assumes John is "[o]ne of the South Carolina bigbugs . . . probably in cotton or turpentine."[101] The potential misreading of the mulato body is what caused anxiety in those determined to protect white purity and privilege. However, part of Chesnutt's point is that the classification of an octoroon—such as John or Chesnutt himself—as black, is an intentional effect of racialization rather than a reflection of reality. Following Chesnutt's own logic, John is not in fact passing.[102] Werner Sollors writes that passing is merely "a social invention" and "a fiction of law and custom" since it "makes one part of a person's ancestry real, essential, and defining, and other parts accidental, mask-like, and insignificant."[103] What is more interesting in terms of ideas of national identity is Sollors's contention that the fiction of passing is "strange in a republican society" because "[i]t runs against the notion that ancestry (after all, an aristocratic concern) should not matter in a true democracy. And even if one cared about ancestry, it would seem to go against any principle of majority rule to let a distinct minority of ancestors 'outvote' the others in a form of ancestor-counting that lacks symmetry."[104] Chesnutt points out the inherent paradox in the United States: that a republic breaking away from the caste system in Europe which emphasized heredity, ancestry, nobility, and blood, would institute a system of slavery and segregation *even more virulently hierarchical* than the system it rejected. In *The House Behind the Cedars*, Chesnutt follows the ideas in his nonfiction regarding how absurd society is in "classifying men fifteen-sixteenths white as black men."[105] Chesnutt allows John to determine his identity, to claim his rights even though doing so means embracing what for American society is not his identity. The conclusion that Chesnutt and his character John come to is one that potentially leads to the precise reality white supremacists feared, namely that their status as those in power would be challenged when it was discovered that the color line was an unworkable fiction which was ultimately impossible to discern or police.

According to the novel, even as a boy John's appearance and bearing made it difficult to identify him as anything other than white. His character is an example of how the mulato troubles the line between black and white, human and not-quite-human. John's mentor, Judge Straight, remembers his first encounter with the boy, emphasizing that "[h]e was no darker than many a white boy bronzed by the Southern sun. His hair and eyes were black and his features of the high-bred, clean-cut order that marks the patrician type."[106] The judge also remarks that John resembles one of his old friends, and it is John's resemblance to a white father who does not acknowledge him that convinces the Judge to help John. Clearly if John had not literally resembled a white man, he would not have been granted the privileges that he was able to get through his association with Judge Straight. John also, according to both the narrator of the novel and Judge Straight, exhibits other characteristics generally associated with whiteness: intelligence, boldness, and charisma. These are similar to the characteristics William Lloyd Garrison attributed to Frederick Douglass and Douglass attributed to Madison Washington. They are characteristics associated with the Western Man. Chesnutt's narrator informs us that John "was a man for whom most people formed a liking at first sight. To this power of attraction he owed most of his success."[107] Here again is the danger in the figure of the mulato, the danger that an individual, despite his/her "invisible blackness," will be misread by society as white.

More important than his actual appearance is John's sense of entitlement—his belief that he should be able to define himself. As Chesnutt argues in "The Future American," the real fiction is that one drop of African blood makes a person black, that someone with the preponderance of white blood is really a black man. John Walden/Warwick feels entitled to the rights and privileges of citizenship. As William L. Andrews writes, John is a "singular figure in American fiction" in that he does not decide to pass so much as he "constructs a legal and moral justification for doing so."[108] In effect John validates his whiteness rather than passing for white; he believes that he has the characteristics that should assign him to the human group and finds a legal argument to support his position. Unlike those on the color line who felt that going north would give them the best opportunity to pass into the white world, John sought his fortune in the South, "the land of his fathers," where he felt that he had an "inalienable birthright."[109] In an analogous way to the manner in which Frederick Douglass and Juan Francisco Manzano write themselves into freedom by appropriating and employing the discourses of whiteness, literacy, and religion, John remakes himself and, in the process, transforms the system of which he is a part.

In actively choosing to be John Warwick and not John Walden, Chesnutt's character defies social custom by deciding that American law and practice are not the highest law and thus are not the factors to determine his identity. His is a self-making akin to that of Manzano and Douglass. Even as a child, John reasons that, "His playmates might call him black; the mirror proved that God, the Father of all, had made him white and God, he had been taught, made no mistakes. Having made him white, He must have meant him to be white."[110] John "stresses the priority of perception and self-identification in the determination of his own race."[111] He reasons that what the eye sees is more important than what society would determine based on legal definitions and the invisible sign of the black blood in his family line. In this passage, Chesnutt also employs religious discourse to counteract the force of the rhetoric of blackness that society attempts to inscribe upon the body of the mulato. The further metaphor of the human family, with God as the "Father of all," not only calls upon Christian ideas, but also gives John a second claim to legitimacy by emphasizing his status as the son of two fathers, both his biological white father and God. In a land where the terms black and mulato are overlain and occupied by negative connotations, John creates an identity which is not black, and which also associates him with the most positive of connotations just as Douglass and Manzano did in their narratives. John insists that both his physical characteristics, the preponderance of white blood in his line, and God's own intention make him white.

Also, just as the slave narrators emphasized literacy as an important aspect of their argument for inclusion in the nation, John's literacy is an important part of his self-making. Kerstin Rudolph comments on "Chesnutt's emphasis on books and fictive stories as tools to be used by white and black characters alike in the making and unmaking of racial identities."[112] The influence of literature is most directly seen in John's appropriation of the name Warwick. But John's literacy also allows him to employ legal discourse in his self-construction. The self-making discourse surrounding John's identity runs in direct opposition to a legal and social system that claims the right to identify, categorize, and place every individual in the system. Despite his belief in his "inalienable" rights from a religious viewpoint, John turns to law in order to justify his choice to live as a white man. When John decides he wants to be a lawyer, it is Judge Straight, his father's old friend, who finds the South Carolina law giving him legal justification for his choice. The law states that not every "admixture of African blood with European" should be considered the same and that "one having all the features of a white" should not be considered a part of "the degraded class . . . because of some remote taint of the negro race"; the law, as Chesnutt's characters report it, says that a jury would "probably be justified" in considering as white any person "in whom the admixture of African blood did not exceed one eighth."[113] Knowing he has one-eighth African blood or less and having already determined to be received into society so that he can exercise the privileges of being a white man, John responds to the judge's reading of the law by stating, "From this time on . . . I am white."[114] While the misreadings of John's body that occur due to the fact that he looks like his father and appears to be of the "patrician type" in and of themselves threaten the stability of a system based on a myth of racial purity, in *The House Behind the Cedars* Chesnutt further challenges the system by depicting a character who is not merely misread, but who actively appropriates religious and legal ideas and writes himself into the white community. Thinking back to the descriptions of Molly's character, it is also important to remember that the fact that Chesnutt depicts a character who manipulates legal rhetoric does not necessarily imply that Chesnutt believes the law is correct. Chesnutt's interest in the "legal stipulations of racial identity is," according to Keith Byerman, "their reasoned arbitrariness"; *The House Behind the Cedars* and other of his novels can also be read, then, as "thought experiments by Chesnutt that track the meaning of such arbitrariness" and highlight race as performance rather than race as biological reality.[115] Through the process of racialization, Chesnutt's society created artificial categories to segregate the population and reserve power and privilege for a select few. Through the character of John, Chesnutt's novel highlights the artificiality of both the process and the categories.

In "The Future American," as Chesnutt gives examples of the "mixing process," he includes the information that many mixed-race individuals negotiate the color line by "fixing their status by the marriages they made."[116] John Warwick has fixed his place in white society by moving to South Carolina and through his marriage to a white woman.[117] The fact that John marries and has a son with a white woman means that although he would be considered a black man by the strict interpretation of Chesnutt's own post–*Plessy v. Ferguson* society, John successfully assumes the place of the white man. He becomes impossible to track, and the invisible blackness gets passed down to his son. John "disappears into (*not* out of) the culture at large" where "(cloaked in whatever new identity he contrives for himself 'elsewhere')" he is "thoroughly underground."[118] The mulato characters in *The House Behind the Cedars* inherently challenge the boundaries of racial categories and social castes. This is particularly true when—as in the cases of John and Rena—the mulato/a characters possess all of the qualities admired and canonized by white society (including white skin). These mixed-race characters overpopulate the color line. Their stories, told in a realistic vein that goes beyond traditional uses of the tragic mulata trope, reinforce Chesnutt's vision as presented in "The Future American": a vision both problematic and hopeful, which undermined the myth of the white nation even as it appeared to reify the value of whiteness as a national signifier. The figure of the mulato has the potential to disrupt white male privilege by usurping the place of the white male; the mulato also threatens white female purity because he becomes the object of and contaminates white women's desire. The mulata, doubly inscribed by race and gender, represents the embodiment of a problematic white desire, but one that can generally be expressed without necessarily corrupting the white man. In many ways, the mulato/a emblematizes the problem of blackness in society. In the United States, "pure" blood—a distinct whiteness to be contrasted to and protected from blackness—is the icon of national identity.

In light of all this, "the novel's final silence concerning John's whereabouts sends a profoundly inflammatory message."[119] John Walden successfully became John Warwick and because George Tryon is not going to expose his secret, he will remain in his new identity. John's story demonstrates to Chesnutt's readers, jealous of the idea of white purity and privilege, that the real fiction is not Chesnutt's novel, but rather the idea that they can identify, place, and control people of African descent and the process of miscegenation to maintain the color line. John stands as a symbol for all of the instances by which "one drop" of black blood has passed silently and invisibly into the "white" bloodstream, echoing Chesnutt's arguments in his nonfiction and presenting a view of the nation in which its citizens may or may not be what they appear to be. It implies that the national family is already miscegenated and makes an argument for a more broadly inclusive idea of national identity.

THE FUTURE CUBAN AND THE FUTURE AMERICAN: THE NEXT GENERATION IN *SOFÍA* AND *THE HOUSE BEHIND THE CEDARS*

Charles W. Chesnutt and Martín Morúa Delgado employ and transform the trope of the tragic mulata, in part by introducing a number of characters whose attributes and actions can serve to challenge ideas of race, caste, and nation. They complicate, rework, and problematize the idea of the national family within their respective nations. Both novels also include a very strong indication of how the future nation might turn out—what the future Cuban or American might be—particularly if things remain as they are.

In the case of a discussion of race and ideas of national identity in *Sofía*, the miscarried child, the product of the incestuous rape of Sofía by Federico, is worthy of note. If the revelation of the hidden evidence that Sofía's mother is white disrupts ideas of national identity based on race, the revelation that Sofía's father is the Unzuázu patriarch, Federico's father Don Sebastián, demonstrates the extent of the danger of continuing to protect white male sexual privilege as it has been protected under slavery and the Spanish colonial system by suggesting how precarious the process of creating a national identity based on both gender and racial privilege can be. The fact that Sofía is pregnant with and then loses Federico's baby raises the horrific specter that under the autocratic Spanish colonial system which jealously privileges whites *and* white male sexual privilege, the new citizen will be the product of incest and may not even be viable; under the totally degenerate Spanish colonial system, the very existence of the next Cuban generation is threatened. The miscarried baby, then, may be the most important character in understanding Morúa's ideas on the need to free Cuba from the oppression of Spanish colonialism. Sofía's child is stillborn due to its fathers' sins: Don Sebastian's sins in engendering Sofía, Nudoso's sins in defining her as a slave (and in abusing his power by beating her), and Federico's violent sin based on considering her an object to be possessed. A Cuban society which allows these sins to continue will find independence stillborn as well. Morúa implies the need to rethink ideas of national identity and forget supposed differences. The decadence and degeneracy of the Spanish colonial system and slavery have led to a dead end. What is needed is the building of the national family Morúa envisions in "Ensayo Político": a unified Cuban nationality built by all of mother Cuba's sons.

Similarly, the most important character in *The House Behind the Cedars* in terms of Chesnutt's ideas about race, racial amalgamation, and national identity, may very well be Albert, the son of John Warwick and his deceased white wife. Wilson points out that one of the reasons Tryon initially rejects Rena is his fear of atavism, that his children with Rena "might reveal the characteristic of Rena's 'degraded people,'" and that Albert is in many ways a counter to that fear.[120] As Melissa Ryan puts it, "[p]aternity, it seems, is a merely symbolic phenomenon; only maternity involves biological processes."[121] The white mother matters more to Albert's identity than John.[122] John and his son represent the reality Chesnutt describes in his essays, that white racial purity is nothing more than a myth. This is particularly evident in the fact that little Albert disappears into the novel with John. Samira Kawash explains that "the mulato body" itself is the thing that destroys the boundary between black and white because, "in the figure of the passing body, the signifiers of race are unloosed from the signifieds; the seemingly stable relation between representation . . . and the real . . . collapses, and representation is suddenly dangerous and untrustworthy."[123] John and his young son, having been divested of the signification of blackness, cannot be identified and excluded. Albert's story demonstrates, as Simmons argues about Chesnutt's novel, that in the future it is not that "race should not matter so much as a statement that race *will* matter *differently* in the future, for better or worse," and further that influencing the assumptions readers make about race and racial identities "might well be a way of nudging some changes along in productive paths."[124] In *The House Behind the Cedars*, Molly represents the fait accompli of miscegenation. Rena represents the attempted exclusion of blackness and the effective exclusion of the female from citizenship, challenges social constructions of racial identity, highlights the performative aspects of all identities, and acts as a smokescreen behind which the story of her brother John is told. John's character and his self-making provide a thorough questioning of the fiction of a pure, white national identity. While critics such as Sally Ann Ferguson and others have discussed John as the "Future American," really Albert is. He is of mixed parentage but looks and will consider himself and call himself white. Unlike his father, Albert will not have to choose or make arguments. He will *be* all that is defined as a true American: a white, human, male, citizen.

For both Martín Morúa Delgado and Charles W. Chesnutt, the future citizen could not be defined based on ideas of racial identities that constructed a false binary in order to negate and exclude those who did not conform to the ideal of the Western Man. Although neither author appears to consider the exclusively male aspect of this ideal or make an argument for the inclusion of women in this paradigm, they both radically expand the idea of the citizen. Morúa's main argument is based on a need to break away from the Spanish colonial model and to find a more inclusive national identity based on the idea of the emerging nation as a mother to all of her sons, a benevolent mother to replace the malevolent Spanish father who created the system he critiques. He also, in making the tragic mulata white, demonstrates the artificial nature of racial identities as constructed in his society. This is one of Chesnutt's main points; the line between human and not-quite-human, and black and white, is fictional. And even if it wasn't a fiction, the line is not truly a line. The second fiction is that otherness can be identified and excluded. The American family is already a miscegenated family. Adapting the trope of the mulato/a allows both of these authors to present visions of more inclusive societies.

NOTES

1. DeCosta-Willis, "Self and Society," 9.
2. Ibid., 16.
3. Julio Ramos, "Cuerpo, Lengua, Sujetividad," *Revista de Crítica Literaria Latinoamericana* 19, no. 40 (1994): 225.
4. Kutzinski, *Sugar's Secrets*, 7.
5. Werner Sollors has a chapter in *Neither Black Nor White* on "Incest and Miscegenation" in which he traces the ways the two ideas have been connected and related to each other both in history and literature.
6. Knadler, "Untragic Mulatto," 441.
7. Bakhtin, "Discourse in the Novel," 299–300.
8. Margaret Toth, "Staged Bodies: Passing, Performance, and Masquerade in Charles W. Chesnutt's *The House Behind the Cedars*," *MELUS* 37, no. 4 (Winter 2012): 72.
9. Handley, *Postslavery Literatures*, 9–10.
10. Ibid., 10.
11. Andrews, *Literary Career*, 137–38.
12. Sommer, *Foundational Fictions*, 29.
13. Ibid.
14. Ibid., 241.

15. Martín Morúa Delgado, *Sofía*, Vol. 1 of *Obras completas de Martín Morúa Delgado* (Havana, Cuba: Comisión Nacional del Centenario de Martín Morúa Delgado, 1957), 7.

16. For explorations of the relationship between *Sofía* and *Cecilia Valdés*, see Rufino Pérez Landa's *Vida Pública de Martín Morúa Delgado*; Lorna V. Williams "Martín Morúa Delgado's *Sofía:* Rewriting *Cecilia Valdés*" in *The Representation of Slavery in Cuban Fiction*; and William Luis' "Time in Fiction: Francisco Calcagno's *Romualdo, uno de tantos* and *Aponte* and Martín Morúa Delgado's *Sofía* and *La familia Unzúazu*" in *Literary Bondage: Slavery in the Cuban Narrative*.

17. Pedro Barreda, *The Black Protagonist in the Cuban Novel*, trans. Page Bancroft. (Amherst: University of Massachusetts Press, 1979), 116.

18. Ibid.

19. Portuondo, *Vigencia política y literaria*, 11.

20. Handley, *Postslavery Literatures*, 83.

21. Barreda, *The Black Protagonist*, 111, 114.

22. Morúa, *Sofía,* 12.

23. Kutzinski, *Sugar's Secrets*, 109.

24. Stephens, *Dictionary*, 238–39.

25. Morúa, *Sofía*, 12–13.

26. Kutzinski, *Sugar's Secrets*, 109.

27. Barreda, *The Black Protagonist*, 110–11.

28. Morúa, *Sofía*, 32.

29. Ibid., 33, 36.

30. Kutzinski, *Sugar's Secrets*, 122.

31. Morúa, *Sofía*, 53.

32. Ibid., 30.

33. Williams, *The Representation of Slavery*, 162.

34. Handley, *Postslavery Literatures*, 84.

35. Kutzinski, *Sugar's Secrets*, 113.

36. Morúa, *Sofía*, 76–78.

37. Luis, *Literary Bondage*, 147.

38. Williams, "Morúa Delgado and the Cuban Slave Narrative," 192.

39. Luis, *Literary Bondage*, 147.

40. Kutzinski, *Sugar's Secrets*, 105.

41. Ibid.

42. Ibid., 111.

43. Ibid., 114.

44. Ibid., 129.

45. Morúa, *Sofía*, 70.

46. Ibid., 65–66.

47. Ibid., 264.

48. Ibid., 52.

49. Ibid., 128–29.

50. Ibid.

51. In the second of Morúa's novels, *La familia Unzuázu*, Magdalena has an affair with Eladislao. They have an illegitimate child and finally marry after his wife dies.

52. Morúa, *Sofía*, 142.

53. Ibid.

54. Ibid., 212.

55. Ibid., 215.

56. Ibid., 219–20.

57. Ibid., 93.

58. Pérez Landa, *Vida Pública*, 142.

59. Morúa, *Sofía*, 114.

60. Ibid., 116–17.

61. Ibid., 117–18.

62. Knadler, "Untragic Mulatto," 438.

63. Chesnutt, *House Behind the Cedars*, 70.
64. Ryan Simmons, *Chesnutt and Realism: A Study of the Novels* (Tuscaloosa: University of Alabama Press, 2006), 12.
65. Anne Fleischmann, "Neither Fish, Flesh, nor Fowl: Race and Region in the Writings of Charles W. Chesnutt," *African American Review* 34, no. 3 (Autumn 2000): 462.
66. Ryan Simmons even argues that the novel is able to provide "a more direct approach to social issues" than the "Future American" essays and that the "level of critique tends to be deeper" in the novel (73).
67. Melissa Ryan explores the difference between male mulato who, as "name," can redefine his identity, and female mulata who cannot escape hers since she is not name, but "body." Melissa Ryan, "Rena's Two Bodies: Gender and Whiteness in Charles W. Chesnutt's *The House Behind the Cedars*," *Studies in the Novel* 43, no. 1 (Spring 2011): 38. Kerstin Rudolph argues that John's whiteness is only possible due to the sacrifice of the black female—that he in fact "exchanges" or sacrifices Rena in order to create and reaffirm not only his whiteness, but also his son's. Kerstin Rudolph, "A Woman of One's Own Blood: John Walden and the Making of White Masculinity in Charles W. Chesnutt's *The House Behind the Cedars*," *American Literary Realism* 46, no. 1 (Fall 2013): 27–46.
68. Wilson, *Whiteness in the Novels*, 77.
69. Ryan Simmons's take on the novel is that it appears to both "subscribe to and to 'illuminate the paradoxes of' the standard conventions for racial fiction at the turn of the twentieth century, especially those concerning mixed-race people" (57).
70. Gillman, qtd. in Wilson, *Whiteness in the Novels*, 66.
71. Chesnutt, *Cedars*, 104.
72. Ibid., 104.
73. Ibid.
74. Ibid., 18.
75. Chesnutt, *Essays*, 126.
76. Sally Ann Ferguson, "Rena Walden: Chesnutt's Failed 'Future American,'" in *Critical Essays on Charles W. Chesnutt*, ed. Joseph R. McElrath Jr., (New York: G.K. Hall, 1999), 199.
77. Wilson, *Whiteness in the Novels*, 69.
78. Ibid., 70, my emphasis.
79. Chesnutt, *Cedars*, 5.
80. Ibid.
81. Ibid., 47.
82. Ibid., 48.
83. Toth, "Staged Bodies," 72.
84. Ryan, "Rena's Two Bodies," 42.
85. Toth, "Staged Bodies," 72.
86. Patterson, *Slavery and Social Death*, 95.
87. Chesnutt, *Cedars*, 42.
88. Ibid., 48.
89. Toth, "Staged Bodies," 87.
90. Ibid.
91. Aaron Ritzenberg, "The Dream of History: Memory and the Unconscious in Charles Chesnutt's *The House Behind the Cedars*," in *Passing in the Works of Charles W. Chesnutt*, eds. Ernestine Pickens Glass and Susan Prothro Wright (Jackson: University Press of Mississippi, 2010), 57.
92. Chesnutt, *Cedars*, 51. Keith Byerman argues that despite the inherent argument in Chesnutt that a person with predominantly white blood, white features, and white manners is white, Rena "might be said to be 'passing' in the sense that she seems to accept the one-drop rule about race. Despite what the law and opportunity say, she troubles herself about whether to reveal her ancestry to Tryon, and she continues to feel a connection to her old home as both domestic and racial space." Byerman, "Performing Race," 87.
93. Anna Shannon Elfenbein qtd. in Sollors, *Neither Black nor White*, 227.
94. Wilson, *Whiteness in the Novels*, 87.
95. Ibid., 78, 87.

96. Ibid., 87.

97. Chesnutt, *Essays*, 126.

98. Ferguson, "Rena Walden," 198.

99. Ryan, "Rena's Two Bodies," 42.

100. Chesnutt, *Cedars*, 195.

101. Ibid., 1–2.

102. Keith Byerman puts it this way: "Having made what he considers a rational decision to be white, he cannot really be thought of as "passing," since the law recognizes his status as legitimate. If the novel is an experiment, then John makes one kind of choice: to accept the identity available to him as an individual and not concern himself with biology or a racial past that was itself arbitrarily assigned" (87).

103. Sollors, *Neither Black nor White*, 249.

104. Ibid.

105. Chesnutt, *Essays*, 68.

106. Chesnutt, *Cedars*, 111.

107. Ibid., 47.

108. Andrews, *Literary Career*, 164.

109. Chesnutt, *Cedars*, 15.

110. Ibid., 107.

111. Kawash, *Dislocating the Color Line*, 125.

112. Rudolph, "A Woman of One's Own Blood," 30.

113. Chesnutt, Cedars, 114. Obviously, it is significant that Chesnutt's novel is set before *Plessy v Ferguson*.

114. Ibid., 115.

115. Byerman, "Performing Race," 84.

116. Chesnutt, *Essays*, 129.

117. Werner Sollors provides an interesting way to look at John's character when he argues that Chesnutt ironically "represented passing in terms of the immigration story" (258) a reading based on the passage in the novel which refers to John as having been "in a figurative sense, a naturalized foreigner in the world of opportunity" and further speaks of South Carolina (or white society, perhaps) as his "adopted country." Chesnutt, *Cedars*, 45. Kerstin Rudolph additionally argues that "John needs and uses his light-skinned African American sister in order to validate his white manhood. This dynamic, which thrives on the sexual barter of women in general, and the symbolic prize of Rena's racially indeterminate blackness that gets handed from John to George in specific, points to African American men's implications into the larger male-dominated sphere or white power." Rudolph, "A Woman of One's Own Blood," 29. Certainly Chesnutt's novel offers no clear critique of the exclusively male nature of constructions of national identity.

118. Charles Duncan, *The Absent Man: The Narrative Craft of Charles W. Chesnutt* (Athens: Ohio University Press, 1998), 15.

119. Ibid., 15–16.

120. Ibid.

121. Ryan, "Rena's Two Bodies," 45.

122. The fact that John passes successfully where Rena cannot and that Albert's future looks bright also relates to Kerstin Rudolph's reminder that since children are classified by their *mother's* racial status, it is easier for males to pass (39).

123. Kawash, *Dislocating the Color Line*, 131–32.

124. Simmons, *Chesnutt and Realism*, 78.

Epilogue

The trajectory of this study traces Afro-Cuban and African American responses to the radical negation brought about by racialization by four nineteenth-century authors writing in a number of genres. While these authors operate within, rather than outside, the process of racialization and participate to varying degrees in the "rituals of Americanization" or Cubanization which loomed large over their own ideas of humanity and citizenship, all of the texts in this book denaturalize constructions of human and national identity based on racialization. The examination of Juan Francisco Manzano's poetry and Frederick Douglass's oratory demonstrates how these authors enter into discourse in order to counter the dehumanizing force of slavery and to destabilize the process of racialization that sought to assign them to the category of nonhuman and exclude them from participation in their homelands. As Manzano writes about his faith, demonstrates the pathos of his tragic fate, and expresses his desire to flee from slavery, he constructs a poetic persona that undermines the racializing assemblages that worked negate his humanity and efface evidence of his intellect and his artistry. Frederick Douglass's speeches were direct and powerful critiques of slavery in the United States, rational discourse that confronted religious hypocrisy, prejudice, and the violence inherent in the slave system. Like Manzano, his texts undermine the stability of a system intended to limit who was defined as human in order to protect the power of the few.

When these two authors wrote the initial versions of their life stories, even the need to accommodate their patrons did not eliminate their ability to negotiate with paradigms of humanity and citizenship and to present their readers with alternate versions of themselves and their nations. They reveal the horrors of slavery, undermine its religious and philosophical justifications, humanize the experience of slavery for the readers, and attempt to renegotiate themselves out of quasi-filial relations with masters in part by creating discourses of identity that demonstrate their very real and significant relation to both masters and the nation. Their examination of the complexity of racial identities in both Cuba and the United States makes yet another argument for their humanity and against the ability for their societies to confidently establish the color line. Perhaps unsurprisingly, both Manzano's *Autobiografía* and Douglass's *Narrative* can be read as reinforcing a racial hierarchy based on the ideology of whiteness, particularly as both authors emphasize their biological identities in order to align themselves with the characteristics generally associated with the Western Man on whom their societies' ideas of humanity and citizenship are based. On the other hand, even within these texts Douglass and Manzano exceed the limits that their patrons attempt to place upon them and become, in Celeste-Marie Bernier's terms, "seemingly transcendent icons of a living, breathing black . . . male humanity, both illusory and mythical but also palpable and historically real."[1] They overpopulated the paradigms of humanity and citizenship of their day and challenged the status quo. This is most evident in their later works, *Zafira* and *The Heroic Slave*, which offer a vision of black male heroism in the struggle against slavery and tyranny. One of the most important things about the black male heroism they construct through Noemí, Madison Washington, and even Douglass himself, is that while these characters do physically resist their subjugation and negation, they are not merely bodies. Their *intellectual* resistance to tyranny and slavery is paramount and has the potential to powerfully alter the conversation about heroism in their nations.

In their nonfiction, postslavery writers Martín Morúa Delgado and Charles W. Chesnutt confront similar complexities of racial identities as well as similarly exclusive paradigms of national identity that relegate people of African descent to the categories of not-quite-human and alien, rather than human and citizen. They most specifically reengage with the thread of the complexity of racial identities. Morúa's vision of mother Cuba as the unifying force uniting all of her sons in a Cuban race regardless of perceived racial identity responds to similar anxieties as Chesnutt's vision of the elimination of difference through miscegenation and the biological construction of an American race. Both authors try to help their nations see past difference and hierarchy and challenge their readers to consider the nation and the body politic in different and more inclusive ways. Their novels reinforce these ideas, Morúa's by providing a cautionary tale regarding what happens if ideas of identity based on racialization continue to allow white males inappropriate levels of power and privilege. He implies that they will not be able to escape the hegemonic power of the colonizer and will find their independence stillborn. For his part, Chesnutt's novel reproduces the argument in his essays, demonstrating the socially constructed nature of racial identities and presenting Albert as the prototypical Future American who, despite the complexities of his heritage, will be white not least of all because he will believe that he is. As with the slave narratives, both Chesnutt and Morúa overpopulate the color line, challenging the racializing assemblages that are meant to enforce it and presenting different ideas of national identity not based on race.

The discourses of identity examined here are not the only possible examples that can be pulled from the archives of Cuba and the United States. Other genres are likely to provide further insight into the ongoing negotiations of personal and national identities by members of the African diaspora in the Americas. There are several potential areas where an examination of texts from the twentieth century might begin. The early twentieth century in the United States saw a blossoming of African American culture, most notably during the Harlem Renaissance, as well as continued efforts on the part of white supremacists to maintain power through mechanisms like Jim Crow and lynching. In Cuba, during the early twentieth century there was a similar blossoming as writers like Nicolás Guillén incorporated African musical and other vernacular traditions into Cuban literature. While there have been a number of works that have begun an analysis of connections within the poetry of Nicolás Guillén and Langston Hughes,[2] there is much more that could be examined in terms of their visions of national identity. Particularly in Cuba, Afro-Cuban cultural forms have been adopted, and sometimes coopted, as being quintessentially Cuban. This reality, however, has not meant that Afro-Cubans have achieved equality. In terms of the first half of the twentieth century, folklore studies like Lydia Cabrera's *Cuentos Negros de Cuba*, Zora Neale Hurston's *Mules and Men*, and Rómulo Lachatañeré's *¡Oh, mío Yemayá! Cuentos y cantos negros* could be read together to examine the ideas of national identity implicit within them.[3] In the second half of the twentieth century, post-revolutionary Cuban culture has incorporated Afro-Cuban literature into key narratives of nationalist identity. In the United States, African American literature has progressively had a larger impact through both a separate African American literary canon and the inclusion of more authors and works in the larger American canon. One genre closely linked to revolutionary nationalism in Cuba is the *testimonio*.[4] Another possible area for comparative analysis would be a comparative reading of Cuban *testimonios* like *Biografía de un cimarrón* and *Reyita, Testimonio de una cubana nonagenaria* against the neo-slave narrative tradition in the United States. There could be fruitful work on Afro-Cuban and African American women's poetry in both nations. What might we discover about race, gender, sexuality, and nation were we to read Afro-Cuban poets like Georgina Herrera, Lourdes Casal, Nancy Morejón, and Soleida Ríos in conversation with African American poets such as Mari Evans, Sonia Sanchez, Nikki Giovanni, Audre Lorde, Lucille Clifton, and Maya Angelou?

The discourses of identity discussed in this book are connected to ongoing struggles in both Cuba and the United States to overcome injustice and racism and create more inclusive versions of national identity. While it is certainly possible to focus on patterns of contradistinction between Cuba and the United States, the examination of these Afro–New World discourses of identity brings into focus that the stories of race and national identity in Cuba and the United States, like the flags of the two countries, reflect each other. Having examined works from the archive of African American and Afro-Cuban literature that gave testimony against such injustices, this book seeks to remind us of a long and powerful tradition of voices crying out against racism in both nations. These texts, as problematic as they may be in some ways, all implicitly argue for the extension of human rights and human dignity to all. It is my hope that this comparative reading of nineteenth-century works from the United States and Cuba allows for a deeper understanding of the socially constructed nature of ideas of racial and national identity and of the very deeply ingrained prejudices that permeate postslavery cultures. The discourses of identity examined in this book were read as important voices from the archive of Afro-Cuban and African American literature that sometimes subtly and sometimes directly create the possibility for new identities by denying the exclusionary nature of the paradigms of identity articulated and enforced by official culture. The works by Manzano, Douglass, Morúa Delgado, and Chesnutt all challenge the radical *othering* of peoples of African descent in post-Plantation America. The bigger question that remains is, how can we continue to interrogate both our past and present to best expose and correct any ways in which our socially constructed ideas of race (or gender or sexuality) cause us to create a vision of the nation and its people that disempowers or excludes anyone who does not fit the established image? How can we resist the temptation to engage in practices that exclude, and choose those which help us to stitch together new banners of national identity that celebrate and embrace all the members of our nation?

NOTES

1. Bernier, *Characters of Blood*, introduction.

2. Previous works most closely related to ideas of the intersections of racial and national identities include Martha Cobb's 1974 essay, "Concepts of Blackness in the Poetry of Nicolás Guillén, Jacques Roumain and Langston Hughes," David Arthur McMurray's 1979 short chapter "Two Black Men in the New World: Notes on the 'Americanism' of Langston Hughes and the Cubanía of Nicolás Guillén," and "'Our America' That is Not One: Transnational Black Atlantic Disclosures in Nicolás Guillén and Langston Hughes" by Monika Kaup (2000).

3. For a discussion of Hurston and Cabrera's use of the folkloric space outside of the modern geopolitical nation to deconstruct gender and racial hierarchies and create the possibility to speak new identities see Karen Ruth Kornweibel, "The Fecundity of Folkloric Space: Revising Hierarchies in Zora Neale Hurston's *Mules and Men* and Lydia Cabrera's *Cuentos Negros de Cuba*," *Comparative American Studies* 2, no. 4 (2004): 403–20.

4. For an examination of *Reyita* as an example of the place of the black woman in the narrative of revolutionary nationalism, see Karen Ruth Kornweibel, "Daisy Rubiera Castillo's *Reyita*: 'Mujer Negra' from Objectified Symbol to Empowered Subject," *Letras Hispanas* 7 (Fall 2010): 67–79.

Bibliography

Allen, Carol. *Black Woman Intellectuals: Strategies of Nation, Family, and Neighborhood in the Works of Pauline Hopkins, Jessie Fauset, and Marita Bonner.* New York: Garland Publishing, 1998.

Anderson, Benedict. *Imagined Communities: Reflections on the Origin and Spread of Nationalism.* New York: Verso, 1991.

Andrews, William L. *The Literary Career of Charles W. Chesnutt.* Baton Rouge: Louisiana State University Press, 1980.

———. "The Novelization of Voice in Early African American Narrative." *PMLA* 105.1 (1990): 23–34.

———. *To Tell a Free Story: The First Century of Afro-American Autobiography, 1760–1865.* Chicago: University of Illinois Press, 1986.

Azougarh, Abdeslam. *Juan Francisco Manzano: Esclavo poeta en la isla de Cuba.* Valencia: Ediciones Episteme S.L., 2000.

Baker, Houston A., Jr. "Autobiographical Acts and the Voice of the Southern Slave." In *The Journey Back: Issues in Black Literature and Criticism*, 27–52. Chicago: University of Chicago Press, 1980.

Bakhtin, Mikhail. "Discourse in the Novel." In *The Dialogic Imagination*. Edited by Michael Holquist. Translated by Caryl Emerson and Michael Holquist. Austin: University of Texas Press, 1981.

Barreda, Pedro. *The Black Protagonist in the Cuban Novel.* Translated by Page Bancroft. Amherst: University of Massachusetts Press, 1979.

Benitez Rojo, Antonio. *The Repeating Island: The Caribbean and the Postmodern Perspective.* Translated by James E. Maraniss. Durham: Duke University Press, 1997.

Berlant, Lauren. "National Brands/National Body: Imitation of life." In *The Phantom Public Sphere.* Edited by Bruce Robbins. Minneapolis: University of Minnesota Press, 1993.

Bernier, Celeste-Marie. *Characters of Blood: Black Heroism in the Transatlantic Imagination.* Charlottesville, University of Virginia Press, 2012, EPUB, EBSCO.

———. "From Fugitive Slave to Fugitive Abolitionist." *Atlantic Studies* 3.2 (2006): 201–224.

Berzon, Judith R. *Neither White nor Black: The Mulatto Character in American Fiction.* New York: New York University Press, 1978.

Blackburn, Robin. *The American Crucible: Slavery, Emancipation and Human Rights.* New York: Verso, 2011.

Blassingame, John W. *The Slave Community: Plantation Life in the Antebellum South*, rev. ed. New York: Oxford University Press, 1979.

Blumenthal, Rachel A. "Canonicity, Genre, and the Politics of Writing: How We Read Frederick Douglass," *Callaloo* 36, no. 1 (Winter 2013): 178–190.

Branche, Jerome. "'*Mulato entre negros'* (y blancos): Writing, Race, the Antislavery Question, and Juan Francisco Manzano's *Autobiografía*." *Bulletin of Latin American Research* 20, no. 1 (2001): 63–87.

Brock, Lisa, and Digna Castañeda Fuentes, eds. *Between Race and Empire: African-Americans and Cubans before the Cuban Revolution*. Philadelphia: Temple University Press, 1998.

Bromell, Nick. "A 'Voice from the Enslaved': The Origins of Frederick Douglass's Political Philosophy of Democracy." *American Literary History* 23, no. 4 (Winter 2011): 697–723.

Burton, Gera C. *Ambivalence and the Postcolonial Subject: The Strategic Alliance of Juan Francisco Manzano and Richard Robert Madden*. New York: Peter Lang, 2004.

Byerman, Keith. "Performing Race: Mixed-Race Characters in the Novels of Charles Chesnutt." In *Passing in the Works of Charles W. Chesnutt*, 84–92. Edited by Ernestine Pickens Glass and Susan Prothro. Jackson: University Press of Mississippi, 2010.

Carbonell, Bettina. "Race/Relations, Acts of Discernment, and Ethical Inquiry in Charles W. Chesnutt's *The House Behind the Cedars*." *African American Review* 45, no. 4 (Winter 2012): 541–556.

Carrión, Juan Manuel. "The War of the Flags: Conflicting National Loyalties in a Modern Colonial Situation." *Centro Journal* 18, no. 2 (Fall 2006): 100–23.

Casanova-Marengo, Ilia. "Desde el *jardín de bellísimas flores:* Entre el silencio y la ruptura en *Autobiografía* de Juan Francisco Manzano." *Monographic Review/Revista Monográfica* 16 (2000): 241–252.

Chávez Alvarez, Clara Emma. "La boradora de la bandera cubana." *Revista de la Biblioteca Nacional José Martí* 1 (January–June 1993): 31–43.

Chesnutt, Charles. *Essays and Speeches*. Edited by Joseph McElrath Jr., Robert C. Leitz, III, and Jesse S. Crisler. Stanford: Stanford University Press, 1999.

———. *The House Behind the Cedars*. New York: Houghton Mifflin, 1900.

Chevigny, Bell Gale and Gari Laguardia. *Reinventing the Americas: Comparative Readings of Literature of the US and Spanish America*. New York: Cambridge University Press, 1986.

Cobb, Martha. *Harlem, Haiti, and Havana: A Comparative Critical Study of Langston Hughes, Jacques Romain, and Nicolás Guillén*. Washington, DC: Three Continents Press, 1979.

Cohn, Deborah N. *History and Memory in the Two Souths: Recent Southern and Spanish American Fiction*. Nashville: Vanderbilt University Press, 1999.

Dathorne, O. R. *Dark Ancestor: The Literature of the Black Man in the Caribbean*. Baton Rouge: Louisiana State University Press, 1981.

Davis, Charles T., and Henry Louis Gates Jr. *The Slave's Narrative*. New York: Oxford University Press, 1985.

DeCosta-Willis, Miriam. "Self and Society in the Afro-Cuban Slave Narrative." *Latin American Literary Review* 16, no. 31 (January–June 1988): 6–15.

Delmar, P. Jay. "Coincidence in Charles W. Chesnutt's *The House Behind the Cedars*." *American Literary Realism* 15, no. 1 (1982): 97–103.

Dizon, Alma. "Mothers, Morals and Power in the Autobiography of Juan Francisco Manzano." *Revista de estudios hispánicos* 21 (1994): 109–17.

Douglass, Frederick. *Autobiographies*. New York: Library of America, 1994.

———. *Frederick Douglass Papers. Series One: Speeches, Debates, and Interviews, Volume I (1841–1846)*. Edited by John W. Blassingame. New Haven: Yale University Press, 1979.

———. *Narrative of the Life of Fredrick Douglass, an American Slave*. New York: Oxford University Press, 1999.

Draper, Susana. "Voluntad de intelectual: Juan Francisco Manzano entre las redes de un humanism sin derechos." *Chasqui: Revista de literatura latinoamericana* 30, no. 2 (November 2001): 102–15.

Duncan, Charles. *The Absent Man: The Narrative Craft of Charles W. Chesnutt*. Athens: Ohio University Press, 1998.

Earley, Samantha Manchester. "Dismantling Master Thought: Discourse and Race in Frederick Douglass' *Narrative*." *Atenea* 21, no. 1–2 (2001): 179–92.

Elder, Arlene A. "MELUS Forum: 'The Future American Race': Charles W. Chesnutt's Utopian Illusion." *MELUS* 15, no. 3 (Fall 1988): 121–29.

Fanon, Frantz. *Black Skin, White Masks*. Translated by Charles Lam Markmann. New York: Grove Press, 1967.

Ferguson, Sally Ann. "Rena Walden: Chesnutt's Failed 'Future American.'" In *Critical Essays on Charles W. Chesnutt*, edited by Joseph R. McElrath Jr., 198–205. New York: G.K. Hall, 1999.

Fleischmann, Anne. "Neither Fish, Flesh, nor Fowl: Race and Region in the Writings of Charles W. Chesnutt." *African American Review* 34, no. 3 (Autumn 2000): 461–473.

Foster, Frances Smith. *Witnessing Slavery: The Development of Ante-Bellum Slave Narratives*, second ed. Madison: University of Wisconsin Press, 1994.

———. *Written by Herself: Literary Production by African American Women, 1746–1892*. Bloomington: Indiana University Press, 1993.

Fox-Genovese, Elizabeth. "Slavery, Race, and the Figure of the Tragic Mulatta, or, The Ghost of Southern History in the Writing of African-American Women." *Mississippi Quarterly* 49, no. 4 (1996 Fall): 791–817.

Fraginals, Manuel Moreno. *El ingenio: Complejo económico social cubano del azúcar*. Havana, Cuba: Editorial de Ciencias Sociales, 1978.

Friol, Roberto. *Suite para Juan Francisco Manzano*. Havana, Cuba: Editorial arte y literatura, 1977.

Gates, Henry Louis, Jr. *The Signifying Monkey: A Theory of African-American Literary Criticism*. New York: Oxford University Press, 1988.

———. *Figures in Black: Words, Signs, and the "Racial" Self*. New York: Oxford University Press, 1987.

Gibson, Donald B. "Faith, Doubt, and Apostasy: *Evidence of Things Unseen in Frederick Douglass's* Narrative." In *Frederick Douglass: New Literary and Historical Essays*, edited by Eric J. Sundquist, 84–98. New York: Cambridge University Press, 1990.

Gilman, Susan. "The Mulatto, Tragic or Triumphant?: The Nineteenth-Century American Race Melodrama." In *The Culture of Sentiment: Race, Gender, and Sentimentality in Nineteenth-Century America*, edited by Shirley Samuels, 221–243. New York: Oxford University Press, 1992.

Gilroy, Paul. *The Black Atlantic: Modernity and Double-Consciousness*. Boston: Harvard University Press, 1995.

Handley, George B. *Postslavery Literatures in the Americas: Family Portraits in Black and White*. Charlottesville: University Press of Virginia, 2000.

Hansen, John. "Frederick Douglass's Journey from Slave to Freeman: An Acquisition and Mastery of Language, Rhetoric, and Power Via the *Narrative*." *The Griot* 31, no. 2 (2012): 14–23.

Hartman, Saidiya V. *Scenes of Subjection: Terror Slavery, and Self-Making in Nineteenth-Century America*. New York: Oxford University Press, 1997.

Hiraldo, Carlos. *Segregated Miscegenation: On the Treatment of Racial Hybridity in the U.S. and Latin American Literary Traditions*. New York: Routledge, 2003.

Hughes, Langston. "The Negro Artist and the Racial Mountain." In *Voices from the Harlem Renaissance*, edited by Nathan Irvin Huggins, 305–9. New York: Oxford University Press, 1995.

Jackson, Richard L. *The Black Image in Latin American Literature*. Albuquerque: University of New Mexico Press, 1976.

———. *Black Writers in Latin America*. Albuquerque: University of New Mexico Press, 1979.

———. "Slavery, Racism and Autobiography in Two Early Black Writers: Juan Francisco Manzano and Martin Morúa Delgado." In *Voices from Under: Black Narrative in Latin America and the Caribbean*, edited by William Luis, 55–64. Westport, CT: Greenwood Press, 1984.

Jiménez, Luis A. "Nineteenth Century Autobiography in the Afro-Americas: Frederick Douglass and Juan Francisco Manzano." *Afro Hispanic Review* 14, no. 2 (Fall 1995): 47–52.

———. "Voces y silencios, y sus vínculos con el poder en la *Autobiografía* de Juan Francisco Manzano." In *Studies in Honor of María A. Salgado*, edited by Millicent A. Bolden and Luis Jiménez, 31–45. Newark, DE: Juan de la Cuesta, 1995.

Johnson, Barbara. "The Quicksands of the Self: Nella Larsen and Heinz Kohut." In *Female Subjects in Black and White: Race, Psychoanalysis, Feminism*. Edited by Elizabeth Abel, Barbara Christian, and Helene Moglen, 37–60. Berkeley: University of California Press, 1997.

Jouve-Martin, Jose R. "En la urna del destino: Zafira y el modo trágico en la obra de Juan Francisco Manzano," *Revista de estudios hispánicos* 43, no. 3 (2009): 501–24.

Kawash, Samira. *Dislocating the Color Line: Identity, Hybridity, and Singularity in African-American Narrative*. Stanford: Stanford University Press, 1997.

Keller, Frances Richardson. *An American Crusade: The Life of Charles Waddell Chesnutt*. Provo, UT: Brigham Young University Press, 1978.

Klein, Herbert S. *Slavery in the Americas: A Comparative Study of Virginia and Cuba*. Chicago: University of Chicago Press, 1967.

Knadler, Stephen P. "Untragic Mulatto: Charles Chesnutt and the Discourse of Whiteness." *American Literary History* 8, no. 3 (Fall 1996): 426–48.

Knight, Franklin W. *Slave Society in Cuba During the Nineteenth Century*. Madison: University of Wisconsin Press, 1970.

Kornweibel, Karen Ruth. "Daisy Rubiera Castillo's *Reyita:* 'Mujer Negra' from Objectified Symbol to Empowered Subject." *Letras Hispanas* 7 (Fall 2010): 67–79.

———. "The Fecundity of Folkloric Space: Revising Hierarchies in Zora Neale Hurston's *Mules and Men* and Lydia Cabrera's *Cuentos Negros de Cuba*." *Comparative American Studies* 2, no. 4 (2004): 403–20.

Kutzinski, Vera. *Against the American Grain: Myth and History in William Carlos Williams, Jay Wright, and Nicolás Guillén*. Baltimore: Johns Hopkins University Press, 1987.

———. *Sugar's Secrets: Race and the Erotics of Cuban Nationalism*. Charlottesville: University of Virginia Press, 1993.

Labrador-Rodríguez, Sonia. "La intelectualidad negra en Cuba en el siglo XIX: El caso de Manzano." *Revista Iberoamericana* 62, no. 174 (January–March 1996): 13–25.

Leante, Cesar. "Dos obras antiesclavistas cubanas." *Cuadernos Americanos* 207 (1976): 175–189.

Lewis, Marvín. "Literature, Black, in Spanish America." In *Africana: The Encyclopedia of the African and African American Experience*, edited by Kwame Anthony Appiah and Henry Louis Gates Jr. New York: Basic Civitas Books, 1999.

Loichot, Valerie. *Orphan Narratives: The Postplantation Literature of Faulkner, Glissant, Morrison, and Saint-John Perse*. Charlottesville: University Press of Virginia, 2007.

Lowe, John Wharton. *Calypso Magnolia: The Crosscurrents of Caribbean and Southern Literature*. Chapel Hill: University of North Carolina Press, 2016.

Luis, William. *Literary Bondage: Slavery in the Cuban Narrative*. Austin: University of Texas Press, 1990.

Manzano, Juan Francisco. *Autobiografía, cartas y versos de Juan Francisco Manzano*. Edited by Jose L. Franco. Havana, Cuba: Municipio de la Habana, 1937.

———. *Autobiografía del esclavo poeta y otros escritos*. Edited by William Luis. Madrid: Iberoamericana Vervuert, 2007.

———. *The Autobiography of Juan Francisco Manzano*. Introduction and modernized Spanish version by Ivan A. Schulman. Translated by Evelyn Picon Garfield. Detroit: Wayne State University Press, 1996.

Martí, José. *Martí Vol. XI: Ismaelillo, Versos Sencillos, Versos Libres*. Habana: Rambla, Bouza y Compañía, 1918.

Martin, Waldo E. *The Mind of Frederick Douglass*. Durham: The University of North Carolina Press, 1986.

McCoy, Beth A. "Race and the (Para)Textual Condition," *PMLA* 121, no. 1 (2006): 156–169.

McWilliams, Dean. *Charles W. Chesnutt and the Fictions of Race*. Athens: University of Georgia Press, 2002.

Miller, Marilyn Grace. "Imitation and Improvisation in Juan Francisco Manzano's *Zafira*." *Colonial Latin American Review* 17, no. 1 (June 2008): 49–71.

Miller, Marilyn. "Rebeldía narrativa, resistencia poética y expresión 'libre' en Juan Francisco Manzano." *Revista Iberoamericana* 71, no. 211 (April–June 2005): 417–36.

Molloy, Silvia. "From Serf to Self: The Autobiography of Juan Francisco Manzano." *At Face Value: Autobiographical Writing in Spanish America.* New York: Cambridge University Press, 1991.

Morejón, Nancy. "Race and Nation." In *Afrocuba: An Anthology of Cuban Writing on Race, Politics and Culture,* edited by Pedro Perez Sarduy and Jean Stubbs, 227–37. Melbourne: Ocean Press, 1993.

Morúa Delgado, Martín. "Ensayo Político o Cuba y la Raza de Color." Vol. 3 of *Obras completas de Martín Morúa Delgado,* 46–107. Havana, Cuba: Comisión Nacional del Centenario de Martín Morúa Delgado, 1957.

———. *Sofía.* Vol. 1 of *Obras completas de Martín Morúa Delgado.* Havana, Cuba: Comisión Nacional del Centenario de Martín Morúa Delgado, 1957.

Mullen, Edward J. *Afro-Cuban Literature: Critical Junctures.* Westport, CT: Greenwood Press, 1998.

Nielsen, Cynthia R. "Resistance is Not Futile: Frederick Douglass on Panoptic Plantations and the Un-Making of Docile Bodies and Enslaved Souls." *Philosophy and Literature* 35, no. 2 (October 2011): 251–68.

Nwankwo, Ifeoma Kiddoe. *Black Cosmopolitanism: Racial Consciousness and Transnational Identity in the Nineteenth-Century Americas.* Philadelphia: University of Pennsylvania Press, 2005.

Olsen, Margaret M. "Manzano's *Zafira* and the Performance of Cuban Nationhood." *Hispanic Review* 75, no. 2 (spring 2007): 135–58.

Paquette, Robert L. "Cuban Whites and the Problem of Slavery." In *Sugar is Made with Blood: the Conspiracy of La Escalera and the Conflict between Empires over Slavery in Cuba.* Middletown, CT: Wesleyan University Press, 1988.

Parkinson Zamora, Lois. *Writing the Apocalypse: Historical vision in Contemporary U.S. and Latin American Fiction.* New York: Cambridge University Press, 1989.

Patterson, Orlando. *Slavery and Social Death. A Comparative Study.* Cambridge: Harvard University Press, 1982.

Pérez, Louis A., Jr. *Cuba and the United States: Ties of Singular Intimacy.* Athens: University of Georgia Press, 1990.

———. *Cuba in the American Imagination: Metaphor and the Imperial Ethos.* Chapel Hill: University of North Carolina Press, 2008.

Pérez Firmat, Gustavo. *Do the Americas Have a Common Literature?* Durham: Duke University Press, 1990.

Pérez Landa, Rufino. *Vida Pública de Martín Morúa Delgado.* Havana, Cuba: Academia de la historia, 1957.

Peyser, Thomas. "An Attack on Christianity in NARRATIVE OF THE LIFE OF FREDERICK DOUGLASS, AN AMERICAN SLAVE." *Explicator* 69, no. 2 (2011): 86–89.

Plessy v. Ferguson, 163 U.S. 537 (1896).

Portuondo, Aleyda T. *Vigencia política y literaria de Martín Morúa Delgado.* Miami: Ediciones Universales, 1978.

Price, Rachel. "Enemigo Suelo: Manzano Rewrites Cuban Romanticism." *Revista Canadiense de Estudios Hispanos* 38, no. 3 (2014): 529–554.

Rama, Angel. *La ciudad letrada.* Hanover: Ediciones del Norte, 1984.

Ramos, Julio. "Cuerpo, Lengua, Subjetividad." *Revista de Crítica Literaria Latinoamericana* 19, no. 28 (1993): 225–237.

———. "La ley es otra: Literatura y constitución de la persona jurídica." *Revista de Crítica Literaria latinoamericana* 20, no. 40 (1994): 305–35.

Ritzenberg, Aaron. "The Dream of History: Memory and the Unconscious in Charles Chesnutt's *The House Behind the Cedars.*" In *Passing in the Works of Charles W. Chesnutt,* edited by Ernestine Pickens Glass and Susan Prothro Wright, 51–66. Jackson: University Press of Mississippi, 2010.

Rodríguez Drissi, Susannah. "Between Orientalism and Affective Identification: A Paradigm and Four Case Studies Towards the Inclusion of the Moor in Cuban Literary and Cultural Studies." PhD diss., UCLA, 2012. http://escholarship.org/uc/item/5ps5d43t.

Rohrbach, Augusta. "'Truth Stronger and Stranger than Fiction': Reexamining William Lloyd Garrison's *Liberator.*" *American Literature* 73, no. 4 (December 2001): 727–55.

Roosevelt, Theodore. *American Ideals.* New York: G.P. Putnam's Sons, 1897.

Royer, Daniel J. "The Process of Literacy as Communal Involvement in the Narratives of Frederick Douglass." *African American Review* 28, no. 3 (1994): 363–74. Accessed July 21, 2015.

Rudolph, Kerstin. "A Woman of One's Own Blood: John Walden and the Making of White Masculinity in Charles W. Chesnutt's *The House Behind the Cedars.*" *American Literary Realism* 46, no. 1 (Fall 2013): 27–46.

Russ, Elizabeth Christine. *The Plantation in the Postslavery Imagination.* Oxford: Oxford University Press, 2009.

Ryan, Melissa. "Rena's Two Bodies: Gender and Whiteness in Charles Chesnutt's *The House Behind the Cedars.*" *Studies in the Novel* 43, no. 1 (Spring 2011): 38–54.

Ryden, Wendy. "Conflicted Literacy: Frederick Douglass's Critical Model." *Journal of Basic Writing* 24, no. 1 (Spring 2005): 4–23.

Saldívar, José David. *The Dialectics of Our America: Genealogy, Cultural Critique, and Literary History.* Durham: Duke University Press, 1991.

Schulman, Ivan A. "Introduction" In *Autobiography of a Slave/Autobiografía de un esclavo,* by Juan Francisco Manzano, 5–38. Translated by Evelyn Picon Garfield. Detroit: Wayne State University Press, 1996.

———. "Invención y disfraz: el discurso cubano de la *Autobiografía* de Juan Francisco Manzano." In *Discursos sobre la 'invención' de América,* edited by Iris M. Zavala, 167–181. Amsterdam, Netherlands: Rodopi, 1992.

Scott, Rebecca J. *Slave Emancipation in Cuba: The Transition to Free Labor, 1860–1899.* Princeton: Princeton University Press, 1985.

Sekora, John. "Black Message/White Envelope: Genre, Authenticity, and Authority in the Antebellum Slave Narrative." *Callaloo* 10, no. 3 (Summer 1987): 482–515.

———. "Comprehending Slavery: Language and Personal History in Douglass' *Narrative* of 1845." *CLA Journal* 29, no. 2 (1985): 157–70.

Selby, Gary S. "The Limits of Accommodation: Frederick Douglass and the Garrisonian Abolitionists." *Southern Communication Journal* 66, no. 1 (2000): 52–66.

———. "Mocking the Sacred: Frederick Douglass's 'Slaveholder's Sermon' and the Antebellum Debate over Religion and Slavery." *Quarterly Journal of Speech* 88, no. 3 (2002): 326–41.

Simmons, Ryan. *Chesnutt and Realism: A Study of the Novels.* Tuscaloosa: University of Alabama Press, 2006.

Sisco, Lisa. "'Writing in the Spaces Left': Literacy as a Process of Becoming in the Narratives of Frederick Douglass." *ATQ* 9, no. 3 (1995): 195–232.

Sollors, Werner. *Neither Black nor White yet Both: Thematic Explorations of Interracial Literature.* New York: Oxford University Press, 1997.

———. "'Never Was Born': The Mulatto, an American Tragedy?" *Massachusetts Review* 27 (1986): 305.

Sommer, Doris. *Foundational Fictions: The National Romances of Latin America.* Los Angeles: University of California Press, 1991.

Sosa, Enrique. "Prólogo a la presente edición." In *El Monte,* by Lydia Cabrera. Havana, Cuba: Editorial Letras Cubanas, 1989.

Starling, Marion Wilson. *The Slave Narrative: Its Place in American History.* Boston: G.K. Hall, 1981.

Stephens, Thomas M. *Dictionary of Latin American Racial and Ethnic Terminology.* Gainesville: University of Florida Press, 1989.

Stepto, Robert B. "Narration, Authentication, and Authorial Control in Frederick Douglass' *Narrative* of 1845." In *African American Autobiography,* edited by William L. Andrews, 26–35. Englewood Cliffs, NJ: Prentice Hall, 1993.

Stoneham, Michael. "Juan Francisco Manzano and the Best of All Possible Worlds." *Journal of Caribbean Literature* 6, no. 1 (Summer 2009): 93–107.

Sweeney, Fionnghuala. "An American Slave: Representing the Creole Self." In *Frederick Douglass and the Atlantic World*, 54–69. Liverpool: Liverpool University Press, 2007.

———. "Atlantic Countercultures and the Networked Text: Juan Francisco Manzano, R. R. Madden and the Cuban Slave Narrative." *Forum of Modern Language Studies* 40, no. 4 (2004): 401–14.

Toth, Margaret. "Staged Bodies: Passing, Performance, and Masquerade in Charles W. Chesnutt's *The House Behind the Cedars.*" *MELUS* 37, no. 4 (Winter 2012): 69–91.

Van Leer, David. "Reading Slavery: *The Anxiety of Ethnicity in Douglass's* Narrative." In *Frederick Douglass: New Literary and Historical Essays*, edited by Eric J. Sundquist, 118–140. New York: Cambridge University Press, 1990.

Vera-León, Antonio. "Juan Francisco Manzano: el estilo bárbaro de la nación." *Hispamérica* 20, no. 60 (December 1991): 3–22.

Walter, Krista. "Trappings of Nationalism in Frederick Douglass's *The Heroic Slave.*" *African American Review* 34.2 (2000): 233–47.

Weheliye, Alexander. *Habeas Viscus: Racializing Assemblages, Biopolitics, and Black Feminist Theories of the Human*. Durham: Duke University Press, 2014.

Welter, Barbara. "The Cult of True Womanhood: 1820–1860." In *Conflict and Consensus in Early American History*, 6th edition, edited by Allen F. Davis and Harold D. Woodman, 247–55. Lexington, MA: D. C. Heath, 1984.

Williams, Lorna V. "Morúa Delgado and the Cuban Slave Narrative." *MLN* 108 (1993): 302–313.

———. *The Representation of Slavery in Cuban Fiction*. Columbia: University of Missouri Press, 1994.

Willis, Susan. "Crushed Geraniums: Juan Francisco Manzano and the Language of Slavery." In *The Slave's Narrative*, edited by Charles T. Davis and Henry Louis Gates Jr., 199–224. Oxford: Oxford University Press, 1985.

Wilson, Matthew. *Whiteness in the Novels of Charles W. Chesnutt*. Jackson: University Press of Mississippi, 2004.

———. "Who Has the Right to Say? Charles W. Chesnutt, Whiteness, and the Public Sphere." *College Literature* 26, no. 2 (Spring 1999): 18–35.

Yarborough, Richard. "'Race, Violence, and Manhood: The Masculine Ideal in Frederick Douglass's 'The Heroic Slave.'" In *Frederick Douglass: New Literary and Historical Essays*, edited by Eric J. Sundquist, 166–88. New York: Cambridge University Press, 1990.

Index

About the Author

Karen Ruth Kornweibel is associate professor of English in the Department of Literature and Language at East Tennessee State University. She has previously published works on Zora Neale Hurston, Lydia Cabrera, Charles W. Chesnutt, Suzan-Lori Parks, and Daisy Rubiera Castillo Bueno.